SECOND EDITION

Creative Speaking

DAVID A. FRANK
Director of Forensics
University of Oregon

Frank, David A.
Creative speaking

National Textbook Company
NTC a division of *NTC Publishing Group* • Lincolnwood, Illinois USA

To my first forensics teacher,
Bob Withycombe

D.A.F.

Acknowledgments for reprinting original material: See page 291,
which is an extension of the copyright page.

Published by National Textbook Company, a division of NTC Publishing Group.
© 1995, 1981 by NTC Publishing Group, 4255 West Touhy Avenue,
Lincolnwood (Chicago), Illinois 60646-1975 U.S.A.
Library of Congress Catalog Card Number 92-80476
Manufactured in the United States of America.

4 5 6 7 8 9 0 VP 9 8 7 6 5 4 3 2 1

Preface

This new and completely revised edition of
Creative Speaking is designed to provide succinct,
comprehensive guidance for those preparing for
individual speech events. This book can also be
used as a textbook for advanced speech courses
designed to give students practical experience in
all of the various forms of speech making.

Though much has changed in the world of
forensics since 1981 when William Buys edited
and coordinated the First Edition, the philosophy
of creative speaking expressed in this new edition
has not. It is still based upon the famous trilogy
of *theory, model,* and *guided practice.* Since ancient
times, speech teachers have believed that the successful presentation of a platform speech or an oral
interpretation of literature is best accomplished
when the presenter has a firm command of the
theories of speech making, is familiar with many
historical models, and has been provided with
guided practice. This new edition updates and
broadens the coverage of the theoretical principles
and guidelines for practice presented in the First
Edition.

Forensics is an academic activity designed to
help students create and present persuasive and
ethical speeches, fostering effective habits of com-

munication. Section One of this handbook explains the educational aims of forensics, the principles and practices of persuasion, and the speech tournament environment. The student who participates in individual events competition has the opportunity to develop good habits of communication by competing in limited preparation public address events (impromptu and extemporaneous speaking), unlimited preparation public address events (oratory, informative, radio speaking, after-dinner/special occasion speaking), and interpretive events (memorized and humorous interpretation as well as prose and poetry reading). These events are discussed in sections two, three, and four.

The chapters that explain the individual events are divided into three parts. First, the educational purpose and rules for each event are discussed. Second, the theories and models of each event are surveyed. Third, concrete suggestions for guided practice are offered.

The central purpose of academic forensics and individual events competition is to encourage students to become knowledgeable, articulate, and ethical individuals. The goal of this text is to provide students with the insights and rules necessary for articulate, ethical and effective speech marking.

Time limits in this book are, generally, based on the rules of the National Forensic League. However, radio commentary and after-dinner or special occasion speaking are not sponsored by the NFL as individual events in national competition. Time limits described for those events are based on the Illinois High School Association guidelines, which are typical of the rules for regional contests.

In regard to interpretation events, NFL rules dictate that humorous and serious interpretation be memorized. Time frames mentioned in Chapter 10 for reading humorous and serious interpretation are based on regional event situations where reading in permitted. Reader's theatre as an event is covered in the appendix. Reader's theatre is not sponsored as an event by the NFL. The time limits mentioned in the appendix are based on Michigan Interscholastic League guidelines, which are typical of regional competition. Participants in any event should consult their coaches regarding the time limits in national, regional, state, or local tournaments.

Mastering the rules of speech making is a necessary first step for the beginning speaker. In this book, the rules and formulas used by successful speakers provide students and teachers with reliable starting points and guidelines. However, students must be encouraged to do more than apply rules and formulas. Truly creative speaking occurs when the rules of speech making guide, but do not bind, inventive impulses. This book is designed to help students become skilled *and* creative speakers.

Foreword

Forensics is a wonderful activity. The teachers and students you meet in forensics will help you become an articulate citizen who enjoys the art of public speaking. You will give your teachers and fellow students much in return. Forensics teachers, coaches, and judges listen to thousands of student speeches each year and learn much from them; they will learn from your speeches as well. You also will teach your fellow students how to strengthen their speeches. When you hear teammates present their oratories and oral interpretations of literature in practice sessions, you will provide them with advice and suggestions on how they might improve. The forensics community is a group of individuals dedicated to increasing the knowledge and eloquence of students and teachers.

Forensics is a powerful skill that will help you form the habits you need to contribute and succeed in our society, in the workplace, and in your private life. At the center of a forensics education is the assumption that you should have knowledge and eloquence. There are people in our society who speak eloquently. Unfortunately, far too often this eloquence is hollow, for it is not accompanied by knowledge. You can gain knowledge by cultivating the habit of reading good books, journal and magazine articles, and newspapers, as well as by watching and listening to television and radio.

Competition in forensics should inspire you to learn how to research a topic with care and thoroughness. If your radio commentary is on health care, or your poetry interpretation is drawn from the poetry of Native Americans, you will want to know more about your topic than any person in your audience. Such knowledge will help you feel comfortable with the conclusions you have reached.

Knowledge *alone* will not help you on your job, with loved ones, in political office—or with your forensics judges. You will also need to know *how* to communicate your knowledge to your audiences. Participating in forensics will strengthen and enhance your habits of communication.

You will learn how to adjust and adapt your ideas to your judges, and your judges to your ideas. Once you have a thorough understanding of your speech and topic, you should think about your audience. Forensics should teach you to keep your audience in mind as you create your speech. In creating speeches for your audiences, you will need to consider their values, emotions, and beliefs. In addition, you will need to adjust your speeches to the immediate surroundings and environment.

If your oratory is designed to persuade your audience that gun control is a good idea, you know that some of your judges will disagree. Forensics should teach you how to adapt your speech to an audience that might disagree with your message. In adapting your speech to such an audience, you will want to identify some common ground that you share with your audience. If you believe gun control will reduce crime, and all reasonable audiences will agree that crime should be reduced, you can provide your audience with persuasive evidence that your thesis is true.

If you deliver your speech in a large room, you will need to adjust your delivery to the surroundings and to your audience. The same is true if you find yourself speaking to an audience in a small room. The creative energy you devote to researching and writing your speech must be duplicated in the delivery and communication of your speech. Participating in forensics should help you develop the habits of effective communication.

Forensics should encourage creative and flexible speech making. You will encounter many examples and models of outstanding individual events speeches in this book. In the forensics program at your school, you will observe many excellent speeches delivered by competitors and teammates. These examples, models, and speeches can give you some insight into what makes up an outstanding speech. Consider these models as guides, but do not try to copy these speeches or use these models as absolute rules that must always be followed. The speeches you deliver are your creations and should reflect your individual personality and spirit. When you use models to the exclusion of your own ideas, creativity, and personality, you become a mirror and an echo.

The best speeches are those that reflect the speaker's personality, intelligence, and unique insight.

Finally, forensics should encourage you to develop strong ethics. Your habits of speech making reveal your character. The evidence you choose, interpret, and present to support your ideas tells your audience much about your ability to be careful and fair. The manner in which you deliver your speech reveals much about your attitude toward your subject and your audience. You should, with your evidence and delivery, seek to improve and enhance the quality of life for your judges and your community.

Speech and action are tightly connected. People take action because of speech. With oratory, government officials can persuade the public to go to war or to make peace. With oratory, speakers can encourage tolerance or perpetuate racism. The link between speech and action underscores the importance of forensics and its ethical significance. Because speech leads to action, your audiences and judges may act on the basis of your speech. Thus you have a responsibility to say what you know and believe to be true. Your speeches should be designed to inspire the best in your audience.

Given this responsibility, in a forensic program you should research, write, and deliver your own speeches. The data or evidence you use should not be twisted to fit your theme. In giving a speech, any ideas, opinions, and evidence drawn from sources outside yourself should be interpreted with care. Similarly, your interpretations of selections from prose, poetry, and drama should be consistent with the literature itself.

The ultimate test of forensics is the good that it does for you, your teammates, your teachers and coaches, and for the local and universal communities to which you belong. Participation in forensics should be fun; there is great joy in winning awards, trophies, and recognition, but fun is not the only end of forensics.

Forensics should also help you develop an understanding of important ideas and an ability to communicate these ideas to a variety of audiences. Forensics should enable you to help others develop these same habits and skills. As you improve your own abilities and you help your teammates develop their habits of research and communication, you are improving your community.

The abiding delight of forensics comes not from the trophies you win. The friendships you form and the habits you develop will remain long after your trophies have found their way into your attic. The permanent benefits of forensics can be seen and heard in the graceful impromptu speeches, oratories, poetry, and prose readings of former individual events speakers whose eloquence continues in later life. Forensics is a rewarding activity. Treat it with the respect it deserves; work hard and with passion.

D.A.F.

Contents

Section Four

The Principles and Practices of Oral Interpretation: The Literary Study and Performance of Prose, Dramatic, and Poetic Literature

SECTION ONE

Background: An Introduction to Forensics and Individual Events

CHAPTER ONE

The Aims of Forensics

Martin Luther King, Jr. and Mario Cuomo, Amy Tan and Saul Bellow, August Wilson and William Shakespeare, Maya Angelou and Robert Frost; these are a few of the many speakers and writers who have inspired audiences with their words. They have moved audiences to feel deeply about social injustice, to think differently about social policies, and to act confidently to change society. All this was possible because of their appreciation of the power and importance of the spoken word.

Forensics should provide you with an appreciation of the spoken word that is crucial to your education and success. While many English courses help students to read and write better, forensics is among the few activities designed to promote the important goal of *oral literacy*. A truly educated person can appreciate and emulate the speeches of the great orators, the plays of noted playwrights, and the poetry of celebrated poets. In addition, a host of studies suggest that businesses and corporations need workers with effective habits of oral communication. Finally, as a citizen in a democracy, you must be able to speak in public, to organize a persuasive speech, and to critically evaluate the oratory of an advocate.

Forensics originated with the writings of the ancients. The ancient Africans, Chinese, Israelis,

Greeks, and Romans understood that an eloquent speaker could gain control over rulers and the masses. Those who taught speech in these cultures emphasized the connection between knowledge and speech, wisdom and eloquence. School forensics activities are a continuation of this tradition of teaching students to connect knowledge with eloquence. Forensics should teach you how to communicate what you know.

Most speech teachers agree that forensics should help students develop critical thinking skills, research abilities, and effective habits of communication. These aims of forensics are crucial if students are to learn and if our culture is to flourish. In addition to these general goals, most speech teachers believe that competition in individual speech events has five educational aims: (1) to strengthen and broaden your knowledge of your topic, (2) to enhance your habits of communication, (3) to teach you to create and deliver arguments for a variety of audiences, (4) to encourage creativity and flexibility, and (5) to teach you ethical speech making.

Understanding Your Topic

Competing in a speech event should inspire you to learn a great deal about your topic. In extemporaneous speaking you are expected to have extensive knowledge about current events. If you participate in oratory, you need to do extensive research on your topic. In the poetry event you should understand the poet's life, the poet's intent, and the time period in which the poem was written. No matter what event you eventually choose, your judges will evaluate your speeches, in part, based on your research and your understanding of your topic.

Studying forensics helps you become familiar with the library and develop the skills necessary to research any topic. The library offers the resources you need to develop topics and then to write your speeches. To prepare for extemporaneous speaking, you should make a habit of reading mainstream periodicals like *U.S. News and World Report, Time,* and *Newsweek.* You should also read progressive and conservative periodicals: *The Nation, Z Magazine, Lies of Our Times, The National Review, The American Spectator,* and *Conservative Digest.* When you research an oratory, you may need to consult the *Journal of the American Medical Association, Scientific American,* or *Psychology Today.*

If you plan to participate in memorized serious, you need to find a cutting from a published novel, short story, or poem. After you select your material, you need to read articles and books that help you understand the author's intent and the social and cultural background of your selection. After you have selected a work of literature to perform, you should research criticism—articles and books about the particular author and the work itself. At least research the background of the writer to understand the context in which he or she wrote the literature at hand. Understanding the time at which the selection was written and published will help you interpret the work effectively. Reading published reviews of the publication will give the necessary background for your oral interpretation.

In researching your speeches you should study opinions from many different sources and perspectives. If you read widely and consult authors who represent different points of view, you will better understand your topics. If your understanding of your topic is limited, your speech may be too narrow for most judges.

Take, for example, the students who won the 1989 national championships in extemporaneous speaking. These students used several magazines in preparing their speeches: *U.S. News and World Report, Newsweek, Current History, Christian Science Monitor,* and *Business Week.* They also cited books they had read: Adam Smith's *The Wealth of Nations,* Zbigniew Brzezinski's *The Grand Failure,* and Richard Nixon's *1989: Victory Without War.*

Successful individual-events students read widely and with care. Unfortunately, some forensics competitors make the mistake of relying on a few sources or a source advocating one perspective. You must develop the habit of reading articles and books written by authors who represent many different viewpoints. For every article written by a conservative author, you should read an article written by a liberal author. After you have studied the opinions of authors with diverse points of view, you can craft your own opinion. You will discover that no one source has a monopoly on Truth.

Studying many sources and developing strong research skills is time well spent. Indeed, many former forensics students report that the research techniques they learned while preparing for individual events competition have served them well in their personal and professional lives. You can acquire these skills too if you take the time to tour the library, meet with the librarian, and learn from more experienced speech students.

Librarians and experienced forensics students will tell you that you need a research plan if you are to find support for your arguments. A research plan lists the resources you need to consult before you write your speech. The research plan also helps you organize your search for information.

Your topic guides the creation of your research plan. If, for example, you want to write an informative speech on earthquakes in North America, you need to consult sources on geology and the earth sciences. If you plan to write a persuasive speech about breast cancer, you should study journal articles and books on biology and oncology (the science and study of cancer and tumors).

Your judges expect that you have read many articles and books on your topic. Some students might find and use one article in *National Geographic* in writing a speech on earthquakes. However, they would not develop a broad or a deep understanding of earthquakes from this one source. Ideally, a speech on earthquakes, or any other topic, should incorporate information from many different sources. If you plan to write a speech on breast cancer, you might start with a magazine article published in *Glamour,* but you would not want to stop there. No matter what your topic, you should find as much useful information on it as you can.

A major aim of the forensics and of participation in individual events is to help students strengthen and broaden their knowledge of important social issues. You need to work hard to locate materials for your speeches because your research will reward you. The best speakers are those who know exactly what they are talking about.

Developing Strong Habits of Communication

We all know people who have great knowledge but are unable to communicate it to other people. While knowledge of your topic is a necessary first step, communicating that knowledge to your audience is the essential second step. Both steps are equally important, for as Cicero and Confucius both recognized, knowledge that is not communicated will not help society, and communication without knowledge can greatly damage society.

Participation in forensics should help you develop the confidence and skills necessary to speak in front of an audience. After you have participated in forensics tournaments and given many speeches, you will have much more confidence in your ability to present your ideas.

Many Americans rank speaking in public as their number one fear! You may have similar feelings. Psychologists and others who have studied stage fright have reached two useful conclusions. First, researchers have found that some nervousness and anxiety are useful and necessary for effective public speaking. Most experienced public speakers report that they often feel slightly nervous before they speak, and that this feeling provides them with additional energy. The second conclusion reached by those who have studied stage fright is that most people rarely speak in front of audiences. Because many people do not have experience speaking in public, they do not feel comfortable in public speaking situations. Your stage fright will be reduced after you have spoken hundreds of times in front of many audiences. Participation in individual events guarantees you many opportunities to speak in front of audiences.

Studying forensics and participating in individual events should also help you improve your habits of communication. Your nonverbal and verbal habits of communication come under scrutiny when you study forensics. Judges and other audiences respond to your delivery, your verbal language, and your body language. An important purpose of studying forensics is to learn the principles of delivery.

You need to pay attention to both the content of your speech and the way you deliver it. The first two aims of forensics and of competition in individual events are equally important. You will want to work hard to discover evidence that supports your opinions and to improve your habits of communication.

Presenting Arguments to Different Audiences

Competing in forensics and individual events should increase your understanding of important social issues and enhance your habits of communication. Participating in individual events should also teach you how to make effective arguments. Learning to construct a strong argument is one of the most valuable skills you can develop, for you will find a need to make arguments throughout your private and public life. Competitors in individual events, from impromptu speaking to poetry reading, design their arguments for their audience.

An argument is an assertion backed by a good reason. For example, if you say, "Eileen Ford is the best modeling agent in the country," you have presented an assertion without a good reason. If you say, "Eileen Ford is the best modeling agent in the country because many famous people work for her," you have presented an assertion and a good reason. Your judges will evaluate your speeches, in part, on the strength of the good reasons you present to support your assertions.

Good reasons come in many forms. Many individual events competitors use examples, statistics, expert testimony, and stories to back up their assertions. In impromptu speaking, a competitor might choose to speak on the following topic: "Consistency is contrary to nature, contrary to life. The only completely consistent people are the dead"—Aldous Huxley, 1894–1963. In presenting this topic, the speaker might use a personal example to develop a theme or an insight.

A good reason can be a statistic. A competitor in extemporaneous speaking might develop a speech on this topic: "Has the American public lost confidence in the institution of marriage?" and argue that "Marriage is less popular than ever before. According to the September 1993 issue of *The Atlantic*, 'about nine million Americans age thirty-five or older have never been married, and every year the number grows.' " In a persuasive speech or radio commentary advocating seat belts for children, a competitor might say, "Seat belts can save lives. According to statistics cited by former Surgeon General C. Everett Koop on February 11, 1992, more than 500 deaths and 150,000 injuries to children could be prevented each year if American children were buckled up." Note here that the statistics form the good reasons backing up assertions.

A good reason can come from expert testimony. For example, an expository speech arguing that ants are one of the most aggressive animals might rely on Harvard scientist E.O. Wilson's statement in the January 21, 1991 *Boston Globe* that ants are "by far the most warlike of social organisms" and "conduct wars which dwarf those of human beings and chimps.'' Because Wilson is an expert on ants, his testimony would be a good reason.

Good reasons can take the form of stories and various stylistic devices. Competitors in oral interpretation use stories and stylistic devices to build their arguments. They use prose, drama, and poetry to make an argument about a theme and a mood. In developing a program for oral interpretation, you might select a scene from August Wilson's play, *Fences*. In this play, the characters develop several themes and arguments about marriage, family, and the African-American culture of the 1950s.

The poems of Archibald MacLeish, Gwendolyn Brooks, Maya Angelou, Denise Levertov, and others make arguments about life, love, and culture. The language of poetry conveys the poet's attitudes, beliefs, and values. A poem is a persuasive argument in favor of attitudes, beliefs, and values. A poem makes an assertion and the language and imagery of the poem make up its good reasons. In this excerpt, ''Reveille,'' from *A Shropshire Lad*, the British poet A.E. Housman makes an argument:

> Up, lad: Thews that lie and cumber
> Sunlit pallets never thrive;
> Morns abed and daylight slumber
> Were not meant for man alive
> Clay lies still, but blood's a rover;
> Breath's a ware that will not keep
> Up, lad: when the journey's over
> There'll be time enough to sleep.

What argument does this poem make? Housman is asserting that life is not in sleep; that if you are not awake when the sun comes up, you are not alive. With his language and imagery, he persuades us to live in the sunlight.

Increasing Creativity and Flexibility

Fortunately, there are rules and principles of speech making that you can follow in creating and presenting a speech. These rules are not laws, nor should they be followed in every situation. Truly creative speaking occurs when the speaker works hard to develop, extend, and modify a speech. On occasion, the speaker may wish to change a speech while it is in progress!

Some believe that good speeches result when speakers follow a set formula. Unfortunately, such formulas, if misused, may stifle creativity and flexibility. Formulas are useful when you are still learning how to construct a speech or need instructions on the basics of speech making. However, formulas may prevent innovation and adaptation.

Take, for example, the organizational pattern frequently used in extemporaneous speaking. Many extemporaneous speakers believe they must have three points that divide the question into past, present, and future. This organizational pattern can help the beginning speaker; however, the more experienced speaker understands that a topic can be organized in many different ways.

Using a formula will not guarantee success. An organizational pattern or set of rules can guide you, but should not bind you to a rigid format as you create your speech. *Creative Speaking* is based on the rules and principles of speech making that have been developed over many centuries, and it requires the speaker to innovate and experiment.

Abraham Lincoln and Martin Luther King, Jr. delivered famous speeches that were eloquent and persuasive. In the "Gettysburg Address" Abraham Lincoln delivered a speech that remains an important statement of American values and dreams. This speech, however, did not conform to the rules audiences expected speakers to follow during the nineteenth century. His speech was uncharacteristically short and did not follow the traditional organizational pattern of the time.

Martin Luther King, Jr.'s "I Have a Dream" speech is an eloquent and uplifting oration that articulates his vision of an America at peace with its diversity. While King delivered this speech from a manuscript, about halfway through the address he deviated from his prepared text and spoke extemporaneously about his dream. Because Lincoln and King were well read and were experienced speakers, they could deviate from the rules and formulas of speech making and audience expectations. Their deviation from rules and formulas enhanced the impact of their speeches.

Lincoln and King could deviate from rules and formulas because they had gained a command of the primary principles of speech making. The beginning speaker should follow the rules and use traditional organizational patterns in creating speeches. The more experienced speaker may wish to deviate from the accepted organizational patterns and ways of presenting a persuasive message. The principles of speech making remain an important foundation for both the inexperienced and experienced speaker, and these general rules should not be abandoned without a good reason.

Ethical Speech Making

Participation in individual events helps you develop important habits of thought and communication. These habits influence the choices you make in public and private life. Develop strong ethics, for the messages and speeches you create influence the choices your audiences makes. If your public speaking skills help you gain a position of respect and authority, you will have greater power to persuade and an increased responsibility to present ethical messages.

For example, if you become a teacher, your students may assume that everything you say is accurate and valid.

Your audiences may use what they learn from your speeches long after those speeches are over. If you teach political science and discuss the life and times of Martin Luther King, Jr. in your class, your students' opinions of King will be influenced by your teachings. If, as you teach, you treat your students with respect and dignity, they will probably use your approach to communication as a model. In short, both what you say and how you say it have important social consequences.

The speeches you make should be based on extensive knowledge. To successfully compete in individual events, you must devote time and effort to library research. Search for new ideas and for innovative techniques for expressing your ideas. As you conduct your research, carefully document the sources of your ideas. Ethical speakers do not claim credit for ideas that they did not create.

Speakers who fail to credit the source of their ideas may be guilty of plagiarism. Plagiarism has destroyed the aspirations of political candidates, the reputations of scholars, and the careers of college students. Competitors in individual events who are found guilty of plagiarism are subject to severe sanctions. These sanctions can range from disqualification from forensics competition to academic suspension. Once you understand and practice the principles of scholarly citation, you need not fear such sanctions.

When you write a research paper for your English or history teacher, you are expected to cite the sources you use. The use of citations is required when you rely on a source outside of your own experience. You should develop the habit of fully listing sources when you borrow ideas from others. This principle is of great importance because you must not claim the ideas of others as your own.

You should also use care in selecting and interpreting books, articles, poems, and other works in your speeches. In selecting and interpreting the work of others, you need to accurately represent their ideas. For example, if you borrow ideas from an article in *Scientific American* magazine to create your oratory, you must be faithful in presenting those borrowed ideas in your speech. You must not take the ideas out of context. In using the ideas of others, ask yourself if the authors you rely on would agree with your interpretation and use of their work.

A number of principles should guide you as you select and use evidence drawn from books, articles, plays, and other sources. We have discussed two general rules: you must cite external sources and interpret them with care. Work with your teacher to identify other principles you need to follow. You should abide by the ethical principles of scholarship in selecting and interpreting external evidence to support your arguments.

Participation in individual events should also help you to develop ethical ways of presenting your message. You should attend to the manner in which you present your speeches. Ethical speakers work hard to display tolerance and to treat their audiences with respect. You may be passionately committed to a position on a given social issue, and you have a right to make this commitment. You should, however, treat the arguments and the positions of those who disagree with respect. The manner in which you treat ideas and opinions different from your own reflects your tolerance.

You should also treat your audience and other competitors humanely. Never dehumanize or denigrate your opponents or your judges. While this expectation may seem obvious, some speakers exhibit disappointingly poor ethical behavior. Whenever possible, you should celebrate the speeches and actions of other competitors and work hard to treat judges and educators respectfully.

Conclusion

You have the privilege of participating in forensics and in individual events competition. The competition can be intoxicating. Have fun and keep in mind why you participate in individual events. Competition in individual events strengthens your knowledge of diverse subjects, including important social issues. Participation in individual events encourages you to conduct thorough and extensive research on your speech topic. Competition in individual events also enhances your habits of communication. As you know, it is not enough to research your topic; you need to communicate what you know to your audience.

A fourth aim of competition in individual events is to encourage creative and flexible speech making. As a beginning speaker, you should start with models and formulas that help you organize your material and ideas. These formulas should never become crutches nor should they stifle your creative impulses. You should become familiar with the traditional rules of speech making and then use them as guides for the artistic choices you make in constructing and presenting your speeches.

Finally, forensics and competition in individual events should teach you ethical speech making. You will learn how to conduct scholarly research and how to select and interpret the evidence you gather for your speeches. In addition, you will learn to communicate humanely and with civility.

The importance of the spoken word has been neglected. Forensics offers you an opportunity to gain an appreciation of the spoken word. Ideally, you will participate in all three categories of individual events and debate. The chapters that follow describe individual events and present suggestions for the practice of these events.

CHAPTER TWO

The Principles and Practices of Persuasion

Your goal as a speaker, regardless of the individual event, is to persuade your judge. In the limited preparation public speaking events (impromptu and extemporaneous speaking), you will draw upon your knowledge of current events, philosophy, and many other subjects to persuade your audience that you have thoroughly and knowledgeably answered the question posed. In unlimited preparation public speaking events (oratory, expository speaking, radio speaking, and after-dinner speaking), you will research and present evidence designed to persuade your judges of your deep understanding of the subject. In the interpretative events, your objective is to persuade the judge that you understand the works you select, and to move the judge with the poetry or drama that make up your program.

Although your goal is to persuade your judge, you need to consider the guidelines and opportunities of each event as you construct your speeches. The guidelines consist of the educational aims of the event, the rules you must follow, and the expectations of the judge. To be successful you will need to work within these guidelines.

While the rules and expectations of these speech events may differ, the principles you should follow in creating a limited preparation, unlimited preparation, or an oral interpretation remain the same regardless of the event in which you participate. These principles have been tested by many speakers before many audiences. In addition, they have been confirmed by social scientific research. Based on experience and careful study, these principles provide a firm foundation for your persuasive efforts.

The Two Proofs Necessary for Persuasion: Artistic and Nonartistic Proofs

For two thousand years, scholars and teachers of speech have counseled students to balance the use of proofs and to choose carefully when selecting evidence to support their arguments. Speeches should consist of a variety of proofs and appeals. The best speeches balance the use of emotion and logic, external sources and personal examples, energetic delivery and solid content.

Scholars and teachers of speech have identified two forms of proof speakers use to persuade an audience. These proofs were first identified by the ancient Greek Aristotle. The first form of proof is artistic proofs, or those that result from the speaker's character and abilities. The second form of proof is nonartistic proofs. Nonartistic proofs are drawn from external sources (books, articles) that the speaker uses to build and strengthen an argument.

Artistic Proofs

Artistic proofs consist of your credibility, your ability to appeal to the emotions of the audience, and your use of logic. As you know, audiences and judges evaluate both the speaker and the speech. Often, the audience's evaluation of the speaker's credibility determines how the audience judges a speech.

Speaker Credibility
Of all the proofs available to you, credibility is the most important. Audiences and judges evaluate your speeches, in part, on the basis of your credibility and reputation. You evaluate other speakers the same way. If you listen to someone you dislike, you may not believe what that person says, even if it is the truth. If one of your friends is an outstanding baseball player, you will tend to believe what she says about baseball. These examples demonstrate that the credibility of a speaker cannot be separated from the speech. A speaker's credibility is made up of the speaker's competence, integrity, and goodwill.

Competence You can establish and strengthen your credibility by building a reputation for well-researched and skillfully presented speeches. Your reputation influences how judges will receive your speeches. Teachers of speech know that your competence, integrity, and goodwill are the keys to establishing your reputation and credibility. There are several steps you can take to build your credibility.

First, you can impress judges with your competence by creating and writing well-documented speeches. A well-documented speech reflects the speaker's thorough research. For example, if your speech includes references to several external sources drawn from many books and magazines, your judges will tend to conclude that you understand your topic. If, however, you rely on one *Reader's Digest* article to support your claim, your conclusions will be less persuasive.

You can also strengthen your audience's perception of your competence by presenting well-organized and well-rehearsed speeches. Successful speakers devote much energy and time to organizing and reorganizing their speeches. They do so because they understand that the form of a speech is as important as the content. Keep in mind that you should know more about your speech than your audience. Your job is to present your speech in a manner that helps your audience understand your major and minor points.

Integrity Successful speakers possess integrity. Think about the people you believe are honest, careful, and trustworthy. Certainly you tend to believe what they tell you. In the same way, your judges will be more likely to believe what you say if they view you as careful, honest, and trustworthy.

Speakers who have integrity have good motives. While competitive success in forensics is an important goal, you should have other, equally important objectives. First and foremost is the desire to tell the truth and to use scholarly care in writing and presenting speeches. Unfortunately, some speakers do not say what they believe, and others invent statistics and quotations to prove their points. Some speakers have no integrity.

Speakers will always be tempted to cut corners to succeed in competitions. However, speakers with integrity avoid shortcuts and strive to speak in a manner consistent with their core beliefs. For example, some speakers might abandon their true political beliefs and rewrite their speeches when speaking before judges whose political beliefs differ from their own. Such pandering does not help build the integrity of these speakers.

How can you be true to your core beliefs and prepare and deliver a speech to an audience that does not share these beliefs? This problem confronts many speakers. The answer is adaptation. You do not need to abandon your core beliefs in order to persuade your judges. Rather, you should search to adapt the way you present your beliefs to your judges. We will return to this point later.

The first component of integrity is honesty. Another important part of integrity, when it comes to writing and presenting speeches, is exercising scholarly care in using external sources in your speeches. Keep in mind that your judges must rely on your interpretation of the sources you use to build your speeches. In using external sources to construct your arguments, you must make sure your interpretations are careful and faithful. Ask yourself this important question when you use articles and books to build your speeches: Would the authors and authorities cited agree with this use of their ideas?

Whenever you borrow ideas from external sources, you should faithfully interpret the ideas and provide accurate citations to the original sources. If you fail to acknowledge the source of an idea or claim another's idea as your own, you are committing plagiarism. As you know, plagiarism can lead to serious consequences. Work closely with your teacher to avoid problems of interpretation and plagiarism.

You need to cultivate and project integrity. Honesty and careful use of external sources are two key components of integrity in individual events competition. You must develop a reputation for integrity, and you can do so by placing honesty and scholarly care above competitive success. In the long run, these values will be more important that any trophies you might win.

Goodwill As you recall, we are discussing credibility. Credibility consists of a speaker's competence, integrity, and goodwill. Credibility is a product of the speaker's character and habits of speech. We already have discussed competence and integrity. We now turn to the third component of credibility: goodwill.

Think of the people you know who display goodwill. You know they intend to do what is right, and they speak to improve themselves and others. When you listen to them, you are not suspicious of their intent; you do not suspect they have ulterior motives. Even if you don't share their view of the world, you know they care for you and for their audiences.

As a competitor in individual events, you can exhibit goodwill in a number of ways. First, you should take forensics and individual event competition seriously. If judges see that your topics are socially significant and well thought out, they will take you more seriously. Your selection of topics will reflect your goodwill and positive attitude toward forensics.

Second, you can display your goodwill by being a good listener. After you participate in oratory, poetry, or some other event, you listen to other student competitors present their speeches and their interpretations. Listen attentively and with courtesy. Compliment the other competitors on the strengths you see in their speeches. When you listen attentively and affirm others, you send a message that you wish the best for your fellow students.

Third, you can be a team leader. All organizations and programs need leadership. You can be a leader by helping your forensics teacher and by serving as an officer for the forensics program. One of the most important ways to help your forensics teacher is to work with new forensics students. You can help new students learn the rules of competition and how to create speeches. In addition, you can assist with fund-raising activities that can help build a healthy budget for your forensics program.

There are many other actions you can take to build a perception of goodwill. Students and judges from other schools hear your speeches and form impressions about you. Your forensics teacher also forms impressions about you. These impressions are important to your success as a competitor in forensics, and you want teachers and other students to believe you are a person of goodwill.

The Speaker's Use of Emotional Appeals

The second artistic proof is the speaker's use of emotions. Think about the best teachers or the best speakers you have encountered. No doubt they made you feel enthusiastic about the topics they addressed. The same is true for your audiences and judges. You will want to move them with your energy and enthusiasm.

Audiences are not moved by scientific logic alone. Human beings are creatures with deep emotions. This does not mean you should abandon scientific and other forms of logic and base your speeches solely on emotional appeals. You should, however, think seriously about how you can incorporate some emotional appeals into your speeches.

As you know, humans have many strong sentiments. Different speeches rely on different emotions. An oratory on child abuse will make your audiences angry and sad. A poem on love may make your audience happy. When you start to work on a speech, identify the emotions you believe will be evoked by your ideas.

Your audiences will have emotional reactions to your speeches. It is important that you present your speeches with feeling and emotion as well. You have heard speakers present ideas in a drab and monotone style. Did this style persuade you? Most likely not. As you work to create and present your speech, make sure you put energy and passion into your presentation. Your audiences and judges will appreciate that energy (if it isn't overdone) and will pay greater attention to your ideas.

One way to bring energy and emotion into your speeches is to choose colorful and powerful words and to use vocal variation when you deliver your speech. If you use colorful language to present your ideas and deliver your speech with energy and with vocal variation, your audience will sit up and pay attention. Your goal as a speaker is to encourage your audience to share your feelings and beliefs. You can accomplish this goal if you deliver your speeches with passion.

At the same time, you should not go overboard and overwhelm your audiences and judges with your enthusiasm. Successful speakers strive for balance. That is why all three components of artistic proofs—credibility, emotional appeals, and logical argument—contribute to the success of every speech you deliver. We can now move to the third component of artistic proof: logical arguments.

The Speaker's Use of Logical Arguments

Speech teachers urge their students to use logical arguments in an attempt to persuade audiences. What are logical arguments? Logical arguments use patterns of reasoning that lead the speaker and the audience to a claim or a conclusion. All speeches designed to persuade rely, in part, on logical arguments. As you construct your speeches, you need to develop strong and convincing logical arguments. Speakers use two forms of logic: inductive logic and deductive logic.

Inductive logic Two fundamental patterns of logic are useful for you to know. The first type of logic is inductive logic. Inductive logic relies on the use of examples to lead a speaker and an audience to a conclusion. The strength of inductive logic is its ability to make your persuasive goal clear and vivid. For example, if you were writing an oratory advocating increased funding for school sports, you might describe how participation in sports kept one of your friends from dropping out of school.

You could offer the story of your friend, told with energy and passion, as proof of why funding for sports should be increased. When you rely on this and other examples to prove your point, you are using inductive logic. As you select examples for your speeches, make sure they are compelling. Well-told examples give your audience and your judges a mental image they can use to follow your reasoning.

Deductive logic Your judges expect you to do more than provide examples for your central point. After listening to the story about your friend and sports, the judges would want to know if your friend's experience is typical. Judges expect you to provide strong generalizations that reflect deductive logic. Deductive logic is a pattern of reasoning that starts with conclusions and generalizations. If you found a study demonstrating that the dropout rate among schools that supported sports was significantly lower than the rate for those that did not support sports, then you could build your speech on this conclusion. You could then use the examples drawn from your experience to illustrate the conclusion.

Inductive and deductive logic work together to help you build powerful arguments. Using logic to create a speech is like using threads to make a rope.

Logic helps bind the parts of a speech together. Ideally, your speeches will use several well-selected examples that are supported by well-documented generalizations or conclusions.

Artistic proofs are those created by the speaker. Such proofs consist of the speaker's credibility, the speaker's use of emotional appeals, and the speaker's use of logical arguments. The successful speaker blends all the elements of artistic proofs. For example, the truly creative speaker knows that good speeches include vivid examples, sound conclusions, and an energetic and eloquent presentation. The second form of proof is nonartistic proofs.

Nonartistic Proofs

Nonartistic, or external, proofs consist of materials you discover in the library and other outside sources you use in your speeches. Articles and books on your topic can provide you with many good ideas to use in developing your speech. Because you always rely, in part, on these ideas, you must select and interpret them with care.

Why are external proofs necessary? Such proofs are necessary because they represent the intellectual work of scholars and writers. Certainly the work of authorities should be scrutinized. However, studying such work is a good starting point for developing strong arguments and powerful speeches.

External sources of proof can be discovered in the library. Every student who competes in forensics and individual events should become familiar with the library. Once you are familiar with the resources available in the library, you can locate articles and books that relate to your speech topic.

Every individual event will require some library work. For example, if you participate in extemporaneous speaking, you need to read about current affairs. If you plan on writing an oratory, you must gather extensive research to support your persuasive effort. If you plan to put together a poetry selection, you need to research the background of the poets you use, and read about the intended meanings of the poems. To be a competent speaker, you must know what you are talking about.

Consult your forensics teacher and the librarian if you need help locating the necessary external sources. You may also need to use the interlibrary loan system or visit a major research library to find the resources you need. To develop your competence on a speech topic, read widely and collect many ideas on the subject. You won't use every idea you discover, but they will help you create your speech.

Once you conduct the necessary research on your topic, your next task is to select external sources to use in your speech. Find the best evidence and the best sources you can to substantiate your speeches. While everyone has a right to an opinion, not every opinion is equal. Work with your forensics teacher to select the strongest opinions from the books and articles you select.

A few rules are helpful as you select sources and evidence. First, look for the opinions of field experts. A field expert is an authority on a specific subject. For example, the Surgeon General is an expert on medicine and health. Obviously, you would not turn to the Surgeon General for information on the meaning of a poem; you would select a professor of poetry and literature instead. When you search for external support, locate the opinions of field experts.

A second rule in selecting sources is to look for recently published materials. The competent speaker is current on the topic of his or her speech and knows about the latest developments in the field. This holds true for all the events. For example, scholars of drama and poetry continue to learn more about the meanings of plays and poems.

Finally, you should follow the rule of explaining and quoting from the experts you rely upon to build your speech. When you rely upon the opinions of field experts, you need to quote them, and explain to your audience how these experts reached their conclusions. Your audience will want to know how the experts reached the conclusions you present. In addition, your audience deserves to know that your interpretation of these conclusions is accurate. You can establish the accuracy of your conclusions by quoting directly from your sources.

Be careful not to overquote field experts or rely too heavily on the ideas of others. Good, creative speeches are more than quotations from experts linked together by transitions. As we noted earlier, effective speeches blend artistic proofs with nonartistic, or external, proofs.

To review, you have learned about the two essential proofs you need to persuade an audience and your judge. These two proofs are artistic proofs and nonartistic proofs. Artistic proofs consist of the speaker's character and ability. Nonartistic proofs consist of external sources you discover in libraries, books, articles, and other sources. Both are necessary if you are to persuade your audience.

You now have a basic understanding of the proofs you need to develop and present. In the next section, you will learn about the principles of persuasion. These principles are rules or standards you can follow to create persuasive speeches. Because speaking is an art, these principles are not intended to be laws. Rather, these principles should help you to make informed artistic choices as you create and present your speeches.

Principles of Persuasion

What is an artistic choice? Speakers make artistic choices when they select among the many ideas, pieces of evidence, and organizational patterns they can use in their speeches. Because speakers have a limited amount of time to present a speech, they must choose the best available ideas, evidence, and structure. When a speaker decides that a chronological organizational pattern is more effective and fitting than a subject organizational pattern, the speaker has made an artistic choice.

You make artistic choices when you select a topic, an organizational pattern, and evidence to support your message. Such choices should not be random and unguided. When you create a speech, you should do so with your judges, the rules of the event, and the principles of persuasion in mind.

Four principles of persuasion are useful in making artistic choices. These principles are accepted by speech teachers and are designed to help you create persuasive speeches.

Adapting Your Persuasive Speech to Your Audience

If your speech is to persuade your judges, you need to choose a topic your judges will find important. Additionally, you need to organize your ideas in a purposeful manner, and adapt your topic and your ideas to your judge.

One of the first lessons you must learn as a speaker is to know your audience. Your audience evaluates your ideas. Your judge ranks your speeches against those of your competitors. When you choose a topic, conduct your research, organize your ideas, and deliver your speech, you do so for an audience and judges. As you gain an understanding of your judges' values and preferences, you learn how to better adapt your ideas to your judges.

Your forensics teacher can give you the best insights into the values and preferences of your judges. Many of your judges will be forensics teachers, others will be students, and some will be drawn from the community. The most successful speakers are those who can adapt their speeches to a broad range of audiences.

How do you adapt your speeches to your judges? First, think about the judges' values. These values help determine their preferences and how they interpret your speeches. Some of your judges may share values and preferences; others may hold very different values and outlooks. As a speaker, you want to create a speech that appeals to judges of all beliefs.

Writing and delivering a speech for judges who may not share your values is difficult, but not impossible. To adapt your speech to these judges, you need to discover the values you and the judges share in common. Once you discover these values, you can build your speech on the values that make up this "common ground."

Adapting your ideas to your judges requires more than identifying shared values. You should also adapt your delivery to your audience. For example, you may need to increase or decrease the volume of your voice depending on the size of the room. The successful speaker adjusts the speech to the physical surroundings.

Among the most important tools you can use to gain insight into the values and outlooks of your judges are the ballots, which your judges write after they hear your speeches. These ballots will provide you with three key pieces of information. First, the ballots let you know how your judges ranked your speech in comparison with the other speeches they heard. Second, your judges praise what you did well. Third, your judges offer suggestions for improvement.

You should read these ballots and, with the assistance of your forensics teacher, identify patterns in the comments made by your judges. Once you detect these patterns, you can gain a better understanding of the values and the preferences of your judges. You can use what you learn from these ballots to improve your speeches.

Persuasive Speeches Address Issues Audiences Find Important

When you select a topic for your speeches, you need to pick a subject that is of importance to you and your judge. People will pay attention to speeches about issues and problems that directly affect them. When you are considering a topic for a speech, ask yourself if your judges will find the subject significant.

Most of your judges will be American citizens familiar with world and national events. When you select topics for your speeches, keep world and national issues in mind. These issues should provide you with many ideas for speech topics.

Many successful speakers choose topics that are significant and well known and attempt to tell the judge something new about the topic. For example, the abortion issue has been thoroughly discussed in this country. You could decide to speak on this topic if you have a new idea to offer, or if you can take a novel approach. Other successful speakers choose topics that have not received the attention they deserve. These speakers alert their audiences to the existence and the importance of a neglected problem.

When you select a topic for your speech, check with your forensics teacher, friends, and others to see if the topic interests them. Judges tend to favor speeches that are significant and that relate to their values and concerns. What may be of importance to you may not be important to your judges. One important goal of the speaker is to make the topic of a speech important to the audience.

Persuasive Speeches Are Well Researched

The library offers many resources on issues of concern to your audience. After you have read widely on your topic, you can develop your position on the topic. As you conduct your research and develop your position, keep your judges in your mind's eye. The successful speaker strives to discover external sources and pieces of evidence that the audience will find relevant. Similarly, as you conduct your research, you want to find books, articles, and other sources your judges will find persuasive.

A well-researched speech will impress your judges and demonstrate to the audience that you are a competent speaker. The most knowledgeable and competent speakers go beyond the standard sources presented by the typical speaker. Competent speakers have read the local newspaper, *Time, Newsweek, U.S. News and World Report.* However, they go far beyond these first-step sources to more specialized materials.

Field experts are the best sources you can use to develop your speeches. You can find the testimony and opinions of field experts in more specialized periodicals and books. If, for example, you are talking about new cancer treatments, you should conduct your research in a medical library where you can consult medical journals like the *Journal of the American Medical Association, Cancer,* and other sources to discover specialized research on cancer treatments.

You should include the best evidence you can find in your speeches. The best evidence comes from sources who demonstrate competence, integrity, and goodwill. You must qualify the competence of the sources you use in your speeches. When you qualify a source, you explain to your audience why they should accept the opinions and conclusions offered by your source.

Some sources are stronger than others. As you gather your research, think about the sources or the field experts that will persuade your judge. Selecting field experts to support your position is of great importance, particularly if you plan to speak before judges who may not agree with your point of view.

As noted earlier, you should explain how your sources reached their conclusions. If your topic is new approaches to the treatment of cancer, you will want to describe the studies that prove (or disprove) the success of these treatments. You should provide your audiences with the reasoning used by your sources.

In summary, when you use the best evidence you can find and explain how your sources reached their conclusions, you create a strong image of competence. As you know, judges place great weight on their perceptions of your competence when they evaluate your speeches.

Persuasive Speeches Are Well Organized

Your speeches should have clear themes, a purposeful order, and sound development. The point and purpose of your speech should be clear to your judges and audiences. Your speeches should have a central idea or theme. Your theme should be expressed and explained by the organizational structure of your speech. Finally, the theme should be amplified in the body of your speech. After you select a topic and discover enough proof to create your speech, you need to organize the topic and the proof. Organizing your speeches strengthens the points you want to make. The organizational pattern you should choose depends on your speech event, your topic, and your evidence. Many organizational patterns are possible.

Speakers often use one of many basic organizational patterns. Most speech teachers agree that all speeches should have a head, body, and tail. The head contains the introduction of the speech; the body provides the major claims in support of the speech; the tail is the summary and the conclusion of the speech.

Why should a speech have a head, body, and tail? Remember the last speech you heard that was unorganized and left you confused. You may have been confused because the speech was disconnected and chaotic. Speakers should organize their ideas in a manner that allows the audience to follow along and to understand the speaker's intent.

Effective speakers tell good stories. Traditional stories have introductions, a plot, and a conclusion. Your audiences and judges are well versed in storytelling. We all have heard and learned from stories others have told us. Human beings are natural storytellers, and when you organize your speeches, you should keep this in mind.

In limited and unlimited public speaking events, many competitors organize their speeches into a central position and three points in support. For example, many extemporaneous speakers answer the question that has been posed and then provide three reasons why their answer is valid. Such an organizational pattern helps speakers organize their thoughts.

Another alternative is to use a chronological organizational pattern. This pattern helps you organize your speeches into time segments. Most often this format involves discussions of the past, present, and future. For example, if you were discussing the state of public education in America, you might present your position and three points. You could organize your three points chronologically. You could discuss the history of education in America, the present state of education, and the future of public education in America.

There are a number of other organizational patterns you might use. A subject organizational pattern allows you to describe the different categories in a given topic. For example, if you were writing a speech on modern music, you might organize your speech into the different types of popular music. In this speech, you might want to talk about Muzak, heavy metal, rap, and so on. You might organize this speech into a pro-con pattern. Your central point might be that modern music is better than traditional music. Using this organizational pattern, you would present the reasons for and against your point. In this speech, you would need explain why you favor one side over another.

No matter what speech event you enter, your speech should have clear themes, a purposeful order, and sound development. The theme, order, and development you choose depend on your event, topic, and evidence.

You know that the topic you select, the evidence you gather, and the organizational structure you use should help you persuade your judge. The next principle of persuasion calls for you to adapt your delivery to your judge. You may have a great topic and strong proof, but if you are not able to communicate this topic and proof to your judge, you will not succeed.

Strong Habits of Delivery Will Persuade Your Audience

Many speakers experience stage fright before they speak in front of audiences. Nervousness is a natural and expected part of public speaking. As you gain experience speaking in front of audiences, you will also gain firm control of your nervous energy. You need such energy to persuade your audience.

The habits you form when you practice your speeches determine, in part, how your speeches are received by your judges. Your posture, gestures, movements, and qualities of voice are the major components of delivery. Your habits of delivery should strengthen, not detract from, the message you are attempting to communicate.

Scholars of human communication tell us that nonverbal communication is the foundation of all communication. Often, nonverbal communication conveys more meaning than verbal communication. Your experience probably bears this out. When you hear a speaker who exhibits good posture, uses effective gestures, moves comfortably, and speaks with a convincing voice, aren't you more likely to accept the speaker's message? To be an effective speaker, you need command of key nonverbal habits of communication.

Posture

The posture you assume sends a message to your audience about your competence. You wish to convey a sense of confidence and conviction when you speak. Whenever possible, adopt a posture that feels and looks comfortable. Assume a posture that allows you to move and gesture. At the same time, stand in a central location so that all members of your audience can see and hear your speech.

Above all, your posture should reflect balance and tone. You should not be too erect or too relaxed. The weight of your body should be evenly distributed between your legs, although some speakers prefer to place more weight on one leg than the other. Your posture should enhance the message you are sending to your audience.

Gesture

No universal principle will tell you how to gesture. Your gestures should not detract from your message; they should be appropriate to your speech and audience, and should not appear contrived or insincere. With practice, you can learn to use gestures that are natural and persuasive.

Many beginning speakers do not know where to put their hands. Because you do not want your gestures to detract from your message, you should leave your hands at your side if they are not in use. Some speakers have been known to play with the change in their pocket. Such gestures lead the audience away from the speaker's theme. Hand gestures should be used purposefully.

Eye contact is another important nonverbal gesture you should consider. Whenever possible, you should achieve and maintain eye contact with your audience. Obviously you do not want to stare at your audience or judge. Rather, with care and discernment you should establish a nonverbal visual connection with your judge and audience.

Body movement

Body movement also helps you deliver an effective speech. Your posture, gestures, and body movement should combine with your verbal messages to convey the theme of your speech. You should move your body with the purpose of underscoring a major point or idea. For example, you may wish to move your body to mark a transition from one point to another. Here, you might walk from one side of the room to the other to visually and nonverbally reinforce the movement from one idea to another.

Vocal qualities

As with posture, gesture, and movement, the vocal qualities that are present when you deliver your speeches should help you persuade your judges. Have you ever had trouble hearing a speaker? Have you ever been bored or excited by a speaker? If so, then you know that volume, pitch, rate, and other vocal factors influence an audience's reaction to a speech.

Your voice is a musical instrument. Great speakers know they must combine their prose with poetry, their science with music. When you deliver your speeches, your voice should reflect the concern you feel for your topic. You can convey your concern by using vocal variety, intensity, and emphasis.

Your audience should hear your message, but should not be made to endure shouting or unnecessarily loud noises. The volume of your voice should vary depending on the point you wish to make. At a minimum, your voice should always remain audible. Some speakers who have soft voices need to "speak up." Other speakers need to "tone down" their volume to accommodate their listeners.

When you deliver a speech, vary the pitch of your voice. Speech teachers recommend that you vary your tone of voice to suit the topic, the audience, and the situation. We have all heard speakers present their themes in a monotone. While their themes may have been interesting, their monotone delivery detracted from their message. Whenever possible, use a variety of tones and pitches in your speeches.

Finally, you should present your speeches at an appropriate rate. Most conversations occur at a rate of 150–185 words per minute. Speakers who talk at rates exceeding 185 words per minute tend to irritate and confuse most audiences. However, speakers who talk at rates below 150 words per minute also risk irritating and boring the audience. As with the other aspects of good speaking, you should strive for balance.

At this point, you see that developing and presenting a persuasive speech is a challenging task. You are right. The forensics activity is designed to teach you the theories of speaking. You should know why a speech is persuasive. Additionally, forensics offers you an opportunity to practice these theories. Guided practice is key to developing effective delivery habits.

Practice and Rehearsal

To gain confidence in your ability to deliver your speeches, you need to practice and rehearse them. Take these practice sessions seriously, for they are crucial to your success. You should set up regular and realistic practice sessions with your forensics teacher and forensics teammates. These sessions should reflect, as closely as possible, the experiences and the climate of the speech tournament.

You will want to establish a calendar for practice and rehearsal. Champion speakers train for tournaments as athletes train for national competitions. Practice sessions should not be crammed together on the night before the tournament. They should be spread out over the days and weeks before the tournament. Practice sessions will be more productive if you treat them seriously. As in athletics and other competitions, champions are made in practice.

In your practice sessions, you should discover how you appear to those who hear you. Important aides you should use are the mirror and videotape camera. With mirrors and videotapes you can see how you might improve your delivery.

In other practice sessions, your forensics coach and teammates can be your audience. Their reactions can help you improve your habits of delivery. When you present your speeches in front of these audiences, be open to constructive suggestions. Practice sessions should be designed to encourage changes in the content and delivery of speeches.

The next section describes the steps you need to take in developing a speech. These steps are based on the principles of persuasion discussed to this point. You can follow the steps outlined in the next section in all the forensics events discussed in this text.

The Practice of Persuasion: The Steps in the Creation of a Speech

There are eleven steps you need to take in the creation of a persuasive speech. These steps should be followed in sequence.

┌─ **Guidelines** ─────────────────────────────────┐

The Steps in the Creation of a Speech
1. Select an event.
2. Learn the rules of the event.
3. Brainstorm about and then select a topic for your speech.
4. Research your topic.
5. Select a theme for your speech.
6. Create an organizational blueprint for your speech.
7. Write a first draft of your speech.
8. Practice your speech.
9. Deliver your speech at the forensics tournament.
10. Read your ballots.
11. Rewrite, revise, and improve your speech.

└──┘

The steps just outlined will help you to build strong speeches.

Select an Event

As a forensic student, you can choose to participate in team policy debate, Lincoln-Douglas debate, and individual events. Speech teachers believe you should have a well-rounded experience in forensics and that you should participate in several forensics activities. The first step you should take when you decide to participate in individual events competition is to select one or more events in which to compete. The next chart lists most of the individual events and their rules.

You should select events that you believe might help improve your research, writing, and speaking skills. During your career as a forensics student, you should compete in a variety of individual events. Competing in a variety of events strengthens your knowledge and abilities.

Learn the rules of the events

Each event has a given aim and specific rules. Before you choose a topic and start writing your speech, you must understand the aims and rules of each event. You must follow the rules of the events, or you may be disqualified.

During practice sessions, make sure that your speech falls within the time limits and meets the goals of the event. If you have questions about the rules, make sure to ask your forensics teacher. The list on page 29 explains some of the rules for these events.

Brainstorm and Then Select a Topic for Your Speech

After you have decided on an event, pick a topic for your speech. Remember that your topic should be significant to both you and your audience. The topic should allow you to develop a persuasive speech.

Before you select a topic, do some brainstorming. A brainstorming session is designed to promote inventive and flexible thinking about the topics you might select for your speeches. You, your forensics teacher, and your forensics teammates should devote some time to listing all the possible topics that might be suitable for speeches.

After you have finished brainstorming, you can select a topic to develop into a speech. Before you settle on a position on the topic, you should do extensive research on the topic.

Conduct Research on Your Topic

This is a key step in the creation of a strong speech. As you know, judges evaluate you and your speech on the basis of your competence. You can establish your competence by having a deep understanding of the subject of your speech. The library should become a second home as you search for all the relevant articles, books, and other materials that relate to your topic.

As you become familiar with your topic, you will become familiar with the issues involved and the writers who are the field experts. When you read articles and books on your topic, take careful notes and, if necessary, make copies of key articles or pages from important books. You will use these notes and copies when you write your speech.

Select a Theme for Your Speech

At this point, you can select a theme for your speech. The theme you select should result from your reading and your discussions with your forensics teacher and others. Your research should support the theme you have identified. This theme should be carefully worded, for your goal is to persuade your judges. The evidence you present in your speech should support your theme and persuade your judges.

Guidelines

Aims and Rules of Individual Events
Limited Preparation Events

1. Impromptu
   Aim: To speak on philosophical topics without benefit of extensive preparation
   Rules: Maximum five (5) minutes

2. Extemporaneous
   Aim: To speak on contemporary issues
   Rules: Maximum seven (7) minutes

Unlimited Preparation Events

1. Expository
   Aim: To inform audience about a topic
   Rules: Maximum five (5) minutes

2. Oratory
   Aim: To persuade audience
   Rules: Maximum ten (10) minutes

3. Radio Commentary
   Aim: To present an opinion on a controversial topic
   Rules: Maximum five (5) minutes

4. After-Dinner Speaking
   Aim: To entertain
   Rules: Maximum eight (8) minutes

Oral Interpretation Events

1. Dramatic Interpretation
   Aim: To select and present a dramatic reading
   Rules: Maximum ten (10) minutes

2. Humorous Interpretation
   Aim: To select and present a humorous reading
   Rules: Maximum ten (10) minutes

3. Poetry
   Aim: To select and present a poetry program
   Rules: Maximum five (5) minutes

4. Prose
   Aim: To select and present a prose program
   Rules: Maximum five (5) minutes

Create an Organizational Blueprint for Your Speech

Once you have selected a theme and have evidence to support it, create an outline of your speech. As you recall, there are a number of organizational patterns you can use. The pattern you select depends on your event, topic, theme, and evidence.

You might test several different arrangements. For example, you might try the chronological organizational pattern. If the chronological pattern doesn't quite fit, you might try a subject organizational pattern. After you select an organizational pattern, you can determine where the evidence you have gathered belongs in the outline.

Write a First Draft of Your Speech

At this point, you have a subject, a theme, research, and an outline. You are now ready to write a first draft of your speech. As you write your speech, try to keep your audience and your judges in mind. In addition, keep in mind that you are writing a speech that will be heard, not read. The speech should have a head, body, and a tail. The speech should also have a central thought and two or three major points in support.

Professional speech writers pay attention to introductions, transitions, and conclusions. You should do so as well. In the introduction, make sure the theme of the speech is clear. When you move from the introduction to the first point, write a transition that helps the judge and the audience see the connection between the theme and the first points of support. Summarize the major points in the speech in your conclusion.

Practice your speech

Once you have finished writing your speech, practice delivering it. You can begin by reading the manuscript out loud to yourself. As you read your speech, listen to see if the speech makes sense. At this stage you should not be reluctant to make major changes in the content and delivery. In fact, many professional speakers make changes in their speeches right up to the moment they speak!

After you feel the speech is ready to be heard by others, practice in front of your forensics teacher. Your forensics teacher will talk with you about the strengths of the speech and how it might be improved. Make sure you use your teacher's advice when you revise your speech.

Your forensics teammates can also provide you with useful reactions to your speech. These reactions may focus on different parts of the speech than those discussed by your teacher. Finally, you may wish to present your speech to your parents or to other people who might provide you with a helpful critique.

The more critiques and reactions you have to your speeches, the more choices you have when you revise your speech.

Deliver Your Speech at the Forensics Tournament

After you have practiced and revised your speech, you are ready for the forensics tournament. Your forensics teacher will register you in your individual event or events before you travel to the tournament. When you arrive at the tournament, you will be scheduled to present your speeches to your judges. The next chapter explains the speech tournament.

You should continue to practice your speech while at the tournament. The best speeches are those that have been constantly revised and improved. When you finish presenting the speech in competition, reflect on what you did well and what you might do to improve.

Read Your Ballots

When you return home from the tournament, your forensics teacher will give you your ballots. These ballots provide useful comments about your speech. Work with your teacher to identify comments you might use to revise your speeches. Be aware that you might be judged by the same judges in the future. These judges will want to know that you have read and have responded to their suggestions.

As you read the ballots, you might keep a list of the comments your judges make about your speech. Once you have compiled this list of suggestions and comments, you can return to the process of revising and improving your speech.

Rewrite, Revise, and Improve Your Speech

No speech is ever perfect. Even if you did very well at the tournament (maybe you won first place!), there is always room to strengthen your speech. After you return from the tournament, use the ballots to guide the revision of your speech. You might decide that a section of the speech needs to be rewritten, that you need more and better research for one of the points you are attempting to make, or that the introduction and the conclusion need revision. All speeches can be improved.

Conclusion

In this chapter, you learned about the principles and practices of persuasion. You can use these principles and practices as guidelines for creating your speeches. As you write and rewrite your speeches, keep the following ideas in mind:

Guidelines

* The best speeches balance the use of emotion and logic, external sources and personal examples, energetic delivery and solid content.
* Your judges evaluate your speeches, in part, on the basis of your credibility and reputation.
* To develop your competence, you must read widely and collect many ideas on your speech topics.
* Persuasive speeches are adapted to your audience and address issues your audience will find important.
* Persuasive speeches are well researched and organized for your judges.
* You should develop habits of delivery that will persuade your audience.
* Remember the eleven steps you should take in preparing, rehearsing, and revising a speech.

The next chapter introduces you to the speech tournament and provides suggestions you can use when you attend a speech tournament.

CHAPTER THREE

Speaking at the Speech Tournament

Forensics teachers created speech tournaments so their students could present their speeches in competition before forensics students and teachers from other schools. The competitive nature of the forensic tournament is intended to motivate students and teachers to achieve excellence in public speaking and oral interpretation. In this chapter, you will be introduced to the speech tournament.

What is a Speech Tournament?

A speech tournament is an organized competition for high school or college forensics students. Most tournaments sponsor competition in debate and individual events. Students involved in individual events prepare and present one or more speeches and compete against students from other schools. All competitors are evaluated and ranked by judges. The terms used to describe speech tournament activities are included in the following list.

Guidelines

Terms Used at Speech Tournaments

Divisions: Categories of competition based on experience

Events: Speech activity with specific educational aims and rules

Grace Period: Time allowed (usually 30 seconds) after the official time has been exhausted

Postings: The sheet listing when and where an event will take place

Panel: The listing of an event, speakers, judge, and room

Speech Tournament: An organized forensics competition

Speech Tournament Locations: Place where tournament is held, usually high school or college campuses

Tournament Director: Person in charge of the speech tournament

Tournament Headquarters: The administrative center of the tournament

Tournament Invitation: Letter inviting forensics program to a speech tournament

Tournament Registration: Form listing the events in which speakers will compete

---

Speech tournaments usually take place at a school. Some tournaments take place at resorts or hotels. Speech tournaments are headed by a tournament director. The tournament director and the director's committee or assistants find the rooms, judges, and the facilities needed to conduct the tournament.

The tournament director sends out invitations to the tournament one to two months in advance. In the invitation, the director includes a description of the events offered, the tournament schedule, a motel list, and other important information. After your forensics teacher receives this information, your teacher will talk with you about the events offered at the tournament.

Your forensics teacher is responsible for sending the tournament director the registration for the tournament. This registration lists the names of the competitors on your team and the events in which they plan to compete. With the advice of your forensics teacher, you select and register for the events that interest you. Once you register, you are committed to these events.

When the tournament director receives the registration forms from all the schools that plan to participate in the tournament, the director organizes the entries. The director determines how many rooms and judges are needed. Some tournaments are quite large.

When the speech tournament takes place, you represent your school in forensics competition. You compete against students from other schools. If you are a new speaker, you compete in the novice division. More experienced speakers compete in the senior and championship divisions.

First, you participate against other speakers in two or three preliminary individual events rounds. A round of individual events involves panels of five to seven speakers and one judge. The judge ranks the speakers and provides each speaker with a rating. Competitors receive a rating from one to four based on the quality of their speeches. The rating allows the judge to compare you to other speakers in your division. After the preliminary rounds are over, the competitors who did the best in the preliminary rounds are advanced to the final rounds.

Speakers who do well in the final rounds are recognized at the awards assembly. Here, the tournament director gives trophies or other awards to speakers who did exceptionally well in competition.

Although you compete as an individual, you also compete as a member of a team. Any competitive success you have contributes to the possibility of winning recognition for your team. Many tournaments offer sweepstakes awards to forensics teams that have competitive individual events speakers and debaters.

After the awards assembly is over, your forensics teacher gives you the ballots the judges have written in response to your speeches. These ballots are important teaching tools, and you should use them to improve your speeches.

How Should You Prepare for the Speech Tournament?

Your goal in preparing for a speech tournament is to have carefully created and well-rehearsed speeches. The best speeches are those that have been revised, improved, and well developed. Before you leave for the tournament, you should have manuscripts for your prepared speeches and your interpretative and poetry programs. If you are participating in limited preparation events, you should hold several practice sessions before the tournament is to begin.

Create a plan for your individual events, detailing the steps you need to take before you depart for the tournament. Your first step is to select the individual events in which you will participate. Your forensics teacher will have a list of the events offered at each tournament.

You and your forensics teacher should select one or more events for you to prepare. For example, you and your teacher may decide that oratory and extemporaneous speaking are right for you. Once you decide to register for these two events, your forensics teacher will place you in a division that fits your experience. If you are new to forensics, you will be registered in the novice, or beginning, division of competition. The more experienced speakers compete in the advanced or championship divisions.

The second step in preparing for the tournament is to plan your speeches. Work with your forensics teacher to create an outline for your unlimited preparation events and for your interpretative selections. If you are registered for a limited preparation event, study the educational aims and rules of these events. When you are familiar with these rules, you can write outlines for potential speeches and think about how you might address impromptu topics and the questions you might face in the extemporaneous speaking event.

The third step you should take is to practice your speeches. As we have discussed previously, you should take practice sessions seriously. Try to make the practice situations resemble the tournament setting. Make sure you space your practice sessions over time. Do not do all of your practicing the day before the tournament is to begin.

You should practice in front of as many audiences as you can find. Keep careful records of the comments these audiences make in response to your speeches. No speech is ever finished, so don't resist changing your speech if necessary. When you need to make a decision about modifying a speech, ask your forensics teacher for advice.

The fourth step you need to take to prepare for a speech tournament is to plan what to wear and what to take. Many students choose to dress formally for tournaments. You want to dress for a speech tournament as if you were going to a job interview, representing a client before a jury, or meeting with colleagues in a professional setting. Many students wear suits and ties, dresses—appropriate professional attire. Judges evaluate you on the basis of your competence, integrity, and goodwill, and you want your clothing to enhance your image.

Remember to bring your speeches and any equipment you need to present your speeches. Some students put their speeches in a briefcase; others put their speeches in notebooks. Given how hard you will work on your speeches, you should make copies. You might give a copy of your speeches to your forensics teacher and a friend. If, by chance, you lost your manuscripts, you could then get a copy from your forensics teacher or your friend.

Students who participate in extemporaneous speaking will prepare "extemp files" (files that contain articles and other materials on extemp questions). Those who participate in expository speaking may bring visual aid materials. If you plan to participate in extemporaneous or expository speaking, bring your extemp file and your visual aids to the speech tournament.

You also may need to bring some money for food. Some forensics programs provide speakers with a daily allowance for food. If not, bring money along so you can maintain proper eating habits during the tournament. Sometimes speakers neglect to eat breakfast or lunch when they are involved in a speech tournament. This is a mistake because your body is under stress when you compete. Regular food and sleep give you the energy and balance you need to do well.

The fifth step you should take is to alert your teachers, and your parents or roommate, to the tournament schedule. They should know when the forensics team will leave for and return from the speech tournament. If you plan to miss classes, let your teachers know and work with them to make up missed assignments. Most teachers support forensics and believe that you will learn many value lessons in forensics. At the same time, you should not neglect your other schoolwork.

If you live at home, provide your parents with a schedule of the tournament. They will appreciate knowing that you have contacted the teachers whose classes you will miss. In addition, they should have the name and phone number for the hotel your forensics team will use while away. Your forensics teacher may send out a letter providing these details.

What Will Happen at the Speech Tournament?

When you leave for the tournament, your forensics teacher will tell you what to expect. If your program is like others, you will travel to the tournament in a bus or in private cars. Make sure you are on time for the departure and have everything you need. The tournament will begin at the time announced in the schedule, so you and your program cannot be late.

Once you arrive at the speech tournament, your teacher will go to the tournament headquarters and pay the registration fees. The tournament will provide your forensics teacher with a schedule of the tournament and a map of the tournament setting. Most tournaments provide enough schedules and maps so that each speaker can have one.

Pay close attention to the schedule your forensics teacher gives you before the tournament begins. Following is a schedule recently used at a forensics tournament.

SAMPLE SPEECH TOURNAMENT SCHEDULE

PATTERN A EVENTS	PATTERN B EVENTS
Extemp	Impromptu
Radio Commentary	Oratory
Expos	Humorous Interp
Serious Interp	ADS

THURSDAY, Feb. 27
- 11:00 - 12:00   Registration
- 12:30 - 1:50   SENIOR LD debate, Round I
- 2:00 - 3:20   JUNIOR LD and ALL CX debate, Round I
- 3:30 - 4:00   ALL DEBATE, Round II
- 5:00 - 6:20   ALL DEBATE, Round III
- 6:30 - 7:20   Break
- 7:30 - 9:00   ALL DEBATE, Round IV

FRIDAY, Feb. 28
- 8:00 - 9:30   CX Debate, Round V
- 8:30 - 9:30   Registration for schools with IEs only
- 10:00   EXTEMP DRAW
- 10:30 - 11:30   Pattern A, Round I
- 12:00   EXTEMP DRAW
- 12:30 - 1:30   Pattern A, Round II
- 1:30 - 2:30   Pattern B, Round I
- 2:45 - 3:30   LD Debate, Round V (both JR & SR)
- 4:00   EXTEMP DRAW
- 4:30 - 5:30   Pattern A, Round III
- 5:30 - 6:30   Pattern B, Round II
- 6:30 - 7:00   Break
- 7:00 - 8:00   Pattern B, Round III
- 8:15 - 9:45   ALL DEBATE, Round IV
- 9:00   IE Semifinal Postings

SATURDAY, Feb. 29
- 7:30   UNIVERSITY CENTER Opens
- 7:45   Debate Outrounds Postings
- 8:00 - 9:30   ALL DEBATE, Octo-finals
- 10:00   EXTEMP DRAW
- 10:30 - 11:30   IE Semi-finals, Pattern A & Pattern B
- 12:00 - 1:00   ALL DEBATE, Quarter Finals
- 1:00   EXTEMP DRAW
- 1:30 - 2:30   IE Finals, Pattern A & Pattern B
- 3:00 - 4:30   ALL DEBATE, Semifinals
- 5:30 - 7:00   ALL DEBATE, Finals
- 8:00   Awards

As you can see, this tournament includes debate and individual events and takes place over a three-day period. The preliminary rounds of both individual events and debate are scheduled for Thursday and Friday. The final rounds and the awards assembly are on Saturday.

Let us assume you register for two events: extemporaneous speaking and oratory. One week or so before the tournament, your forensics teacher registers you in these two events.

As you can tell from the schedule, extemporaneous speaking is in pattern A and oratory is in pattern B. A pattern consists of events that are conducted during the same time slots. At many tournaments, you can only participate in one event per pattern. For example, you could not participate in both extemporaneous speaking and expository speaking because both are pattern A events and are scheduled during the same time slot.

After you arrive at the speech tournament and receive a schedule, you must prepare for your first round. As you look at the schedule, you note that your first round will begin at 10:30 on Friday. Because you are competing in extemporaneous speaking, you and your teammates who participate in extemporaneous speaking need to remember the extemp file. You also need to remember your oratory manuscript.

As soon as you are at the tournament, find out where the tournament director has posted information about individual events. A posting lists when and where an event will take place. A posting also lists the order in which the speakers will present their speeches and the name of the judge. The following is a sample posting:

Checklist

Extemporaneous Speaking
Novice Division
Friday, Feb. 28
10:30–11:30
Pattern A, Round I
Judge: John Rindo, Hinterlands Academy
Room: 1204 Preiss Hall

Speaker One: Sweeney, North team
Speaker Two: Hunt, South team
Speaker Three: Richardson, East team
Speaker Four: Hanson, Central team
Speaker Five: **YOU**, Jefferson team
Speaker Six: Stolp, Southeast team

Let us assume that you are speaker five. You will speak on one of the three extemporaneous questions given to speaker five.

Speaker Five, Extemp
1. Will the Arabs and Israelis achieve lasting peace?
2. Who will be our next president?
3. Will disco make a return?

You have thirty minutes to choose a topic, prepare your speech, and find 1204 Preiss Hall. Your judge, Mr. Rindo from Hinterlands Academy, will be in this room. Mr. Rindo will have listened to four speakers before he hears your speech. After he listens to your speech, he will evaluate your effort in comparison to the other speeches he has heard.

He will fill out a ballot for all six speakers. You will receive this ballot after the tournament is over. Mr. Rindo will rank and rate you in comparison to the other speakers, and provide his reactions to your speech, including some suggestions for improvement. He will then turn his ballot in to the tournament headquarters.

Examine the sample ballot on the next page.

He awarded you a one in the round. This means that Mr. Rindo ranked you above the other five speakers, and concluded that you were the best speaker in the round. The rating allows the judge to compare you to other competitors in the novice division of extemp. He gave you a rating of twenty-five, which means that, in comparison to other speakers in novice extemp, he felt you were a strong speaker.

Your ranking may not always reflect your rating. For example, all six speakers might present outstanding speeches for students in novice division. Unfortunately, Mr. Rindo would have to award three of the six speakers a ranking of four. However, Mr. Rindo could give all the speakers a rating of twenty-five.

Again, you will not read Mr. Rindo's ballot or learn how he ranked and rated your speech until after the tournament. When you finish your first round, you need to look at your schedule to see when you will speak next. The schedule tells you that your next speech will take place between 12:30 and 1:30 (pattern A, second round). Your extemp draw will take place between 12:00 and 12:30.

Return to the room or location where the tournament headquarters is posting panels and other information. The second round of pattern A will be posted by 12:00. Let us assume you are the second speaker in round two. Since you are the second speaker, you must select one of the topics given to the second speaker. You have thirty minutes to prepare your speech and to find 12 John Hall. When the round is over, Ms. Boling will rank and rate you

┌─ **Checklist** ─┐

Speech Tournament Individual Events Ballot
Event: Novice extemp
Round One
Time: 10:30–11:30
Room: 1204 Preiss Hall
Judge: J. Rindo, Hinterlands Academy

Speaker Five: **YOU**, Jefferson team
Rank (1–4) 1
Rating (15–30) 25

Comments:
You did a fine job in analyzing your topic. I particularly like the chronological organization you used. I also like the external sources you used to prove your points: You sure have done a lot of reading on this topic! You quoted from *Nation*, *The Economist*, *U.S. News and World Report*, and *The Progressive*. I appreciate the variety of sources you used in this speech. Your conclusion was well constructed and well supported.

Keep working to improve your delivery. On occasion, you spoke too quickly and you stumbled over some words. Also, you should feel comfortable using gestures on occasion.

Overall, a good speech.

Judge's signature _____
Judge's school _____

---

and the other five speakers. As with the judge in the first round, Ms. Boling will write a ballot explaining in detail why and how she ranked and rated you.

When you finish round two of pattern A, you need to move, quickly, to round one of pattern B. You can view this posting where the others are posted. In this pattern, you present your oratory. Your judge will compare it to the five or six other oratories she hears in the round. Unlike the extemp round, you are expected to arrive before the first speaker speaks. You will hear all the speakers present their oratories.

Listen carefully and respectfully to the oratories delivered by the other competitors. When it is your turn to speak, make sure to achieve eye contact

```
┌─ Checklist ─┐──────────────────────────────────────────┐
│             └─────                                      │
│                                                         │
│  Extemporaneous Speaking                                │
│  Novice Division                                        │
│  Friday, Feb. 28                                        │
│  12:30–1:30                                             │
│  Pattern A, Round II                                    │
│  Judge: K. Boling                                       │
│  Room: 12 John Hall                                     │
│                                                         │
│  Speaker One: Jennings, Kennedy team                    │
│  Speaker Two: YOU, Jefferson team                       │
│  Speaker Three: Smith, Truman team                      │
│  Speaker Four: Jones, Roosevelt team                    │
│  Speaker Five: Wu, Washington team                      │
│  Speaker Six: Garcia, Adams team                        │
│                                                         │
└─────────────────────────────────────────────────────────┘
```

with everyone in the room. Although the judge evaluates you and writes your ballot, your competitors should also be targets of your persuasive efforts. After evaluating your speech, Ms. Watanabe might make comments on the ballot. (See page 45.)

You now have over an hour before your extemp draw at 4:00. During this break between rounds, you might eat lunch, revise your oratory, or watch round five of Lincoln-Douglas debate. If one of your teammates is competing in this event, he or she might appreciate your support. Before you attend a teammate's debate, make sure to ask. Sometimes debaters do not want teammates to watch their debates.

At 4:00 you must select an extemp topic for the third round of pattern A. As with the previous two rounds, look at the posting to find the room where the event is to take place:

You have thirty minutes to prepare your speech and to find 103 Friendly Hall. This round you are the sixth and the last speaker. Your judge prepares this ballot explaining the rankings and ratings you earned.

When you finish with this round, you need to hurry to your next round. As you can tell from the schedule, the next event is the second round of pattern B. This is your second opportunity to present your oratory.

You can tell from the posting that you are the third speaker.

As with the previous oratory round, you will listen to the other five speeches. If, during the break, you made revisions in your speech, you might incorporate them into your presentation. Don't forget to listen, with care, to the other

---

Checklist

Speech Tournament Individual Events Ballot

Event: Novice extemp
Extemporaneous Speaking
Novice Division
Friday, Feb. 28
12:30–1:30
Pattern A, Round II
Judge: K. Boling
Room: 12 John Hall

Speaker Two: **YOU**, Jefferson team

Rank (1–4) 2
Rating (15–30) 23

Comments:

Your organizational pattern was excellent. A pro-con structure fit this topic. You gave good reasons for both sides of this issue. (I do, however, agree with your bias.) You should use more external sources. You relied heavily on your own opinion.

You don't seem to have your hands under control. Your hand movements distract from your speech. Otherwise, your analysis was strong.

Judge's signature _____
Judge's school _____

---

speeches. The judge will watch to see how you perform as a speaker and as an audience member.

As your judge listens to your speech, he or she writes comments on the ballot. On occasion, the judge writes as you are speaking. Do not let this bother you. The judge may be writing positive comments in response to your speech. After the speech tournament is over, you can use all the judge's comments to improve your oratory.

When the sixth speaker has completed his or her speech, leave the round and return to the headquarters area. You have a thirty minute break. During this break, you might eat a snack, talk with your friends, and prepare for your last preliminary round.

Your final preliminary round is in pattern B, which involves your oratory. As you read the posting, notice that you are the second speaker.

```
┌─ Checklist ──────────────┐─────────────────────────────┐
│                                                          │
│  Persuasive Speaking                                     │
│  Novice Division                                         │
│  Friday, Feb. 28                                         │
│  1:30–2:30                                               │
│  Pattern B, Round I                                      │
│  Judge: J. Watanabe                                      │
│  Room: 308 Chapman Hall                                  │
│                                                          │
│  Speaker One: YOU, Jefferson team                        │
│  Speaker Two: Pope, Jefferson team                       │
│  Speaker Three: Ally, Truman team                        │
│  Speaker Four: Nakamura, Roosevelt team                  │
│  Speaker Five: Bowie, Washington team                    │
│  Speaker Six: Bond, Adams team                           │
│                                                          │
└──────────────────────────────────────────────────────────┘
```

By this time, you should be familiar with the setting and the expectations. Note that you will hear Nakamura's speech (speaker five) for the second time. You might hear the same speaker two or three times during a tournament. If this happens, you should still pay close attention to the speaker and the speech.

Experienced competitors know that each round is important. The rankings and ratings you earn over the three preliminary rounds will be averaged. Speakers with the highest averages will be advanced to the semifinal and final rounds. Do your best in all three rounds.

As you can tell from the ballot, the judge was impressed with the speech.

When the sixth speaker finishes, walk back to the tournament headquarters and talk with your teammates about the speech tournament. As you can tell from the schedule, a debate round will take place between 8:15 and 9:45. The postings of those who are being advanced to the semifinal round of individual events goes up at 9:00. Again, you have a choice: you can either watch a debate round or wait for the individual events semifinal postings.

Competitors who receive the best rankings and ratings are advanced to the semifinal rounds. The tournament director and the director's assistants total the rankings and ratings of all the speakers in each individual event. For example, in the extemp event, you earned a one ranking and a twenty-five rating in the first round, a two ranking and a twenty-three rating in the second round, and a two ranking and a twenty-seven rating in the third round. In extemp, you earned a five ranking and seventy-five ranking.

In the oratory event, you earned a two ranking and a twenty-six rating in

---

Checklist

Event: Persuasive Speaking

Time: 1:30–2:30
Room: 308 Chapman Hall
Judge: J. Watanabe

Speaker One: **YOU**, Jefferson team

Rank (1–4) 2
Rating (15–30) 26

Comments:

Your topic is significant and compelling! You have certainly identified an important problem. Excellent problem-solution organizational pattern. This pattern lets me know what the causes of the problem are and what we might do to solve the problem. Good support for your claims. Your research is solid.

Here are some suggestions for what you might do to improve your speech. First, you should do some more reading on this issue. You relied heavily on one *Newsweek* article. Certainly there are more articles on this topic. Second, make sure you use all of your time. The speech is short. You could use this time to build your argument. Third, keep working to improve your delivery. At times, you didn't look as though you knew what to do with your hands.

Judge's signature _____
Judge's school _____

---

the first round, a three ranking and a twenty-five rating in the second round, and a one ranking and a twenty-eight rating for the third round. In oratory, your total ranking after three rounds was six and your total rating was a seventy-nine. After tournament headquarters determines the cumulative rankings and ratings for the competitors in all events, speakers with the best scores will be advanced to the semifinals.

Let us assume there were forty competitors in extemp and thirty-five in oratory. The headquarters needs to advance approximately fourteen students to the semifinal rounds. There will be two semifinal panels in each event. After the cumulative rankings and ratings are calculated for all the students in each event, the fourteen students with the best scores in each event are placed into these panels.

```
┌──────────────────┐─────────────────────────────────┐
│  Checklist       │                                 │
└──────────────────┘                                 │
│                                                     │
│  Extemporaneous Speaking                            │
│  Novice Division                                    │
│  Friday, Feb. 28                                    │
│  4:30–5:30                                          │
│  Pattern A, Round III                               │
│  Judge: M. Brand                                    │
│  Room: 103 Friendly Hall                            │
│                                                     │
│  Speaker One: Garcia, Adams team                    │
│  Speaker Two: Smith, Bellevue team                  │
│  Speaker Three: Boyd, Hastings team                 │
│  Speaker Four: Kim, Madison team                    │
│  Speaker Five: Thomas, Sprague team                 │
│  Speaker Six: YOU, Jefferson team                   │
│                                                     │
└─────────────────────────────────────────────────────┘
```

In the extemp event, you earn a cumulative ranking of five (you were ranked one in the first round, two in the second round, and two in the third round). Let us assume that out of the forty competitors, your ranking is the ninth best overall. You are a semifinalist in extemporaneous speaking!

In the oratory event, you earned a cumulative ranking of six (a two in the first round, a three in the second round, and a one in the third round). When this score is compared to those earned by other students, you have tied with two other students for the fourteenth position. The tournament headquarters breaks the tie by using the cumulative ratings. Because your cumulative ratings are higher than those of the other two competitors, you are advanced to the semifinals of oratory.

At 9:00 a list of the semifinalists goes up, and you see your name on the semifinalist lists for both extemp and oratory. When you and your forensics team return to the tournament on Saturday, you might attend an octo-final round of debate and then find the postings for your semifinal rounds.

You are in semifinals in two events that take place during the same hour. The tournament director schedules your speeches at different times during that hour. The extemp posting begins at 10:00, and because you are the first speaker, you select a question from among the three offered to the first speaker.

You may have three judges in your round, and a small crowd of supporters and other students.

You prepare your speech and then find 1207 Preiss Hall. You are scheduled to speak at 10:30. When you finish, explain to your judges that you are a

---

Checklist

Speech Tournament Individual Events Ballot
Event: Novice extemp
Friday, Feb. 28
4:30–5:30
Pattern A, Round III
Judge: M. Brand
Room: 103 Friendly Hall

Rank (1–4) 2
Rating (15–30) 27

Speaker Five: **YOU**, Jefferson team

Comments:

I really liked your introduction. You captured my attention with the example you used! Your organizational structure wasn't as clear as it might have been. Were you using a geographical pattern? I wasn't clear. You presented some good external sources in support of your ideas. The *New York Times* article provided you with some excellent backing for your ideas.

Your delivery was solid, but make sure you keep your hands under control. Also, you should reduce the distance between you and your audience. This is a big room. Move closer to your audience the next time you speak in a big room.

Judge's signature _____
Judge's school _____

---

semifinalist in oratory, and that you must leave. The oratory semifinal round is scheduled in 1200 Preiss Hall.

Another student may be speaking when you arrive, so you should wait for this student to finish before you walk into the room. Since you are the last speaker in this semifinalist panel, you will listen, with courtesy, to all the speakers and then deliver your speech. When the round is over, return to the tournament headquarters area to learn if you have been advanced to the final rounds.

As with the preliminary rounds, the tournament headquarters creates cumulative ranking and rating scores for all competitors in the semifinal rounds. The students with the top six scores are advanced to the final rounds.

Checklist

Persuasive Speaking
Novice Division
Friday, Feb. 28
5:30–6:30
Pattern B, Round II
Judge: J. Stanley Gray
Room: 207 Villard Hall

Speaker One: Warren, Kennedy team
Speaker Two: Scott, Gonzaga team
Speaker Three: **YOU**, Jefferson team
Speaker Four: Walsh, Fairview team
Speaker Five: Twohy, Capital team
Speaker Six: Nakamura, State team

Let us assume that in the extemp semifinal round, the first judge gave you a two ranking, the second judge gave you a one ranking, and the third judge gave you a one ranking. Your total score is a four. This ranking earns you a spot in the final round.

Let us assume that in the oratory semifinal round, the first judge gave you a three ranking, the second judge gave you a two ranking, and the third judge gave you a four ranking. The cumulative total is an eight. Unfortunately, this does not earn you a spot in the final round of novice oratory.

The finals postings go up around 12:30. Because you are in the final round of novice extemp, you note that the extemp draw will begin at 1:00. The final round will take place between 1:30 and 2:30.

As with the semifinal round, you speak before three judges and other observers. You should feel proud to be in the final round, and you should feel confident in your abilities to create and deliver your speeches. Your speech will be evaluated by your judges, and you will learn of their decision at the awards assembly.

When the final round is over, there is some time for you to eat and to watch a debate round. You might do homework or walk around the campus. Make sure to let your forensics teacher know where you will be. At 8:00, the awards ceremony takes place.

The awards ceremony is designed to recognize students, forensics teachers, and the tournament director and assistants for outstanding performances and contributions. The tournament director and tournament management staff

---

Checklist

Event: Persuasive Speaking

Time: 5:30–6:30
Room: 207 College Hall
Judge: J. Lichtenstein

Speaker Five: **YOU**, Jefferson team

Rank (1–4) 3
Rating (15–30) 25

Comments:

This is a great topic area! I share your concern. I particularly liked your problem-solution format. It really fit your topic area. While I don't agree with your solution, I think you have made some good points. You depend on a writer from *Newsweek* to support your conclusion. You might find better proof here.

You should keep working on your delivery. Either keep your hands at your side or use them to help you make your point. Your hand gestures and body movement distract from your major points. Keep working on this.

Judge's signature _____
Judge's school _____

---

acknowledge the efforts of judges and forensics teachers. You should thank your forensics teacher and judges for the energy and effort they have devoted to you.

Be courteous and professional at the awards assembly. You will sit with your team during the assembly, and you should feel free to cheer and clap if one of your teammates wins an award. Congratulate other students you know when they are recognized, and applaud to acknowledge the achievement of every speaker who receives an award. Try not to talk too much during the awards assembly so that others can hear what the tournament director and staff are saying.

You may receive a trophy for being a semifinalist in oratory, and you may earn a first place trophy in extemp! If you receive an award, you should be proud of your accomplishment and smile when the tournament director or staff hands you your trophy. Many students do not win trophies, so your pride should not be mistaken for arrogance.

┌─────────────────┐
│ **Checklist** │
└─────────────────┘

Persuasive Speaking
Novice Division
Friday, Feb. 28
7:00–8:00
Pattern B, Round III
Judge: J. Weston Walsh
Room: 202 Baxter Hall

Speaker One: O'Rourke, Twin Falls team
Speaker Two: **YOU**, Jefferson team
Speaker Three: Iverson, Jamestown team
Speaker Four: Johnstone, East team
Speaker Five: Nakamura, State team
Speaker Six: Bile, Southeast team

What Should You Do After The Tournament?

When the awards assembly is over, your forensics teacher thanks the tournament director for hosting the tournament and gets your ballots. Make sure not to leave anything behind. As you return to your bus or car, check to see the extemp file is with the team and that you have your own belongings and the speech materials you brought with you.

Your forensics teacher will give you your ballots soon after the tournament is over. Read these ballots with care, for they will give you useful insights that you can use to revise your speeches. Your forensics teacher can help you to interpret the ballots. At the end of the tournament, you will be tired, but you will have learned a great deal.

Conclusion

The speech tournament is an exciting event. You should devote time and energy preparing and practicing for tournaments. When you arrive at the tournament, follow the tournament schedule. If you have prepared and practiced your speeches, you will be capable of competing with the other speakers. While one goal of the tournament is competitive success, competition should help to provide you with the motivation to learn.

After the tournament is over, you can reflect on what you learned. Your judges' comments and the experience of the speech tournament should help

---

Checklist

Persuasive Speaking

Novice Division
Friday, Feb. 28
7:00–8:00
Pattern B, Round III
Judge: J. Weston Walsh
Room: 202 Baxter Hall

Speaker Two: **YOU**, Jefferson team

Rank (1–4) 1
Rating (15–30) 28

Comments:

You have a catchy introduction; I liked your problem-solution format. I agree completely with your solution. Your analysis of the problem is very persuasive to me. I hope that others will hear your speech and agree that we need to do something. I also liked the evidence you used to create your speech. Overall, this was a fine speech.

Judge's signature _____

Judge's school _____

---

you become a better speaker and a more articulate citizen. In the chapters that follow, you will learn about the rules that regulate forensics individual events, you will encounter models of outstanding speaking, and you will receive instruction on how to practice individual events. Learning how to write and present individual event speeches may be one of your most valuable educational experiences.

```
┌──────────────────────────────────────────────────────┐
│  ┌─────────────────┐                                  │
│  │   Checklist      │                                 │
│  └─────────────────┘                                  │
│                                                        │
│  **Extemporaneous Speaking**                          │
│  Novice Division                                       │
│  Semifinal Round                                       │
│  Judges: John Rindo, Hinterlands Academy              │
│          Jessica Stolp, Evergreen team                │
│          Rick Hanson, Western team                    │
│                                                        │
│  Room: 1207 Preiss Hall                               │
│                                                        │
│  Speaker One: **YOU**, Jefferson team                 │
│  Speaker Two: Tree, South team                        │
│  Speaker Three: Bray, South team                      │
│  Speaker Four: Berbue, McKay team                     │
│  Speaker Five: Church, Springfield team               │
│  Speaker Six: Wright, Mill team                       │
│                                                        │
└──────────────────────────────────────────────────────┘
```

```
┌──────────────────────────────────────────────────────┐
│  ┌─────────────────┐                                  │
│  │   Checklist      │                                 │
│  └─────────────────┘                                  │
│                                                        │
│  **Oratory**                                          │
│  Novice Division                                       │
│  Semifinal Round                                       │
│  Judges: John Rindo, Hinterlands Academy              │
│          Jessica Stolp, Evergreen team                │
│          Rick Hanson, Western team                    │
│                                                        │
│  Room: 1200 Preiss Hall                               │
│                                                        │
│  Speaker One: Jacobson, Sweethome team                │
│  Speaker Two: Collins, South team                     │
│  Speaker Three: Borhis, East team                     │
│  Speaker Four: Taylor, Brigs team                     │
│  Speaker Five: Martinez, Jefferson team               │
│  Speaker Six: **YOU,** Jefferson team                 │
│                                                        │
└──────────────────────────────────────────────────────┘
```

Checklist

Extemporaneous Speaking

Novice Division
Final Round
Judges: Hung lu Troc, St. Mary's team
        Jason Dasso, Evergreen team
        Charles Cleveland, Western team

Room: 1312 Preiss Hall

Speaker One: Wu, South team
Speaker Two: Pacehco, South Bend team
Speaker Three: Johnstone, East Creek team
Speaker Four: Perelman, Kennedy team
Speaker Five: Burke, Springfield team
Speaker Six: **YOU**, Jefferson team

SECTION TWO

Limited Preparation Events: Impromptu Speaking and Extemporaneous Speaking

These events are designed to help speakers present their ideas on topics and questions for which they have limited time to prepare. The best impromptu and extemporaneous speakers are those who are well read and well informed on current events before they arrive at the tournament. These speakers develop habits of reading and discussion that allow them to present informed opinions on a host of topics and questions.

The impromptu event draws upon the speaker's

ability to organize and present information with limited preparation time. Speakers who excel in impromptu are those who devote considerable amounts of time to reading, writing, thinking, listening, and discussing important subjects.

The extemporaneous speaking event allows the speaker thirty minutes to prepare a speech. Again, speakers who excel in extemporaneous speaking are well read and use the thirty minutes not to learn about a subject from scratch, but to organize and polish their ideas. Participation in impromptu and extemporaneous speaking prepares students for situations they may one day encounter when they enter the professional world and are required to speak immediately on an issue, without benefit of extensive preparation.

CHAPTER FOUR

Impromptu Speaking

The educational aim of impromptu speaking is to help you develop the ability to prepare and deliver a speech with little advance warning. Most of your preparation takes place before you arrive at the speech tournament to participate in the impromptu event. Your preparation for this event occurs when you think, read, discuss, and argue about important philosophical questions.

Before you participate in impromptu speaking, you should know the rules of the event and what your judges expect. The rules of impromptu speaking are clear and not the focus of much controversy. Judges have fairly uniform expectations of what the impromptu speaker should accomplish. After you learn about the rules and expectations of the event, you will see how successful impromptu speakers prepare and present their speeches.

Rules of Competition and the Impromptu Round

The rules of the impromptu event vary; however, many tournaments require the following:

Guidelines

Rules of Impromptu

Topic Areas: Most tournaments use philosophical words and phrases.

Length: Most tournaments allow five (5) minutes with a thirty-second grace period. A timekeeper or judge may use cards or hand signals to alert the speaker to the time remaining. For example, the timekeeper may hold up four fingers at four minutes left, and three fingers at three minutes left.

Procedures: Most tournaments outline the following procedures:

1. The contestant will draw three topics, replace two, and keep one as the subject of the speech.

2. The speaker may read the topic selected to the judge(s) or may include the topic in the speech.

3. The speaker will begin to speak immediately without time for preparation.

4. No materials, such as notes or speech outlines, will be allowed as the speaker presents the speech.

5. Contestants are not to hear the speakers who speak before them. When the speaker has finished his or her speech, the speaker may remain in the room to hear the other speakers.

These rules are enforced by the judges and the tournament director and staff. Competitors who violate these rules risk have their rankings and ratings reduced. Some violations occur because competitors do not know the rules and therefore fail to follow them. The rule most often violated in impromptu speaking is the time limit. Competitors are often penalized because they go over the time limit.

The impromptu round

As a competitor in the impromptu event, you are one of five to seven speakers evaluated by a judge. Let us assume you are speaker one in the first round of

```
┌─ Checklist ─┐──────────────────────────────────┐
│             └──────┘                            │
│                                                 │
│  Postings                                       │
│  Impromptu speaking                             │
│  Novice Division                                │
│  Round One                                      │
│  Judge: Hung lu Troc, St. Mary's                │
│  Room: 1310 Preiss Hall                         │
│                                                 │
│  Speaker One: YOU, Jefferson team               │
│  Speaker Two: Kim, South team                   │
│  Speaker Three: Larson, Northeast team          │
│  Speaker Four: Cross, Southwest team            │
│  Speaker Five: Gonzales, Central team           │
│  Speaker Six: Jones, Lincoln team               │
│                                                 │
└─────────────────────────────────────────────────┘
```

novice impromptu speaking. All the speakers will wait outside the door until individual speakers are called in by the judge. When you finish your speech, you should stay and watch the other competitors.

When you enter the room for an impromptu speaking event, the judge gives you three slips of paper with philosophical statements or words on them. They may appear in the following form:

Whenever a friend succeeds a little something in me dies.
Gore Vidal (b. 1925)
American novelist

Consistency is contrary to nature, contrary to life. The only completely consistent people are the dead.
Aldous Huxley (1894–1963)
British author

Art is I; Science is We.
Claude Bernard (1813–1878)
French physiologist

Guidelines

Traditional Impromptu Organizational Pattern

I.   Introduction
    A. Presentation of Topic
    B. Presentation of Theme
    C. Preview of Body
       Transition

II.   Body
    A. Point One:
       Support
    B. Point Two
       Support
    C. Point Three
       Support
       Transition

III. Conclusion
    Review and summary

You must select one of the three topics, and place the others back on the table or desk. You may think for a moment about the theme you wish to develop and the two or three points you plan to make in support of the theme. Because impromptu speeches are limited to five minutes, with a thirty-second grace period, you should begin the conclusion of your speech when you see that you have about one minute to thirty seconds remaining.

Most impromptu speakers use a traditional organizational pattern. This pattern includes an introduction in which the topic, theme, and an organizational preview are offered, the body of the speech with supporting proof, and a conclusion that summarizes and reviews. If you are new to this event, you should follow the traditional organizational pattern above.

After you finish speaking, sit down and listen to the other five speakers. Notice how they develop their themes and supporting points. As always, you should be a good listener. When the round is over, the judge will rank and rate and write ballots for all the speakers.

Judges' Expectations of the Impromptu Speaker

Many judges would agree with this statement made by a forensics teacher, Clark Olsen [from "Judge Ballot" in the *1989 Championship Debates and Speeches* (Annondale: SCA, 1991) p. 116.].

> I want to learn something new from an impromptu speech, not just hear common information eloquently presented. [I appreciate] unique examples, those that go beyond the stereotypic politics, entertainment/ literature, and a personal application. Finally, speakers, especially in a final round, should look like they want and deserve [first place in the round].

Judges look for insightful thought and speech about the topic you select.

Most judges have at least five questions they ask when evaluating your speech: Did you follow the rules? Did you address the quotation directly and insightfully? Did you organize your impromptu? Did you provide adequate support for your points? Did you deliver your speech clearly and eloquently? Let us take each of these questions in turn.

Did you follow the rules?

The rules for this event are clear. You must select one of three philosophical statements or words. You must develop and present a speech that lasts five minutes, with a thirty-second grace period. The rules explicitly prohibit the use of notes or other materials.

Judges enforce these rules. If you are overtime (beyond the grace period), your judge may disqualify you or reduce your score. When you violate a rule, most judges lower your score regardless of the quality of your speech. Judges must be fair to all competitors, so they will apply all rules equally.

Did you address the philosophical statement or words directly and insightfully?

The philosophical statement or quotation that you select must be at the center of your speech. Judges lower your rankings and ratings if you speak around the topic, or if you develop points that are not directly relevant.

Your main point, your organizational pattern, and your supporting evidence should all be related to the topic. At the end of your speech, your judge considers whether you have spoken to your topic. If you have, your rank and rating will benefit.

Judges want you to do more than just address your topic, however. They also expect you to provide them with an insightful commentary on the topic. An insightful commentary on your selected topic allows your judge to see your topic from a new perspective. Think hard about your topic, and give your judge your best thoughts.

Did you organize your impromptu?

Judges expect you to organize your speech. Your impromptu should have a central theme and two or three supporting points. When you select your topic, identify a theme that addresses the philosophical statement you chose, and use this theme to organize your speech.

Judges evaluate your speech, in part, on your ability to organize your thoughts. Whenever possible, be explicit about the organizational pattern you use. Successful impromptu speakers often preview their organizational pattern and review later to remind the judges of the major points.

Did you provide adequate support for your points?

Judges also listen for the support you use to back up your points. The best impromptu speakers cite books and articles they have read that help them interpret their topics. Such citations may not be needed in every impromptu speech, but all judges expect you to explain your interpretation of the topic.

Did you deliver your speech clearly and eloquently?

Outstanding impromptu speakers have an engaging style. Judges give a higher rank to speakers who can communicate their ideas with clarity and conviction. The nonverbal messages you send when you gesture and move your body should underscore your verbal messages. Your vocal tone and rate of speech also play a role in the judge's evaluation of your speech.

Judges evaluate the content and the delivery of your speech. Both are important, and you should work on both during practice sessions. With these questions in mind, we now turn to the steps you can take to prepare and present successful impromptu speeches.

Guidelines and Models for Impromptu Speaking

When you present an impromptu speech to a judge, the judge evaluates the speech by posing several questions: Did you follow the rules? Did you address

---

Guidelines

Steps in Creating and Presenting an Impromptu Speech

Before The Round

1. Develop the habit of reading, writing, thinking, listening, and talking about important subjects.
2. Practice impromptu speaking.

During the Round

3. Select the topic that you can best develop; you must present an insightful theme with two to three points of support.
4. After you have selected a topic, develop a theme with two or three major points.
5. Present the topic to your judge.
6. Present your theme.
7. Preview the organization of your speech.
8. Develop the points that support your theme.
9. Conclude your speech.

---

the quotation directly and insightfully? Did you organize your impromptu? Did you provide adequate support for your points? Did you deliver your speech clearly and eloquently? You want your judge to answer these questions with a resounding "yes." To accomplish this goal, use the above guidelines when you prepare for and present impromptu speeches.

Before the Round

There are two steps you can take to prepare for competition in impromptu speaking: develop the habit of reading, writing, thinking, and talking about important subjects; and practice impromptu speaking.

Develop the habit of reading, writing, thinking, and talking about important subjects

Speakers who gain an understanding of philosophy and current affairs can speak to almost any topic. You can develop such an understanding if you read books and articles on philosophy and current events. If you are a good student, you write well-researched term papers that also may be helpful in an impromptu speech.

You can also think about the meanings of key words and concepts. When people talk about issues such as justice, peace, or equality, listen carefully to their ideas. Finally, talking about important subjects can help you to develop your thoughts and opinions on a variety of issues.

Practice impromptu speaking

You and your forensics teacher should set up practice sessions to help you prepare for competition. In these practice sessions, follow the rules of the event and speak on topics that you might face at the tournament. As you practice your speeches, ask those who hear you if you have addressed the topic insightfully. These practice sessions prepare you for the tournament. More specific advice on how to practice impromptu speeches is provided next.

During the Round

Select the topic that you can best develop, presenting an insightful theme with two to three points of support

The rules for impromptu state that the "contestant will draw three topics, replace two, and keep one as the subject of the speech." You need to make an artistic choice from among the three topics. If you are a beginning speaker, choose the topic that you know something about. As you gain experience, you will have the ability to speak on any of the three topics. When you are more experienced, you will choose the topic that best fits your knowledge, the judges, and the situation.

Assume that you had to pick one topic from the following three:

Whenever a friend succeeds a little something in me dies. Gore Vidal (b. 1925) American novelist

Consistency is contrary to nature, contrary to life **The only completely consistent people are the dead.** Aldous Huxley (1894–1963) British author

> **Art is I; Science is We.**
> Claude Bernard (1813–1878)
> French physiologist

Which one should you pick? Select the topic from which you can create the most insightful theme with two or three supporting points.

You can develop several themes in response to the first topic. The theme of jealousy is an obvious implication. If you select this topic, you can talk about the meaning of jealousy and develop two or three points about jealousy.

The second topic invites you to develop a theme about consistency. Here, you can develop the idea that people should be inconsistent about consistency. What two or three points might you develop about this topic?

The third topic asks you to consider the meaning of art and science. What theme might you develop? What two or three points might you present to build your theme?

After you have selected a topic, develop a theme with two or three major points

After you select your topic and return the other two options, you should create a theme and an organizational pattern. Present the theme at the beginning of the speech, and preview the points you wish to use to develop your ideas. The theme is the anchor and the center of your speech, and your speech should develop the theme.

For example, if you selected the first topic by Gore Vidal, you might develop the theme that jealousy and competition are sometimes part of a friendship. Your three points might relate to jealousy and competition between friends in the international sphere (between nations), professional relations (between colleagues), and personal affairs (between sweethearts). Your theme development outline might look like that in the guidelines box on page 66.

Your goal is to specify a theme and develop points to back it up. Your speech should have an introduction, a statement of your topic and theme, a preview of your major points, the presentation of your points, and a summary.

Present the topic to your judge

Your judge wants to know which topic you have selected. The rules for impromptu speaking state: "The Speaker may read the topic selected to the judge(s) or may include the topic in the speech." You may choose either option. The first option allows you to read the topic you have selected directly to the judge. For example, if you selected the topic by Aldous Huxley, you would read the topic to the judge: "Consistency is contrary to nature, contrary to life. The only completely consistent people are the dead."

Guidelines

Topic: Whenever a friend succeeds a little something in me dies.

Gore Vidal (b. 1925)
American novelist

Theme: Jealousy and competition are sometimes part of a friendship.

Point One: International sphere (between nations).

Point Two: Professional relations (between colleagues).

Point Three: Personal affairs (between sweethearts).

Your other option is to integrate the topic into your introduction. For example, you might begin your speech on the Huxley quotation in this manner:

> I have a friend who is known for her consistency and judgment. However, sometimes her judgment leads her to conclude that consistency is not always the best course of action. Perhaps Aldous Huxley was thinking along these lines when he stated that: "Consistency is contrary to nature, contrary to life. The only completely consistent people are the dead." My friend and Mr. Huxley would agree that sometimes it is good to be inconsistent about consistency.

In this introduction, you told your judge which topic you selected and the theme you wish to develop.

Which option is better? More experienced impromptu speakers tend to weave the topic into the introduction of the speech. This approach pleases judges, for it demonstrates the speaker's ability to make gentle connections. The other approach (reading the topic to the judge) allows the speaker to be clear and explicit about the topic under discussion. This option is often useful for the less experienced speaker.

Present your theme

All impromptu speakers should use the topic to develop a central theme. A theme consists of the primary idea, central concept, and foundation of your impromptu. Your judge should be clear about the theme you wish to develop. The theme should be drawn directly from the words and the meaning of the topic you selected. To this point, you have seen two themes taken from the first two topics. The Gore Vidal statement might lead to the theme that jealousy and competition are sometimes part of a friendship. The Huxley statement

---

Checklist

Guidelines for Choosing a Theme
1. Use what first comes to mind when you read the topic.
2. Focus on the subject of the statement.
3. Refer to the background and the experiences of the statement's author.

---

might inspire the theme that sometimes it is good to be inconsistent about consistency.

The theme must come from the topic you select. As you attempt to draw a theme from a topic, there are several guidelines you can follow. First, what ideas come to mind first when you read the topic? These first impressions should help you to form a central idea. Again, make sure your ideas are related to the topic, for the judge expects you to address and develop the topic.

One way to guarantee that your ideas are related to the topic is to identify the subject of the philosophical statement. The subject of the statement should form the core of your speech. The subject of Vidal's statement is friendship, the subject of Huxley's statement is consistency, and the subjects of Bernard's statement are science and art.

You will impress your judge if you can develop your theme by referring to the author of the statement you select. For example, Gore Vidal is a famous American author, commentator, and playwright. If you had read one of his books (*Lincoln: A Novel, 1876: A Novel, The Decline and Fall of the American Empire*), you could use Vidal's writings to develop your theme. Vidal is known for his caustic comments about people and relationships, and reference to his works would enhance your credibility.

Aldous Huxley's statement about consistency is consistent with his philosophical and literary works. You may have read his book *Brave New World* in an English literature class. The theme of the novel concerns the power of science and technology and their capacities to destroy human liberty, freedom, and creativity. In developing a theme about consistency, you could refer to Huxley's novel and his concerns about unbridled science, technology, and consistency.

Claude Bernard, the author of the "Art is I; Science is We" statement, is the founder of experimental medicine. He also wrote comedies and vaudeville plays. He was both a scientist and an artist. If you made use of Bernard's biography in constructing a theme on this topic, your judges would be most impressed.

Preview the organization of your speech

After you present the topic and the theme to the judge, give your judge an overview of your speech. A preview helps you create an organizational pattern for your speech. A preview also helps the judge understand your theme and the points you wish to develop.

If you have two or three points in support of your theme, give your judge a brief summary of the points you will present. You might tell your judge the topic and theme of your impromptu and then say, "I'd like to present three points in support of my theme. First, ... Second, ... Third . . . ." After you present the preview, move to your first point.

Develop the points that support your theme

At this point, you have an introduction that includes the topic you selected, the theme you developed, and a preview of the points you will offer in support of your theme. When you finish the preview, begin discussing the first point that supports your theme.

Present your first point clearly. Your points should be supported with examples and other evidence. When you finish your first point, use a transition to bridge your first point with your second point. A transition statement summarizes what has been said before and helps the audience to the next idea. When you finish with the major points in support of your theme, you should move to your conclusion.

Conclude your speech

The focus of an impromptu speech should be the topic. In concluding an impromptu speech, direct your attention to the topic. Summarize what you and the judge have learned from your analysis of the topic. This summary should consist of a restatement of the theme and a brief review of the points you made in support of it. When you finish your speech, return to your seat so you can hear the other competitors.

After the Round

After the impromptu round is over, review your performance and think about what you might do to improve. Ask yourself the same five questions that the judges use to evaluate impromptu speeches: Did you follow the rules? Did you address the quotation directly and insightfully? Did you organize your impromptu? Did you provide adequate support for your points? Did you deliver your speech clearly and eloquently?

If you had the opportunity to watch the other competitors, you should compare your speech with the others you heard. You can learn from other competitors, and make use of what you learn to improve. Some speakers use vivid examples to illustrate their points. Other speakers use strong organizational patterns that you might also use.

When you return from the tournament, you should analyze the ballots your judges have written, noting both compliments and constructive criticism. Both are important if you are to improve.

You now know the rules of the impromptu event and the steps you can take to prepare and present a successful impromptu speech. In the next section, you will analyze a model impromptu speech.

A Model Impromptu

Now that you understand the theory of impromptu speaking, you can consider models of impromptu speaking that vividly illustrate what you might do in your own speeches. The impromptu speech we will consider here illustrates the guidelines discussed in this chapter. The speaker selected the statement written by Claude Bernard, "Art is I; Science is We."

This speech followed the traditional organizational pattern:

Guidelines

Traditional Impromptu Organizational Pattern

I.   Introduction
   A. Presentation of Topic
   B. Presentation of Theme
   C. Preview of Body
     Transition

II. Body
   A. Point One
     Support
   B. Point Two
     Support
   C. Point Three
     Support
     Transition

III. Conclusion
    Review and summary

The speech we will consider was delivered by Cort Sylvester of Concordia College, and he won the national championship in impromptu speaking with it. Sylvester's speech contains all the important components of an impromptu speech.

The Introduction

An introduction should have three parts: a presentation of the topic, the theme, and a preview of the speech. The introduction should make the judge want to hear the speech. Consider Cort Sylvester's introduction from a championship speech:

> One of the most popular shows ever produced, both in its initial run and in syndication, is "Star Trek." And one of the most popular characters in that series is Mr. Spock, the half-human, half-Vulcan first officer of the *Enterprise*. [A common theme on] "Star Trek" . . . is the conflict within Spock between his human emotional side and [his] Vulcan logical side, which attempts to push emotion into the background and rely only upon . . . intellect. Spock often explains that his emotional side must [be confined] within himself, whereas his rational side is what must be applied to help the collective hope, to help his shipmates and the society in which he lives to become much more progressive and much more successful. . . . it is this same conflict that Claude Bernard addressed when he noted that "Art is I; Science is We."

The first part of the introduction accomplishes two goals set out for an introduction. First, he incorporates the topic into his analysis: ". . . it is this same conflict that Claude Bernard addressed when he noted that 'Art is I and Science is We.' " Second, he identifies the theme he plans to develop from the topic: "[A common theme on] Star Trek . . . is the conflict within Spock between his human emotional side and [his] Vulcan logical side, which attempts to push emotion into the background and rely only upon. . . intellect."

The judges applauded the use of "Star Trek" and Mr. Spock. One judge wrote: "Great example (Mr. Spock) for this quotation. Clever and effective." Another judge wrote "[Good use of] Mr. Spock to illustrate the conflict in the Bernard quotation. Fine explanation of your interpretations of the quotation." A third judge wrote that "Dr. Spock is a great example of this quote." The Mr. Spock examples provide the judges with an interesting and vivid illustration of the topic, thereby fulfilling an important principle of persuasion.

Cort Sylvester's introduction suited the third purpose of an introduction: it gave the judges an overview of the speech. In specific terms, Sylvester stated that he would use three points to explain the meaning of the Bernard quotation:

> First of all by realizing that indeed, scientific process is often a societal endeavor; second, by realizing that the artistic and emotional endeavors are individualistic; and finally, by realizing that we must strike a balance between those two aspects of our personality in order to make society prosper.

With this preview, the judges understand what he intends to do with his topic and theme. The preview made for a nice transition to the body of the speech. One judge observed that the "Logical progression in the body of the speech made it easy to follow—good organization."

The Body

The body of the speech should be designed to develop the topic and the theme. The theme of this speech was based on three points. In turn, the speaker stated the point he wished to develop and then offered support for the point. Because impromptu speeches should center on the topic and the theme, the speaker should try to connect all the points to the central theme. Let us examine how the speaker developed his three points.

The scientific process is often a collective endeavor

When an impromptu speaker chooses a topic, he or she must develop a theme and supporting points. The first point Mr. Sylvester makes in support of his theme is that the scientific process is a collective endeavor. Note how this first point is intended to develop the "Science is we" part of the topic.

> Initially it seems quite clear that as Bernard suggested, scientific process is often a collective endeavor. . . . . A. Pascarella, a theorist in techno-logical applications . . . . . . suggests that when we make technological breakthroughs, what we are attempting to do is not only make our own lives much easier, through. . . labor-saving technology, but also [pro-mote] economic and societal growth within the system. That is, we at-tempt to free up more time within the society to address problems that we could not address if we took the time that the labor saving devices allow us to conserve. . . .

At this point in his speech, Sylvester has presented his first idea in support of his theme, connected it to the topic ("it seems quite clear that as Bernard suggested"), and quoted an external source (A. Pascarella) in support of his idea. In further developing his first point, he states:

> Hawthorne, in his famous short story "The Birthmark," addressed the

societal implications of technological problems when he examined the implications of a scientist attempting to remove a birthmark from his wife's face. Eventually he realized that the only scientific endeavor that was fruitful was that which attempted to solve a useful problem within the scope of scientific investigation, because what we must do is not to make our individual selves better but, through science, to make the society in which those individual selves operate, much more smooth.

Sylvester does a nice job of using a scientist and a novelist to build his first point. One judge agreed and wrote: "Very nice juxtaposition of literary writer with (a) theorist in science." In addition, Sylvester cited the story from which Hawthorne's theme is taken. Finally, the story is vivid and illustrates the need for science to concern itself with the social and not the personal.

Transition
In moving from the first point to his second point, Sylvester uses the following transition: "At the same time, however, what drives us to perform scientific investigation is quite often our individual drives . . . . those individual drives are most accurately expressed not through scientific investigation, but through artistic endeavors. And that is how we must now examine Bernard's statement."

This transition provides two specific links. First, the transition links his first point to his second point. His audience can see the connection between the first point on the scientific process as a collective endeavor and the second point that artistic endeavors are individualistic. The second link he provides is to the statement and theme. As with the first point, he reminds his audience that his second point is meant to explain the Bernard statement.

Artistic endeavors often come from within ourselves
With his second point, Cort Sylvester addresses the other part of the Bernard quotation: "Art is I." Here, he refers to a short story and a pop artist to establish his point:

> . . . artistic endeavors, even if they are expressed in several technological fashions, often come from within ourselves. In Hawthorne's short story, we find that [the scientist] actually destroyed the balance within his life . . . by attempting to solve his wife's cosmetic problems. In actuality, he needed to take into account his wife's inner desires. She liked her face as it was, and the scientist should have appreciated that as well. Pop artist Andy Warhol often indicated that the only art that was truly meaningful was that which the artist within him or herself believed was valuable. Of course, most of us in looking at his paintings of Campbell Soup labels probably agree with Warhol that we can't find value in it unless it strikes at something we ourselves have experienced. . . .

With this statement, Sylvester provides his judges with the reasoning for his second point. He does a nice job connecting Hawthorne's short story and Warhol's observation to the Bernard statement. He continues to develop his second point as follows:

> . . . . we express our individual desires through artistic endeavors. Hawthorne wrote in order to express those thoughts that were most important to him. Warhol painted to do the same thing. Thus, through our artistic endeavors, we express those emotional desires, those intellectual pursuits that are most important to us on an individual level, which would eventually drive technological progress. And it is for that reason that we must now address the third aspect of Bernard's quotation. . . .

Mr. Sylvester weaves the Hawthorne and the Warhol experiences together to build a conclusion that artistic impulses take place at an individual level. When he finishes this second point, he has addressed the two parts of the Bernard statement. With his first point, he has interpreted and explained the "science is we" statement. With his second point, he has interpreted and explained the "art is I" statement.

Transition

In moving from his second point to his third point, he states: "And it is for this reason [point number two] that we must now address the third aspect of Bernard's quotation, that is, that in order to be truly successful, we must strike a balance between these two aspects of our personalities." This is an excellent transition, for it reminds the judges that the first two points provide the foundation for the third point. The third point, in turn, restates and develops the theme Sylvester takes from the Bernard statement.

We must strike a balance between the scientific and the artistic aspects of our personalities

In this third point, Sylvester returns to the theme of his speech. He also returns to the introduction and his use of Mr. Spock:

> Spock was able to operate in the confines of the *Starship Enterprise* because he did strike a balance. Within the confines of his own cabin, he played his broken harp, expressing the musical, emotional, and artistic drives which pulled at him from his human side. But, when in contact with the rest of the ship, he was able to repress those emotional drives. He was able to balance the aspects of his personality to allow the intellectual and the emotional side to surface when they were most appropriate.

This point is nicely developed, and Spock is the perfect illustration. Mr. Spock is a wonderful example of the emotion-logic tension. In further developing this third point, Sylvester returns to an external source introduced earlier:

> Pascarella, in his writings on the humanization of technology, addresses the same issue on a societal level [when] he points out that technology, if misapplied, or if applied only [to human problems], can often be destructive. However, if we apply that emotional side of ourselves, those individualistic drives [we can] make them much more appropriate for the situation in which we exist.

This reference to Pascarella reminds the listeners of the first point of the speech and provides them with a nice transition to the conclusion.

Transition from point three to conclusion
Sylvester is near the end of his speech. In moving from his third point to the conclusion, he states: "Clearly then, humanity as a whole, much like Spock, must strike a balance between two aspects of our personality." This transition allows him to connect his theme to his major example (Mr. Spock) and to the Bernard quotation.

Conclusion
In the conclusion of an impromptu speech, the speaker should return to the topic and the theme taken from the topic. If possible, the speaker should use the examples developed in the body of the speech to tie the speech together. In this speech, Sylvester returns to the topic and theme of the speech. He also uses the example he offered at the beginning of the speech to tie the speech together:

> Clearly then, humanity as a whole, much like Spock, must strike a balance between two aspects of our personality. Bernard realized that this is balance between the individual and the collective and the fact that it is expressed through emotional, artistic, or intellectual and rational drives, only proves that any of our personalities can have some important content and only by balancing them properly can we apply this to the society in which we exist.

With this conclusion, Sylvester summarized the theme of his speech. The theme, that a balance should exist between the art as I and science as we, is a direct analysis of the Bernard quotation. In many ways, this impromptu speech is an excellent model.

Judges' Reactions

The judges were pleased with his speech. One judge wrote that Cort Sylvester "demonstrated a subtle structure, and wove a single example throughout his speech, making reference to it many times, which showed creative analysis. He also demonstrated the confidence of a national champion." Another judge wrote: "Beautifully structured transitions. Fine use of the references for philosophical, theoretical, and scientific examination of the elements inherent in the concept."

However, the speech was not perfect. You might agree with the following assessment made by one judge: "Some very complex and compound sentences . . . at times this can be hard to follow. . . . The link between art and science is a bit vague—I would like to have heard you develop the link even more than you did."

One judge commented on Sylvester's use of the quotation: "I would prefer that you place the quotation on the desk. This allows you to gesture more freely. Don't gesture with the card!"

As you examine the structure and the content of this speech, you can see why judges gave this speech outstanding rankings and ratings. The examples Sylvester used, the transitions he offered, and the structure and the content of the speech should provide you with a model for your impromptu speeches. With such models in mind, you should put your knowledge into practice.

Practicing Impromptu Speaking

You now know the steps you need to take to create and present a winning impromptu speech. At this point, you can visualize how these steps fit together and how an impromptu speech should be organized. Following are some concrete suggestions for preparing to compete in impromptu speaking.

Develop the habit of reading, writing, thinking, and talking about important subjects

Read widely

The best impromptu speakers read articles and books written by authors who represent different and diverse points of view. You should read your daily local newspaper, a daily national newspaper, and one of the news weeklies (*U.S. News and World Report, Time, and Newsweek*). Given that these newspapers and news weeklies may not represent diverse points of views, you should also read selections from the alternative press. For example, *Nation, The Progressive,* and *Mother Jones* magazines present ideas and perspectives not seen in the mainstream press.

You should also take classes that address philosophical and literary topics. The more you know about philosophy and important philosophers, the better you will be at developing and presenting philosophical topics and themes. In the same light, the more you know about literature, the better you will be at analyzing literary passages. You learn much by reading philosophy and literature.

Write outlines of impromptu topics

In order to prepare for impromptu speeches, you should take philosophical statements and quotations you might receive in impromptu rounds and write outlines of speeches you might deliver using these statements and quotations. The *Concise Columbia Dictionary of Quotations* is an ideal source for philosophical statements and quotations. Take two or three topics from this dictionary and outline possible impromptu speeches.

When you write your outlines, use the traditional organizational pattern. It is appropriate for almost any topic and is ideal for the beginning impromptu speaker. Make sure you use the topic to identify a clear theme and two or three supporting points.

Think, listen, and talk about important subjects

To prepare for the impromptu round, think, listen, and talk with friends and others about important subjects. Listen carefully to those whose opinions on contemporary events are well supported and developed. As you think and listen to others, keep in mind what impromptu judges look for: "I want to learn something new from an impromptu speech, not just hear common information eloquently presented."

The conversations you have with your teachers, friends, and parents will prepare you for the impromptu round. If, for example, one of your friends asks your opinion on gun control, your answer will resemble an impromptu speech. In many ways, the conversations you have on such topics help you to develop well-supported opinions that you may use in the impromptu round.

Practice

As you prepare for competition in impromptu, you should create a practice schedule. Include in this schedule time for solitary practice, practice in front of your friends, and practice in front of your forensics teacher. When you practice by yourself, you should design the practice sessions to resemble the actual impromptu round. Select three topics from the *Concise Columbia Dictionary of Quotations* and choose one as the subject of an impromptu speech.

You should time your speech and make sure that you follow the other rules of the event. Your speech should have a theme and two or three points in support of the theme. When you finish, you should ask yourself the five questions that judges use to evaluate impromptu speeches. Finally, you might want to tape record your practice speeches so you can hear what you have done.

Solitary practice is not enough. Your practice schedule should include prac-

Checklist

Checklist for Impromptu Speaking

Before Practice

1. Know the educational aims of impromptu speaking.
2. Know the rules of the impromptu speaking event.
3. Understand what will happen in the impromptu round.
4. Understand what judges expect of impromptu speakers.
5. Visualize the steps you should follow in selecting a topic.
6. Understand how to develop a theme from a topic.
7. Know how to develop points that support the theme.
8. Develop introductions, transitions, and conclusions.
9. Consider models of outstanding impromptu speaking.
10. Establish practice schedules.

During Practice

11. Practice by yourself.
12. Practice in front of friends.
13. Practice in front of your forensics teacher.

At the Tournament

14. Select the best topic.
15. Organize your speech around a theme and two or three points.

After the Tournament

16. After the tournament, read your ballots and use the comments to improve.

tice sessions in front of your friends. Again, you should strive to create a situation that resembles the actual impromptu round. After you finish your speech, ask your friends for constructive criticism.

Finally, your forensics teacher should listen to you develop and present an impromptu speech. As an expert and an educator in forensics, your coach will offer guidance you and your friends cannot provide. Because your forensics teacher's suggestions will reflect the opinions of your judges, you should write them down.

As you practice for impromptu speaking, use the checklist above.

CONCLUSION

Competition in impromptu speaking should help you develop the ability to organize your thoughts and speak clearly at a moment's notice. It should also give you greater understanding of philosophical words and phrases. If you know the rules of the event, if you practice, and if you work hard to improve, you will earn success in this event. Impromptu speaking is a challenging event that you will enjoy if you practice and strive to tell your judge something new.

CHAPTER FIVE

Extemporaneous Speaking

The educational aim of extemporaneous speaking is to help you develop the ability to organize your thoughts and prepare a speech on an important current event in a short time. In this event, you are allowed thirty minutes or longer to prepare. You may use books, magazines, and other materials to prepare your speech. You are not to talk with other people about your topic before you speak.

Before you participate in extemporaneous speaking, you should understand the rules of the event and your judges' expectations. The rules of the extemporaneous event are well established, and judges use a shared set of standards to evaluate extemporaneous speeches. After you learn about the rules and expectations of the event, you will see how successful extemporaneous speakers prepare and present their speeches.

Rules of Competition and the Extemporaneous Round

The rules of the extemporaneous event vary; however, many tournaments require the following:

Guidelines

Rules of Extemporaneous Speaking

Topic Areas: Most tournaments use questions related to current events. The National Forensic League has two divisions of extemporaneous speaking. One division is the United States division that involves U.S. domestic and foreign policy. The second division covers the domestic and foreign affairs of all countries. The question is presented in the form of a question.

Preparation: Depending on the tournament, speakers are allowed thirty (30) minutes or an hour to prepare. During the preparation time, extemp speakers may be assigned to an "extemp prep room" (a room designed for extemp preparations).

Length: Most tournaments allow seven (7) minutes with a thirty-second grace period. A timekeeper or judge may use cards or hand signals to alert the speaker as to the time remaining. For example, the timekeeper may hold up four fingers at four minutes left, three fingers at three minutes left, and so on.

Procedures: Most tournaments outline the following procedures:

1. The contestant selects one of three questions one hour or thirty minutes before the round is to begin. When the contestant has selected the topic, the contestant prepares the speech using books, magazines, and other materials. Prepared notes are not to be used. The contestants draw at intervals of seven minutes.

2. The speaker may read the topic selected to the judge(s) or may include the topic in the speech.

3. The speaker may use notes during preparation time. Some tournaments allow contestants to use notes during the speech; others forbid use of notes.

4. Contestants are not to hear the speakers who speak before them. When the speaker finishes his or her speech, the speaker may remain in the room to hear the other speakers.

Checklist

Postings

Extemporaneous speaking
Novice Division
Round One
Judge: D. Wong
Room: 102 Preiss Hall

Speaker One: Rindo, Hopkins team
Speaker Two: Smith, Madison team
Speaker Three: Arnold, Thurston team
Speaker Four: **YOU**, Jefferson team
Speaker Five: Tre, Wright team
Speaker Six: Phillipi, College Grove team

These rules are enforced by the judges and the tournament director and staff. If you violate these rules, you risk having your rankings and ratings reduced, so learn the rules and follow them consistently. The most common violations concern time limits and the use of notes and materials. Make sure you remain within the time limits set forth by the tournament. You should also remain aware of the rules relating to notes and other materials.

The Extemporaneous Round

Let us assume that you plan to compete in the extemporaneous event at the speech tournament described in the last chapter. The tournament schedule lists the times competitors draw their questions. According to the schedule, you will draw your questions at 10:00, 12:00, and 4:00.

As in every event, you need to find the posting area to determine where your rounds are scheduled and what three questions you have as options for your speech.

Let us assume that you are scheduled as speaker four in the first round of novice extemporaneous speaking, as shown in the postings above.

When you find the extemp posting area, you need to wait until the tournament management posts your questions. Remember, there will be three speakers before you. The tournament staff posts the questions at seven-minute intervals. The first speaker receives his questions at 10:00, the second speaker receives her questions at 10:07, the third speaker receives her questions at

10:14, and you receive your questions at 10:21. Once your questions are posted, you have thirty minutes to prepare a speech on one of them.

Round One
Speaker Four
1. Will the Arabs and Israelis achieve a lasting peace?
2. Will the President's health care plan work?
3. How can government attract and retain quality people for public service?

Let us assume that you have the three questions shown above.

Write these questions on a piece of paper, and then select one as the topic of your speech. You should select the question you think you can best answer. As soon as you select your question, you need to begin preparing your speech. In preparing your speech, you need to consult your extemp files.

An extemp file consists of copied articles and other materials, organized according to questions. The typical extemp file would contain information on the Arab-Israeli conflict, the President's health care plan, and issues relating to public service. Once you select your questions, consult your extemp file for information and opinions that will help you start outlining your speech.

Most extemporaneous speakers use the traditional organizational pattern explained in the last chapter. To review, this pattern includes an introduction in which the question is presented, an answer or theme that addresses the question offered, and an organizational preview outlining the speech. The body of the speech follows with two or three points and supporting proof. Last is a conclusion, which summarizes and reviews the speech. If you are new to this event, you should follow this traditional organizational pattern.

Outline the major points of your speech (See guidelines on page 83.) and then look in your extemp file for supporting evidence. Do not take time to write out your speech or prepare a manuscript. You will speak from your outline. After you have devoted twenty minutes or so to preparing your speech, you need to find 102 Preiss Hall. When you find the room, you must wait until the third speaker finishes and the judge calls for you.

The judge tells you when to begin. Make sure you stay within the time limits and follow the extemp rules established for the tournament. The three speakers who spoke before you may also be in the room, and you should include them in your speech with your eye contact and delivery.

When you finish your speech, sit down and listen to the two speakers who will follow you. As you listen to these speakers, consider what they do well and what you might learn from them to improve your next speech.

Guidelines

Traditional Extemporaneous Organizational Pattern

I.   Introduction
    A. Presentation of question
    B. Presentation of answer or theme
    C. Preview of body
        Transition

II. Body
    A. Point One
        Support
    B. Point Two
        Support
    C. Point Three
        Support
        Transition

III. Conclusion
    Review and summary

Judges' Expectations of the Extemporaneous Speaker

Judges expect you to develop an intelligent and, when possible, original answer to the question you select. The best extemporaneous speakers rely on more than one *Time* magazine article or *U.S. News and World Report* editorial for their thoughts and ideas. Judges reward speakers who rely on numerous sources and present novel insights.

Judges require you to address the question you have drawn. Your rankings and ratings suffer if you shift to a topic or idea unrelated to the question. You should develop a central theme that answers the question. While you are not required to take a personal stand on a controversial issue, judges do expect you to answer the question directly.

Keep in mind the five questions judges ask when they evaluate your speech: Did you follow the rules? Did you address the question directly and insightfully? Did you organize your extemporaneous speech? Did you provide adequate support for your points? Did you deliver your speech clearly and eloquently? Let us take each of these questions in turn.

Did you follow the rules?

The rules for this event are clear. You are to select one question from three options. Your speech should last seven minutes, with a thirty-second grace period. Many tournaments explicitly prohibit the use of notes or other materials.

Judges enforce these rules. Your judge may disqualify you or reduce your score if you violate the time limit, regardless of the quality of your speech. Judges must be fair to all competitors, so they apply all rules equally.

Did you address the question directly and insightfully?

Focus on the question you selected and keep it at the center of your speech. Judges lower your rankings and ratings if you speak around the issue or discuss irrelevant ideas. Your major point, your organizational pattern, and your supporting evidence should all relate directly to the topic. At the end of your speech, the judge considers whether you have spoken to your question. If you have, your success will be reflected in your rank.

Judges expect you to do more than just stay on the subject, however. Judges also expect you to provide them with insightful commentary on the question you select. Your speech should allow your judge to view your topic from a new perspective. Try to tell your judge more than what you read in one of the news weeklies. Judges reward you for presenting your own insights and perspectives, if you are well informed.

Did you organize your extemporaneous speech?

As in every event, judges listen to be sure your extemporaneous speech is carefully organized. You must answer the question you select, and include two or three supporting points. As soon as you select your question, invent an answer and a central thought in response to it. Your answer and central thought form the core of your speech.

Judges evaluate you, in part, on your ability to organize your thoughts. Whenever possible, be explicit about your organizational pattern. Successful extemporaneous speakers usually preview their organizational pattern and then review, reminding the judges of the major points in the speech.

Did you provide adequate support for your points?

Judges also listen for the proof you offer in support of your ideas. The best extemporaneous speakers cite books and articles to support their response to the question selected. Such citations may not be needed in every extemporaneous speech, but all judges expect you to explain your interpretation of the topic.

Did you deliver your speech clearly and eloquently?

Outstanding extemporaneous speakers have an engaging style. Judges give you a higher rank when you communicate your ideas with clarity and conviction. Remember that your gestures, movements, vocal tone, and rate of speech all contribute to your judge's evaluation of your speech. Judges evaluate the content and the delivery of your speech. Be sure that your delivery reinforces your ideas.

With the judges' expectations in mind, review these guidelines for preparing and presenting extemporaneous speeches. Consider how successful extemporaneous speakers have followed these guidelines.

Guidelines and Models for Extemporaneous Speaking

There are two techniques you can use to prepare for competition in extemporaneous speaking. You can develop the habit of considering current events, and you can create an extemp file. (See guidelines on page 86.)

Develop the habit of reading, writing, thinking, and talking about current events

The best extemp speakers read widely on current events. If you wish to do well in extemp, you need to develop the habit of reading newspapers, magazines, and books in which the authors analyze and explain domestic and international affairs. In addition, as you listen to the radio and watch television, you should pay attention to the news. The more you know about current events, the better your extemp speeches will be.

You can start by reading your local newspaper and a national newspaper. Your local newspaper features stories about your local community; national newspapers provide information about national and international issues. Here are some well-known newspapers you should consult on a regular basis:

New York Times
Wall Street Journal
Christian Science Monitor
USA Today
Washington Post

Guidelines

Steps in the Creation and Presentation of the Extemporaneous Speech

Before the Tournament

1. Develop the habit of reading, writing, thinking, and talking about current events.
2. Create an extemp file.
3. Practice extemporaneous speaking.

During the Tournament

4. Select the question that provides you the best opportunity to develop and present an insightful theme with two to three points of support.
5. After you have selected a question, develop an answer and a central thought with two or three major points.

During the Speech:

6. Present an introduction that includes your question, answer, and theme, and a preview of the organization of your speech.
7. Develop the points that support your theme.
8. Conclude your speech.

After the Speech and Tournament

9. Listen, if possible, to the other speakers.
10. After the tournament, read your ballots and use the comments made by your judges to improve your next speech.

The best extemp speakers read magazines and journals as well. You should read general circulation magazines, and, on occasion, specialized journals. Here are some well known magazines and journals you should consider:

Time
Newsweek
U.S. News and World Report
New Republic
Harpers'

Mainstream newspapers and magazines, such as the *New York Times* and *Time,* can provide you with popular opinions. To broaden your understanding of current events, you should read magazines that present ideas different from those featured in the mainstream press. Read magazines with both conservative and liberal editorial slants. For traditional and conservative viewpoints, you should read some of the following:

Commentary
American Spectator
The Economist
Business Week

To analyze views at the other end of the political spectrum, you should also read some liberal and progressive magazines, such as these:

Nation
Progressive
Tikkun
Z magazine

If you want to gain additional information about foreign affairs, there are many important newspapers, magazines, and journals for you to consult. Here are three good examples:

International Herald Tribune
World Press Review
Foreign Affairs

You should also listen to radio and television programs that feature discussions about current events. Often, experts on a given topic give their opinions on such programs. While there are many programs you might consider, here are some that many informed people take in:

"All Things Considered" on National Public Radio
"The MacNeil-Lehrer News Hour" and "This Week in Review" on the Public Broadcasting System
"Face the Nation" on NBC
"Meet the Press" on CBS
"Nightline" on ABC
"World in Review" on CNN

If you regularly read and observe all the sources listed here, you will be well on your way to developing the broad understanding that extemp speakers need. However, you need to do more than read newspapers and watch and listen to news programs. You should develop the habit of talking about current affairs with friends and others. Through conversation, you can develop your ideas and opinions about current events. These dialogues allow you to test the logic and soundness of your opinions.

As you develop good habits of reading and conversation, you should also think and write about current affairs. If you have an assignment in a history class, you might choose to develop a theme that relates to a current event. Whenever possible, make your academic work and your forensics experience work together.

The best extemp speakers are constantly thinking about how they would answer the questions posed to them in extemp competition. For example, when you read an article about the President's health care plan, you should think about how you might use the opinions expressed by the author in an extemp speech. Reading and thinking about current events will strengthen your extemp speeches.

Practice extemporaneous speaking

As with any speech event, you and your forensics teacher should set up practice sessions to help you prepare for extemp competition. In these practice sessions, follow the rules of extemporaneous speaking and address questions you might face at the tournament. Practice your speeches in front of others and ask them if you have addressed the question in a meaningful and insightful manner. These practice sessions prepare you for the tournament. More specific advice on how to practice extemporaneous speeches is provided later in this chapter.

Select the topic that provides you with the best opportunity to develop and present an insightful theme with two to three points of support

The rules for extemporaneous state that you must select one of three questions as the focus of your speech. If you are a beginning speaker, choose the subject you know best. As you gain experience, you will be able to address any of the three questions. Experienced speakers select the topic that best fits their knowledge, the judges, and the situation.

Round One

Speaker Four

1. Will the Arabs and Israelis achieve a lasting peace?
2. Will the President's health care plan work?
3. How can government attract and retain quality people for public service?

Assume that you had to pick one topic from among the three above. Which one would you pick? You should select the question from which you could create the most insightful answer with two or three supporting points.

The first question asks that you discuss the attempts to end the Arab-Israeli conflict. This conflict has ancient roots, and your judge would expect you to have a basic understanding of the issues dividing the Israelis and the Arabs as well as their recent promise to resolve their differences. You would need to have good information to provide your judge with a solid answer. Here, newspapers such as the *New York Times* and journals like *Foreign Affairs* would help you form an answer to the question.

The second question asks if the President's health care plan will work. This question requires you to understand what the president intends to do about the health care crisis and asks you to judge the effectiveness of his strategy. Magazines like the *Progressive* and *Business Week* would provide you with some well-reasoned opinions that would help you answer this question.

The third question asks that you tell the judge how the government might attract and retain quality people for public service. The point of this question is to inspire the speaker to discuss the quality of public service. Answers to this question might be found in news weeklies, such as *U.S. News and World Report* and *Nation*.

After you select a question, develop an answer or theme with two or three major points in support

When you select a question, you should identify an answer to it that you can use as the theme of your speech. Focus on the answer or answers to the question in your speech, and create an organizational pattern with two or three major points to support your view.

For example, if you select the first question on the Arab-Israeli peace agreement, you might answer, based on our reading, that the 1993 peace agreement will bring lasting peace to the region. In the body of your speech, you could identify the two or three reasons for your answer. To support your answer, you might rely on articles published in the *Washington Post* and *Tikkun*.

An outline of this speech might look like this:

Question: Will the Arabs and Israelis achieve a lasting peace?
Answer: The 1993 peace agreement will bring lasting peace to the region.
Point One: The Israelis want peace now.
Point Two: The Arabs want peace now.
Point Three: The international community wants peace now.

Your goal is to specify an answer to the question and to present points to back up your answer. Your speech should have an introduction, a statement of your topic and theme, a preview of your major points, the presentation of your points, and a summary.

Integrate external sources into your speech

Your judge wants evidence that you have done some reading and thinking on these issues. To demonstrate that you understand the topic, you should consult your extemp file for articles and other materials on the Arab-Israeli conflict. Ideally, you will have done a great deal of reading on this topic before the tournament. You should use the extemp file to address the specific question you selected and refine your understanding of the theme you wish to develop.

The best extemp speakers use between ten and twenty external sources. You should use external sources to build the answer to the question you select and to provide evidence that supports your major points. For example, if you read an article in the *Washington Post* that says most Israelis are pleased with the peace treaty, you might use this as proof for the point that the Israelis want peace now. If you use the *Washington Post* article as proof, you need to refer to it in your speech.

You have several choices on how to cite proof from external sources. One choice is to quote directly from the sources. If you wish to provide proof for your second point that the Arabs want peace now, you might quote the author of an article in *Foreign Affairs* magazine on this issue. For example, you could state that "Arabs appear to want peace with Israel. According to . . ."

You can also paraphrase an external source. A paraphrase is a summary of another's idea or opinion. In order to develop the third point of the speech, you might paraphrase from the *Washington Post*. Here, you might say that "Recent editorials in the *Washington Post* observe that the international community intends to help the Arabs and the Israelis implement the details of the peace accord." This paraphrase helps you build support for your answer.

Keep in mind that any idea you borrow from an article or other source needs to be cited in your speech. You cannot claim someone else's ideas as your own. If you fail to credit the source of your ideas, you may be guilty of plagiarism, of presenting the ideas of others as if they were your own. You should also qualify, whenever possible, the external sources you rely on in your speech. When you qualify a source, you explain why the source is credible. Try to use competent and knowledgeable sources with expertise about the question you selected.

Using your answer as the focus of your speech, create a speech that has a head (the introduction), body, and tail (the conclusion)

At this point you have an answer to the question, two or three points, and external sources that support your answer. Now you need to use these elements

---

Checklist

Goals of the Introduction
1. Set tone of speech
2. Present question
3. Answer question/present theme
4. Preview body of speech

---

to construct your speech. Your speech should have an introduction, a body, and a conclusion.

The Introduction
The introduction should accomplish four goals. If you accomplish the four goals above, your judge will want to listen to the body of your speech and will have a clear idea of what you intend to say.

Set tone of speech. The judge's first impression is crucial. Judges draw conclusions about you based on your posture, speaking rate, and attitude. Walk up to the podium with confidence. As you begin your introduction, demonstrate that you are confident and knowledgeable about your subject.

Present extemp question. You need to let your judge know which question you selected. Most extemp speakers weave their question into their introduction. For example, if you selected the question "Will the Arabs and Israelis achieve lasting peace?" you might integrate the question into your introduction as follows:

> The Arabs and the Israelis have fought several wars since the founding of Israel in 1948. However, because of the historic 1993 peace accord, there is hope that the two sides will at last resolve their differences. This raises the question "Will the Arabs and Israelis achieve lasting peace?"

As you read this introduction, notice that the speaker tells the judge why the question is significant. The first two sentences of the introduction alert the judge that the focus of the speech is the Middle East. The second sentence sets the direction the speaker might take in the speech: the violence may finally end because of the 1993 peace agreement. The third sentence clearly identifies the question the speaker selected. With these three sentences, the speaker provides the judge with the focus of the speech, the direction the speech will take, and the question the speaker selected.

Present an answer or theme. Your judge knows that you must select a question from among three. After you select and present a question to your judge, you need to answer the question or develop a theme based on it. Most extemp speakers choose to answer the question, although the event rules do not require the extemp speaker to take a position on an issue.

Whether you take a stand or not, you must always supply evidence from the articles and other external sources you have read. Think carefully about the question you select and then develop an answer you can support with evidence and analysis.

Presentation of preview. After the judge knows your question and the answer or theme you wish to develop, you should provide the judge with a preview of your speech. In this preview, you will give your judge a "road map" of your speech. The preview should be a clear outline of your speech.

For example, if you selected the question about the Arab-Israeli peace accord, your preview might look like this:

> I believe there are three reasons why the Arabs and the Israelis will finally resolve their differences. First, the Israelis want peace now. Second, the Arabs want peace now. Third, the international community wants peace now. Let us move to the first point.

This preview offers the judge a good sense of the direction you plan to take.

The Body

In the body of the speech, you develop the two or three reasons that support your answer or theme. Your reasons should be well organized and carefully presented. For example, if the first point in support of your speech is that the Israelis want peace now, then you must provide evidence of their desire for peace. Again, this point is one of three points that compose your answer to the question.

How do you "prove" this point? You can prove it by using external sources (books, articles, etc.) that address the Israeli position on peace in the Middle East. *World Press Review, The New York Times,* and *Nation* might provide you with proof for this point. From these sources, you might gather statistics, quotations, and other forms of evidence to build your argument.

Use the best evidence you can discover when you develop an extemporaneous speech. Your evidence should come from experts in the field and from the most recent sources available. Recent evidence and opinions are vitally important when you speak on current events, which are timely and subject to frequent changes.

The body of your extemp speech should be a carefully constructed and organized set of points, transitions, citations of external sources of evidence, and summary statements as shown in the following guidelines.

Experienced extemp speeches identify the specific points they wish to make ("Israelis want peace now"). After presenting the point, they create a transition between the point and the external source ("This is true because many public

```
┌─ Guidelines ──────────────────────────────────────────────┐
```

Steps to Take in Creating the Body of the Extemp Speech

Point: The major issue or ideas you wish to present
Example: "Israelis want peace now."

Transition: The bridge between one point and the next point.
Example: "This is true because many public opinion polls prove
that most Israelis support the peace agreement."

External Source of evidence: An authority outside the speaker
Example: "According to the *Washington Post* October 1, 199X" a
majority of Israelis are pleased with the details of the new peace accord."

Summary: Conclusion and recapitulation
Example: "Given this expression of support for the peace
agreement, we can conclude that the Israelis will keep their word.
Fortunately, the Arabs are ready for lasting peace now as well."

opinion polls prove that most Israelis support the peace agreement"). The
external source proves the point. Here, you might quote from a national
newspaper to prove your point: ("According to the *Washington Post* October
1, 199X a majority of Israelis are pleased with the details of the new peace
accord.").

The summary step allows you to recap and tie together the point you wish
to establish ("Given this expression of support for the peace agreement, we
can conclude that the Israelis will keep their word. Fortunately, the Arabs are
ready for lasting peace now as well."). The summary step should contain a
bridge, a transition, between the point made and the point about to be made.

The two or three points you present to build your answer or theme should
contain well-stated positions, transitions, external sources, and summaries. If
you have strong and well-supported points, the judge will see that you know
a great deal about the subject. By the time you are ready to conclude your
speech, the points you presented should allow you to turn back to the extemp
question with a well-developed answer or theme.

The Conclusion

In the conclusion of your extemporaneous speech, you should return to the
question. Remember, your judge expects you to address the extemp question
throughout the speech. The conclusion should allow you to summarize and
pull together the points you made. Your conclusion should review for the

judge how the introduction, body, and conclusion establish an answer to the question.

Many extemp speakers begin their conclusions by restating the question ("Now we can return to the central question: Will the Arabs and Israelis achieve a lasting peace?). This step alerts the judge that the speaker is not off track. Once you restate the question, the judge will expect an answer ("Based on the three points I have presented, we can predict that the Arabs and Israelis have good reasons to abide by the peace agreement in the near future."). The answer results from the points presented in the body of the speech.

Finally, many extemp speakers return to their introduction for guidance in developing their conclusion. For example, the speaker might begin her speech with a story or a parable and then return to the story or parable in the conclusion. Regardless, the conclusion should allow the judge to see how all the parts of the speech fit together as an answer to the extemp question.

After the Speech and Tournament

When you finish your speech, return to your chair. As always, you should listen, with care, to the other speakers and take notes on what they do well. Listen for their use of external sources, their introductions and conclusions, and their speaking style. As you listen, compare and contrast your speech with those of your competitors. As you compare and contrast the speeches, you can evaluate your own performance for strengths and weaknesses.

After you return from the tournament, analyze your ballots for patterns. Do your judges applaud your introductions and conclusions? Do they suggest you might speak more clearly? Your ballots are always among your best sources of information about your speaking performance.

You now know the rules of the extemporaneous event and the guidelines you should follow in preparing and presenting your speech. In the next section, you will analyze a model extemporaneous speech.

A Model Extemporaneous Speech

Now that you know the theory of extemporaneous speaking, you can consider models or examples of extemporaneous speaking that vividly illustrate what you might do in your own speeches. The extemporaneous speech we will consider here illustrates the steps discussed in this chapter. The speaker is Suzie Sprague. In 1989 she won the national championship in extemporaneous speaking with her speech on the former Soviet Union. In this speech, she answered the question: "Can the Free World count on Gorbachev to take peace off the list of impossible dreams?"

Ms. Sprague's speeches followed the traditional organizational pattern.

Guidelines

Traditional Extemporaneous Organizational Pattern

I. Introduction
    A. Presentation of topic
    B. Presentation of theme
    C. Preview of body
        Transition

II. Body
    A. Point One
        Support
    B. Point Two
        Support
    C. Point Three
        Support
        Transition

III. Conclusion
     Review and summary

All the basic components of a successful extemporaneous speech were present. We will consider each of these components.

The Introduction

Remember that the introduction should set the tone of the speech, identify the extemp question, specify an answer or theme, and preview the body of the speech. The introduction should inspire the judge to listen. Consider the story Ms. Sprague uses to begin her speech:

> P.T. Barnum, one of the greatest show men of all history, used to display what he termed "The Happy Family." Now this family consisted of a lion, a tiger, a bear, a wolf, and lamb all in the same cage. "Remarkable," said one visitor to Mr. Barnum. "How long have they been there together?" "Seven years," Barnum replied. "But occasionally we have to replace the lamb." Now Mr. Barnum exhibited the classic example of the saying "Appearances can be deceiving." For while it appears that these animals were as happy as "Wild Kingdom," every evening the lion, the tiger, the bear, and the wolf had lamb chops for

dinner. The . . . success of Mr. Barnum's exhibits were based upon his philosophy that there's a sucker born every minute.

With this story, Sprague introduces the theme of the speech: that appearances can be deceiving, and that suckers are born every minute. Her transition between the Barnum story and the extemp question linked the theme to the behavior of the Soviet Union:

Unfortunately, we can apply this philosophy to the modern-day political spectrum, for as we turn our eyes to the Soviet Union, it might appear that the recent withdrawal of the Soviet Union from Angola and from Afghanistan signals a new liberalism in their military policy and [that] the free world can count on peace from them. However, if we leave the suckers behind and delve into the reality of the situation, we will find that the truth is far different.

This is an excellent transition, for it connects the P.T. Barnum story and statement about "suckers," the classic saying that appearances can be deceiving, to the subject of the Soviet Union. With this introduction, Sprague highlights truths that some believe to be universal, and she links them to the actions of the Soviet Union.

In her next statement, she invites the judges to consider the motives and behaviors of Mikhail Gorbachev:

Now it is very important for the United States to examine whether or not Mikhail Gorbachev, the leader of the Soviet Union, is really going to stick to his policy of peace throughout the world. Because as leaders of the free world, it is necessary for us to make sure that he does not remain a constant threat to democracy and that the capitalist economies in the world are secure.

With this statement in mind, she identifies and introduces the question she selected:

Therefore, it becomes very important to us to ask the question: "Can the free world count on Gorbachev to take peace off the list of impossible dreams?"

At this point in her speech, she has established her theme and presented the question she wishes to answer. In her next statement, she gives the judges her answer to the question, along with a preview of her speech:

Well, unfortunately for the free world, we are going to have to continue to dream the impossible dream and answer "no" [to] this question. First, because of the opposition within the Soviet Union. [Second], because Gorbachev remains a constant threat to democracy. And finally, because of his continued economic imperialism.

In this introduction, Sprague sets the tone of the speech with the P.T. Barnum story, identifies the extemp question, answers the question, and previews the body of her speech. With this introduction given, she can now move to the body of the speech.

The Body

In the body of the speech, she presents and develops three points: (1) that the opposition within the Soviet Union will prevent peace, (2) that Gorbachev remains a threat to democracy, and (3) that Gorbachev's economic imperialism will prevent peace. Note how she states her points, provides transitions between her points and external sources of evidence, and then provides summary statements as follows:

The opposition within the Soviet Union will prevent peace

In her first point, she establishes her first reason why the free world cannot count on Gorbachev to take peace off the list of impossible dreams:

> But first, [we turn] to the resistance within the Soviet Union to Mikhail Gorbachev's supposed policies of peace. It seems that Gorbachev has been walking a political tightrope in his nation with these policies because there is not very much agreement within the hierarchy of the Soviet government. In his book *1989: Victory Without War,* former President Richard Nixon looks toward the Soviet Union and tells us that in the Soviet Union you can't teach an old bureaucrat new tricks.

Note how Plano provides her judges with a transition between the introduction and her first point: "But first, [we turn] to the resistance within the Soviet Union . . . ." With this first point, she uses an external source, Richard Nixon, to suggest that the Soviet bureaucracy would prevent policies of peace. She strengthens this point by making use of a second external source taken from *U.S. News and World Report:* "As *U.S. News and World Report* tells us (May the thirteenth), it is the Soviet bureaucracy that is the biggest obstacle to true peace within the entire world." She concludes her first point in this manner: ". . . as a result [of the Soviet Bureaucracy] the free world cannot count on Gorbachev because Gorbachev cannot count on his own people." This conclusion reminds the judges of the extemp question (Can the free world count on Gorbachev to take peace off the list of impossible dreams?) and provides a transition between her first and second points.

Gorbachev remains a threat to democracy

In her second point, Sprague establishes another reason why Gorbachev should not be trusted: "But the second reason why . . . the free world can't count on Mikhail Gorbachev to . . . give peace to the entire world is due to the fact that he remains a constant threat to democracies around the world." She does a nice job, once again, connecting her points to the question. Remember that the question reads "Can the free world count on Gorbachev . . . ." By using the language of the extemp question in the points she makes, she keeps her focus on her main theme.

She used two external sources, Richard Nixon's *1989: Victory Without War* and a *U.S. News and World Report* article, to build her first point. She uses two external sources to build her second point as well. To prove that Gorbachev remains a constant threat to democracies around the world, she states:

> The columnist John Hughes explained in the *Christian Science Monitor* on May the twenty-third that Communism is still a threat to the United States because Mikhail Gorbachev continues to give economic and military support to such nations as Cuba and Nicaragua. At the same time he also poses a threat to Africa where his constant domination of the Ethiopian government and active involvement within Southern Africa also makes it very difficult for fledgling democracies to exist there. And if we look toward southeast Asia we find the same philosophy through his constant [support of] the North Korean government.

With this point, Plano provides proof for her answer to the extemp question. The details she offers are strong. Because of Gorbachev's policies, communism remains a threat in Cuba, Nicaragua, Ethiopia, Southern Africa, and North Korea. Judges look carefully at the proof you provide for your points, and the more detailed your proof is, the stronger your points are.

To strengthen this second point, she states:

> According to *Current History* magazine of September of 1988, [Gorbachev] remains a threat to Western Europe. For although the recent agreements have existed between the Soviet Union and the United States, he will never completely withdraw his troops from Eastern Europe, and as a result, the importance of NATO remains constant.

By using two well respected external sources, *The Christian Science Monitor* and *Current History,* Sprague gives her judges good reasons to accept her position on Gorbachev. The third reason she presents in favor of her answer builds upon the first two points.

Gorbachev's economic imperialism will prevent peace

The third reason she offers for answering "no" to the extemp question is based on three external sources and conclusions drawn from these sources. In developing this third point, she states:

> But the third and final reason why the free world can't count on Gorbachev to take peace off the list of impossible dreams is because of his

continued economic imperialism throughout the world. Unfortunately for most nations, it has been a Marxist form of economic imperialism. Groucho Marx, that is.

This is a clear and a clever statement of her third point. Once again, she restates the question and her conclusion. The third point, about economic imperialism, is well defined. Even more important, however, is her use of humor. There is no doubt that she is against communism. Her reference to Groucho Marx, the famous comedian known for his absurd humor, cleverly underscores her point that Marxism is a bad economic system.

She uses three external sources to establish her third point, and provides her judges with clear explanations of her perspective:

> As former presidential aide Brzezinski writes in his most recent book, *The Grand Failure,* . . . because the economy in the Soviet Union is failing, Mikhail Gorbachev wants to take down the economies of all the other nations that he can possibly find.

This external source provides her with Gorbachev's motivations. She continues building her third point with proof from *Newsweek* and *World Monitor* magazines:

> On October the seventeenth, *Newsweek* magazine tells us that the recent involvement of the Soviet Union in Southeast Asia is purely to help the Soviet Union's own economy. And he is trying to impress his own economic opinions onto these nations. *World Monitor* tells us in April of this year that the same holds true for Eastern Europe. For although these nations are trying to reform their economies to a more democratic style, the Soviet version of reform is only harming these nations as it brings the economies into a plummeting abyss.

Sprague provided well-supported evidence for her third point. She concludes by noting that Gorbachev has reduced Soviet military involvement: "He is increasing economic intervention and continuing the communist doctrine of imperialism." With the establishment of her third point, she moves to her conclusion.

Conclusion

In the conclusion of an extemp speech, the speaker should return to the question he or she selected. The judge expects you to maintain your focus on the extemp question throughout the duration of your speech. The conclusion should show the judge how all the points presented in the introduction and the body of the speech provide strong proof for the answer to the extemp question.

In this speech, Suzy Sprague reviews the three points presented in the body of her speech and returns to her introduction and the P.T. Barnum "Happy Family" story:

> So although it might appear on the outside that the recent withdrawal of the Soviet Union from Afghanistan and Angola . . . is truly going to help peace for the United States and the entire free world, if we delve into the reality of the situation, we will find that this is not the truth for three reasons. First, [there] is the lack of support in the Soviet Union. [Second], because he remains a threat to democracy. And finally, because of his continued economic imperialism. Although the appearance might be one thing, if we delve into the reality, we find that the reality is very similar to P.T. Barnum's happy family.

Sprague includes the elements of a conclusion. First, with the first sentence of the conclusion, she reminds the judges of the question that was the subject of her speech. Second, she reviews the three reasons developed in the body of her speech that support her answer. Third, she returns to her introduction when she referred to the reality-appearance distinction and the P.T. Barnum happy family story.

Judges' Reactions

As you can tell, there are many good reasons why Suzy Sprague won the national championship with this speech. While the judge's reactions and ballots are not available, can you identify the reasons for the judges' favorable response to this speech?

Overall, the speech met the rules of the event, and developed a well-supported answer to the extemp question.

Sprague directly answers the question she selected. She does not shift to a topic or an idea unrelated to the question: "Can the free world count on Gorbachev to take peace off the list of impossible dreams?" She follows the rules of the event, organizes her speech, provides adequate support for the speech, and delivers her speech with clarity and occasional humor. Some strengths of this speech stand out.

First, Ms. Sprague develops an intelligent and a well-supported answer to the question. She does more than rely on one *Time* magazine article. In fact, she relies on seven external sources. Two of these seven external sources are books (Richard Nixon's, *1989: Victory Without War* and Zbigniew Brzezinski's *The Grand Failure*). The other five sources are magazines and a newspaper: *Newsweek, World Monitor, U.S. News and World Report, Current History, Christian Science Monitor*.

Second, the organization of this speech is strong. Her introduction provides a theme that she uses to connect the three points developed in the body of the speech. The sayings and stories in the introduction reappear in her conclusion. She uses brief but effective transitions between her points, and her speech has a strong sense of purpose and direction.

There are some weaknesses in this speech as well. First, nearly all the books and articles she uses were written by conservative authors. Extemp speakers should read widely and draw their ideas from across the political spectrum; this speech relied too heavily on conservative sources. Had she included sources from liberal and progressive authors, her speech would have reflected a broader vision.

Second, although she does answer the question, she does not say what the United States and the "free world" should do to counter the Soviet economic threat. Many judges would be curious to know. She does say that Gorbachev and the Soviet threat remain threats to world peace. If this is so, what should policy makers do to counter this threat?

Regardless of these weaknesses, the speech was a success. It was well organized and presented, and it offers a good model for your efforts. As you work to create introductions, bodies, and conclusions for your speeches, examine this speech for clues and insights into how you might put your extemp speeches together.

Practicing Extemp Speaking

You now know the rules of extemp speaking and have analyzed model extemp speeches. With these rules and models in mind, you can now develop a system for practicing extemp speaking. Having a system helps you prepare for the forensic tournament and for the extemp round.

Practice writing extemp questions and then outlining responses

Many extemp questions are taken from the headlines of newspapers and news magazines. You can anticipate the questions you might face at tournaments by reading the headlines of local and international newspapers and the headlines in *Time, Newsweek,* and *U.S. News and World Report.* On occasion, you might see an extemp question that is taken directly from the title of a *Newsweek, Time,* or *U.S. News and World Report* article. After you have written some extemp questions, practice outlining answers to these questions.

The two examples that follow on page 102 would be outlined as follows: By outlining responses to potential extemp questions, you will be better prepared for the tournament setting.

As you read books, magazines, and journal articles, look for evidence and proof you can use in your speeches. In addition, it is crucial that you create and maintain an extemp file.

Question: Will the Arabs and Israelis achieve a lasting peace?
Answer: The recent peace agreement will bring lasting peace to the region.
Point One: The Israelis want peace now.
Point Two: The Arabs want peace now.
Point Three: The international community wants peace now.

Question: "Can the free world count on Gorbachev to take peace off the list of impossible dreams?"
Answer: No.
Point One: Opposition within the Soviet Union
Point Two: Gorbachev remains a threat to democracy
Point Three: Gorbachev's continued economic imperialism

Building an Extemp File

As you read earlier in this chapter, an extemp file contains articles and other materials on the extemp questions you might face. You and your teammates should work together to create a comprehensive and a well-organized extemp file. Your forensics team may have subscriptions to journals and magazines that you can use to find articles for your extemp files.

Most extemp files are arranged topically. If you choose a question about the Middle East, you can consult your extemp file on the Middle East to get current and useful information. With this information in hand, you can create a carefully documented speech.

Practice your Extemp Speeches

Your extemp outlines and the work you do on the extemp file help you prepare for the forensic tournament. You also need to practice your extemp speeches, both in front of others and when you are alone. The old adage "Practice makes perfect" applies here, for your practice sessions should be as realistic as possible.

You can practice extemp speeches when you are alone. Select a question that might appear among your choices when you compete at the next tournament. After consulting your extemp file, create an outline of your speech. After you have finished with the outline, build an introduction, body, and conclusion for the speech. Then, stand and present the speech as you would if you were speaking to a judge.

You might choose to audio or video tape your speech to see how you appear to others. Make sure to follow the rules of the event and, in particular, to obey the time limitations. Then review your performance to identify the strengths of your speeches and areas that need attention.

You should also speak in front of your friends and your forensics teacher. Your friends can provide reactions to your delivery, analysis, and presentation. Your forensics teacher can point out the strengths and weaknesses of your speech.

Read Your Ballots and Record Suggestions for Improvement

You already know that you should read your ballots carefully because they contain useful suggestions from your judges that you can use to improve your speeches. Your friends and forensics teacher can also help you to improve, and you may wish to record their suggestions in a notebook. Keeping track of these suggestions is a good way to improve your impromptu speaking.

The checklist on page 104 will help you prepare and practice for competition in extemporaneous speaking.

CONCLUSION

Competition in extemporaneous speaking should help you develop the ability to speak about current events. Extemporaneous speaking is designed to help you learn more about international, national, and cultural issues. The habits you develop as a successful extemporaneous speaker will make you a better student and a more responsible citizen.

Checklist

Checklist for Extemporaneous Speaking

Before Practice

1. Know the educational aims of extemporaneous speaking.
2. Know the rules of extemporaneous speaking.
3. Understand what will happen in the extemporaneous round.
4. Understand what judges expect of extemporaneous speakers.
5. Visualize the steps you should follow in selecting a topic.
6. Understand how to develop an answer from the extemp question.
7. Know how to develop points that support the question.
8. Develop introductions, transitions, and conclusions.
9. Consider models of outstanding extemporaneous speaking.
10. Establish practice schedules.

During Practice

11. Practice by yourself.
12. Practice in front of friends.
13. Practice in front of your forensics teacher.

At the Tournament

14. Select the best topic.
15. Organize your speech around a theme and two or three points.

After the tournament

16. After the tournament, read your ballots and use the comments to improve.

SECTION THREE

Unlimited Preparation Events

> Original Oratory

> Expository Speaking

> Radio Commentary

> After-dinner Speaking

Unlike impromptu and extemporaneous speaking, the events discussed in the next four chapters allow you an unlimited amount of time to prepare your speech. In addition, you may choose the topics for these speeches. If you compete in these events, you will have time to conduct extensive research on your topic and to practice delivering your speeches over the course of the forensics season.

The oratory event is among the oldest of all forensics activities. The rules of the event require competitors to identify and discuss a problem of social significance. Many orators advocate a solution for the problem they identify. The best orations are well documented with external sources and are delivered with passion. The habits and skills you learn in this event can be applied to almost any speaking situation.

The expository event is intended to inform an audience about something. Unlike the oratory event, the speaker does not set out to persuade. The topic of an expository speech should interest the audience. Like the oratory event, the best expository speeches are well documented with external sources and are energetically delivered. Many competitors use visual aids in this event. Visual aids help the audience picture the subject of the expository speech. The informative event helps you develop teaching and leadership skills.

The radio commentary event is structured to resemble television and radio news commentaries. Radio commentaries are to be original analyses of current events. Competitors in this event prepare a script and read their commentary from this script. Because the event is intended to resemble the conditions of broadcast journalism, competitors must finish their commentaries at a definite time (usually between 4:45 and 5:15 minutes). Good radio commentaries develop an idea or two with insightful analysis and adequate support from external sources.

The after-dinner speaking event is also known as speech to entertain or special occasion speaking. As the second name suggests, after-dinner speaking is intended to entertain the audience during a special event. While tasteful humor is the key technique of an after-dinner speaker, the speaker should present a serious theme or subject. The best after-dinner speeches are witty, sparkling works that enlighten and entertain.

Participation in the four unlimited preparation events should help you develop habits and skills you can use in almost all speaking situations. You should, at some point in your forensics experience, participate in all of the events. Regardless of the speaking situation, you need to be persuasive, informative, analytical, and humorous.

CHAPTER SIX

Original Oratory

The educational aim of the original oratory event is to allow you to develop a persuasive argument about a problem you believe is important. Judges expect you to select a socially significant problem, and many judges anticipate that you will offer a solution to the problem. Judges also expect you to offer proof to support your arguments, and to present a well-organized and delivered speech.

The best orators balance and integrate examples with generalizations, emotional appeals with logical analysis. Most judges agree that the best orators also use an inspired and, on occasion, a dramatic speaking approach. To succeed in this event, you must understand what persuades an audience.

The rules of this event are simple and straightforward. The vast majority of student orators follow these rules without any problem. Those who do violate the rules sometimes go over the time limit (ten minutes), fail to provide the proper citations to quoted materials, or exceed the amount of quoted material allowed in this event. Make sure you understand and follow the rules of this event.

Rules of Competition and the Original Oratory Round

The rules of the original oratory event may vary; however, many tournaments require the following:

Guidelines

Rules of Original Oratory

Topic Areas: Students may select any topic that is significant. Many orators use the problem-solution format, but this organizational pattern is not required. The speech must be the original creation of the student. Many tournaments impose a 150 quoted-word limitation on the student orator. In other words, original oratories must not contain over 150 quoted words.

Length: Most tournaments allow ten (10) minutes with a thirty-second grace period. At the speaker's option, a timekeeper or judge may use cards or hand signals to alert the speaker to the time remaining. For example, the timekeeper may hold up four fingers at four minutes left, three fingers at three minutes left, and so on.

Procedures: Many tournaments employ the following procedures:

1. A manuscript of the speech must be available to the judge and to other appropriate individuals. A bibliography of the external sources used in the speech should be included.
2. Memorization of the speech is allowed.
3. Other tournament-specific rules may apply.

These rules are enforced by the judges and the tournament director and staff. Competitors who violate the rules risk having their rankings and ratings reduced. Pay close attention to the rules for original oratory for each tournament you attend because they may differ. Always make sure you and your forensics teacher have manuscript copies of your oration, that your speech does not include more than 150 quoted words, and that your speech is less than ten minutes and thirty seconds in length.

The Original Oratory Round

The tournament schedule on page 110 lists the times you are to present your oratory.

According to the schedule, original oratory is a pattern B event. You will present your oration three times on Friday, at 1:30, 5:30, and 7:00. If you do well in these three rounds, you may present your oratory at 10:30 (semifinals) and at 1:30 (finals) on Saturday.

When you arrive at the tournament, you need to find the area or room where the tournament staff is posting. Find out early where your rounds are scheduled to take place.

Let us assume that you are speaker two in the first round of novice original oratory.

You need to find Deady Hall. Try to arrive ten to fifteen minutes before the round starts. When the judge and other competitors have arrived, speaker one (Palm from Westbrook) will be the first to speak. While Palm and the competitors speak, be a good audience member. Always pay attention to the speaker and the speech, and provide positive and warm reactions whenever possible.

As you listen to your competitors, try to identify what they do well and what you can learn from their orations. You might ask yourself: How do they introduce their oratory? What organizational pattern do they use? What sources of proof do they offer to establish their argument? The answers to these questions may inspire you to consider changes in your oratory.

Most orators use the problem-solution organizational pattern. This organizational pattern encourages you to identify a significant concern that is important to you and your audience. After you identify the problem, propose a solution to it. As in any event, you must offer good support for the claims you make in your speech. A successful oration includes support from the best external sources, and reasoned analysis. As always, your audience and your judges have expectations about what you should and should not do with your original oratory.

Judges' Expectations of the Original Oratory Speaker

Judges of the original oratory event use common standards when they evaluate student competitors. At a minimum, judges want to hear oratories that are socially significant, well supported with internal analysis and external sources,

SAMPLE SPEECH TOURNAMENT SCHEDULE

PATTERN A EVENTS
Extemp
Radio Commentary
Expos
Serious Interp

PATTERN B EVENTS
Impromptu
Oratory
Humorous Interp
ADS

THURSDAY, Feb. 27
  11:00 - 12:00 Registration
  12:30 - 1:50 SENIOR LD debate, Round I
   2:00 - 3:20 JUNIOR LD and ALL CX debate, Round I
   3:30 - 4:00 ALL DEBATE, Round II
   5:00 - 6:20 ALL DEBATE, Round III
   6:30 - 7:20 Break
   7:30 - 9:00 ALL DEBATE, Round IV

FRIDAY, Feb. 28
   8:00 - 9:30 CX Debate, Round V
   8:30 - 9:30 Registration for schools with IEs only
  10:00   EXTEMP DRAW
  10:30 - 11:30 Pattern A, Round I
  12:00   EXTEMP DRAW
  12:30 - 1:30 Pattern A, Round II
   1:30 - 2:30 Pattern B, Round I
   2:45 - 3:30 LD Debate, Round V (both JR & SR)
   4:00   EXTEMP DRAW
   4:30 - 5:30 Pattern A, Round III
   5:30 - 6:30 Pattern B, Round II
   6:30 - 7:00 Break
   7:00 - 8:00 Pattern B, Round III
   8:15 - 9:45 ALL DEBATE, Round IV
   9:00   IE Semifinal Postings

SATURDAY, Feb. 29
   7:30   UNIVERSITY CENTER Opens
   7:45   Debate Outrounds Postings
   8:00 - 9:30 ALL DEBATE, Octo-finals
  10:00   EXTEMP DRAW
  10:30 - 11:30 IE Semifinals, Pattern A & Pattern B
  12:00 - 1:00 ALL DEBATE, Quarter-finals
   1:00   EXTEMP DRAW
   1:30 - 2:30 IE Finals, Pattern A & Pattern B
   3:00 - 4:30 ALL DEBATE, Semifinals
   5:30 - 7:00 ALL DEBATE, Finals
   8:00   Awards

Checklist

Postings
Original Oratory
Novice Division
Round One
Judge: Watanabe
Room: 101 Deady Hall

Speaker One: Palm, Westbrook team
Speaker Two: YOU, Jefferson team
Speaker Three: Durrant, Lakeview team
Speaker Four: Jackson, Wright team
Speaker Five: Trond, Sanford team
Speaker Six: Boyd, Kennedy team

Guidelines

Organizational Pattern
I. Introduction
    A. Presentation of problem
    B. Presentation of possible solutions
    C. Preview of Body
       Transition

II. The problem
    A. Identification of problem
    B. Explanation of the nature of the problem

III. Possible Solutions
    A. Possible solutions offered
    B. Possible solutions evaluated
    C. Best solution proposed

IV. Conclusion
    A. Review and summary
    B. Call to Action

and delivered in a conversational style. As you write and present your oratories, keep these expectations in mind.

Most judges have at least six questions they will ask when they evaluate your speech: Did you follow the rules? Did you identify a significant problem? Did you identify a workable solution to the problem? Did you organize your speech? Did you provide adequate support for your points? Did you deliver your speech clearly and eloquently? Let us take each of these questions in turn.

Did you follow the rules?

Judges expect you to know and to follow the rules of this event. Depending on the violation, judges may penalize you for failing to comply with the rules. While some tournaments have different sets of rules for oratory, you must always stay within the time limit of ten minutes with a thirty-second grace period. In most tournaments you may not quote more than 150 words, and you must make a manuscript of your speech available to the judge and tournament staff.

The rules for district and state tournaments may differ from those used by in school-sponsored tournaments. For example, the oratory you present at a district tournament may need to be the same oratory you present at the state tournament. Make sure to check with your forensics teacher for the rules for individual tournaments.

Did you identify a significant problem?

Judges expect you to choose a problem of social significance. If you want to persuade your judge, you must select a topic that will interest your judge. A socially significant topic is one that your audience views as important. Many judges prefer that student orators speak to issues of national consequence.

At the same time, keep in mind that many judges have heard thousands of oratories on issues of social significance. These judges may be weary of issues like capital punishment, abortion, or drunk driving. Although some judges may be weary of these topics, don't automatically avoid choosing them. Rather, if you do select a topic like capital punishment or abortion, try to say something novel about it.

Did you identify a workable solution to the problem?

The rules of the event do not require you to present a solution to the problem that is the focus of your speech. However, many judges do expect a problem-solution format. Your solution should help reduce the frequency and the severity of the problem you identify. Judges expect your solution to be workable, affordable, and without undesirable side effects. They want to know why the solution you propose has not been adopted already.

Here are some examples of how judges might evaluate the workability of a solution. Suppose you argue that Americans own too many handguns. You also say that handgun ownership leads to many violent deaths each year. To solve the problem, you believe that the government should not allow citizens to own handguns. Clearly, judges will expect you to demonstrate that the government could realistically outlaw handgun ownership. They will also expect you to prove that your solution—outlawing handgun ownership—would reduce the number of deaths by handguns. Judges apply similar expectations to any solution you might offer.

Did you organize your speech?

Judges expect you to organize the ideas and proof you use to construct your oratory. Beginning student orators should use the traditional problem-solution method. The great advantage of this method is that it is simple and fits most subjects. Once you understand this approach, you can use it to create a clear and persuasive speech.

Remember there are other organizational patterns that you might use. Given the topic, problem, and solution you develop, you may wish to use a topical organizational pattern, a cause-effect approach, a chronological approach, or another organizational method. Work with your forensics teacher to select and apply the most appropriate organizational structure for your oration.

Did you provide adequate support for your points?

Your judges expect you to have a good understanding of the problem and solution you select for your oratory. Such an understanding is a result of extensive library research. The library research you conduct on your topic should lead you to the best and most recent sources on your subject. By relying on the best sources, you can create an oratory that meets the judges' expectations.

Judges listen for the evidence when you make a point. Be sure to qualify the evidence you present in the body of your speech. For example, if you say that restrictions on gun ownership will reduce handgun violence, then you will need to have evidence to support this claim. Your evidence might be an expert who offers concrete proof that a ban on handgun ownership would reduce crime.

Finally, the best student orators create speeches that draw upon many varied sources. Judges tend to give lower rankings to orators who base their claims on one or two articles or sources. Orations based on several books and articles tend to be better received than those that depend on one *Newsweek* article and one *Time* article.

Did you deliver your speech clearly and eloquently?

Judges will reward you for presenting your speech with clarity and in a conversational mode. Talking with, not at, the judges tends to improve your score. At the same time, most judges appreciate an energetic and engaging delivery. The best orators maintain a balanced delivery, adjusting their volume, pace, and tone according to the judge, the room, and the situation.

Some orators go overboard and are too loud, too energetic. Others speak too softly and fall into a monotone. Most judges enjoy and look for a style and presentation that is moderate and in control. They will lower your scores if you are overly dramatic or, at the other extreme, if you don't seem to care about the speech.

Creating an Original Oratory

With judges' expectations in mind, let us move to the steps you need to take in creating and presenting your oratory:

These guidelines are designed to help you select, develop, and present your oratory. Each step is important if you are to create a persuasive speech.

Brainstorm topics for your oratory

You need to find a topic for your oratory that appeals to you and your judges. Your oratory reflects your personality and values. As you select a topic for your oratory, try to pick a problem that is significant and intriguing, and one that offers you the opportunity to say something new.

The process of brainstorming is designed to provoke a wide-ranging discussion between you, your forensics teacher, and your teammates on possible speech topics. While brainstorming, search for any topic that sounds even remotely interesting. At this stage, you should write down all the topics that come to mind. Let us say the brainstorming produced the topics in the following checklist.

As you examine these topics, notice that several are the focus of continual discussion: abortion, capital punishment, the electoral college. While these topics are important, let us say that you find the lottery and urban gangs the most interesting topics. After researching both topics, you decide to speak about the lottery. You discover, as a result of your research, that your state has decided to use the lottery to fund education. You also discover that lotteries

---

Guidelines

Steps in the Creation and Presentation of the Original Oratory

Before the Tournament

1. Brainstorm topics and subjects for your oratory.
2. Conduct research on the topic you have selected.
3. Identify a theme and organize your research into a problem-solution format.
4. Write the first draft of your speech.
5. Practice your speech.

During the Tournament

6. Present your speech to your judges.
7. Listen to the other speakers.
8. Make modifications in your speech as necessary.

After the Speech and Tournament

9. After the tournament, read your ballots and use the comments made by your judges to improve.
10. Conduct additional research and practice your speech.

Checklist

Results of the Brainstorming Session

Abortion	Urban gangs	Drug abuse
Capital punishment	Palestinian refugees	Medical system crisis
Euthanasia	Gun control	Energy crisis
Electoral college	Recycling	Lotteries
Teen pregnancy	Sewage crisis	Cruelty to animals

---

have some undesirable consequences that, you believe, make them a bad policy option.

After talking with your teammates and your forensics coach about the topics from the brainstorming session, you are persuaded that the lottery is the best subject to pursue. Your next step is to conduct extensive and thorough research on the lottery.

Conduct research on the topic you select

Once you have selected the lottery topic, you need to discover books, articles, and other materials on the topic. Read books and articles from a number of authors and sources representing a broad spectrum of perspectives. You should read articles that both celebrate and condemn the lottery as a money-raising vehicle. As you read these materials, you may change your opinion about the lottery. The articles you read may persuade you that the lottery is an ultimate benefit to society.

Read the literature on your persuasive topic with an open mind. Your oratory will be stronger if you understand the opposing side and can see that there may be reasonable positions different from your own. However, you need to take a stance. Do so after you have discovered solid proof, drawn from external sources, in favor of your position.

As you read books and articles on the topic of your oratory, look for quotations you might use in the body of your speech. You may use these quotations to establish a point or to bolster one of your claims. Record these quotations on notecards. The sources of the quotations should be recorded on your notecards and in your bibliography. Take care when you record quotations from external sources, for you are responsible for not altering or distorting the authors' meanings. After you have enough research to make a strong argument, you need to organize your ideas and your research.

Identify a theme and organize your research into a problem-solution format

Once you pinpoint a topic and gather enough evidence from external sources to form an opinion, you need to identify a central thought or theme and then organize it. That central thought or theme forms the core of your speech. For example, the core of the lottery speech might be the following: The lottery promotes gambling, and gambling is destructive to society. You could build your speech on this central thought.

You need to organize your central thought and research into a persuasive pattern. The most popular organizational pattern is the problem-solution format. The problem-solution format shown on page 117 might be used to organize the lottery speech.

The problem-solution organizational pattern should be used to divide the speech and place ideas and quotations in their proper place. Note how the pattern is sequential, moving from the problem to the solution. You can arrange the ideas and quotations you gather in this sequential order. At this

---

Guidelines

Problem-Solution Organizational Pattern

Central thought: The lottery promotes gambling, and gambling is destructive to society.

1. A problem, concern, or issue is identified.
    Example: Lotteries promote gambling. Gambling is destructive to society.

2. The nature of the problem, concern, or issues is outlined.
    Example: Gambling is addictive, exploits the lower class, and promotes organized crime.

3. Possible solutions are offered.
    Example: Governments should not use lotteries to raise revenue.

4. Possible solutions are evaluated.
    Example: In comparison to revenues raised by the lottery, sin taxes (taxes on cigarettes, alcohol) are better sources of government revenue.

5. The best solution is proposed.
    Example: Lotteries should not be used to raise governmental revenue; sin taxes are better options.

---

stage in the creation of an oratory, you need to develop a detailed outline for your speech. With the outline in hand, you can write the first draft of your speech.

Write the first draft of your speech

Most experienced orators write many drafts of their speeches. The first draft should not be the draft you use at the tournament. Use your outline, with the central thought and the problem-solution format, to write your speech. As with any speech, your oratory should have an introduction, a body, and a conclusion.

Experienced speech writers keep their audience in mind as they write their speeches. You should do the same. Adapt the introduction, body, and conclusion of your speeches to your audience. Your goal is to persuade them. Good speech writers think hard about what means of persuasion will win over their audiences.

Write the introduction with your audience in mind. The introduction should give your audience a good reason to listen to the rest of your speech.

Most audiences will listen to a speech if the topic is of social and personal importance and interest. Begin by explaining the significance of the subject in a way that will capture the audience's attention. Most important, your introduction should contain the central thought or theme of your speech.

In the body of the speech, outline the problem and suggest some possible solutions; present evidence and analysis to support your opionions. As with any other speech, the body of your oratory should be designed to advance a central thought or theme.

In concluding your speech, you need to summarize and review. Most orators use the conclusion to call their audiences to action. If your description of the problem is vivid and compelling and your proposed solution seems workable, your audience will want to act on your solution. The conclusion of the speech should be designed to inspire your audience to act.

Remember that your first draft should not be your final draft. In fact, your speech should go through many drafts. When you conduct more research and present your speech to a variety of audiences, you will discover that sections and sentences in the first draft need to be modified. Your speech should be in a constant state of evolution.

It is crucial to continue to modify your speech over the course of the forensics season. Judges provide many good comments on how you can improve your speech. Take the time to modify your speech on the basis of these suggestions, and you will become a better speaker as a result.

Practice your speech

You need to establish a practice schedule to determine whether listeners find your speech persuasive. Take these practice sessions seriously, and make them resemble the tournament environment as much as possible. Your should practice alone, in front of your friends, and with your forensics teacher.

Use the responses of these and other audiences to improve your speech. The responses of these audiences give you important clues about how the judge will receive your speech at the tournament. Your forensics teacher can give you good advice on how to adapt your speech to your audiences. You should seek out critiques of your speeches, for the more constructive criticism you receive, the stronger your speech will be.

Present your speech to your judges

By the time you arrive at the tournament, your speech should be in good order. You have at least two or three opportunities to present your speech to judges. While you may have practiced your speech many times, make sure that you deliver the speech as if it were the first time. Judge give you higher scores if you appear to be sincerely interested in your speech.

Don't be too concerned about mistakes you might make. Often, the judge will never know you forgot a sentence or a paragraph of your speech unless you reveal the error through your facial expression or posture. If you do make a mistake, don't stop speaking. Many speakers, both beginning and experienced, make mistakes. The goal is to continue speaking and to finish making your point.

Listen to the other speakers

Before and after you speak, listen carefully to the speeches of your competitors. As you know, you should strive to be a good audience member. This means treating the other speakers as you would want them to treat you. If you disagree with the speaker's perspective, do not give the speaker negative nonverbal reactions. Remain a civil and a polite audience member.

You can learn much from the speeches delivered by your competitors. You should take notes on what they do well and how they organize and present their speeches. Their speeches can provide you clear examples of effective and not-so-effective oratories. After the tournament is over, you may wish to use these examples as models for improving your speech.

Modify your speech as necessary

Your speech should be in a constant state of evolution. You may decide after your first round that some minor changes need to be made. For example, you may decide to change the wording of the introduction or to use a different piece of proof for one of the points in the solution section. You should, however, wait until the tournament is over to make major changes in your speech because you need time to think through any major alterations in your speech. Make sure to talk with your forensics teacher or an experienced team member if you think your oratory needs significant change.

After the tournament, read your ballots and use your judges' comments to improve

When the tournament is over, your forensics teacher will give you the ballots your judges wrote in reaction to your speech. These ballots will tell you how your judges ranked and rated you in comparison to your competition, and will record what your judges felt were the strengths and weaknesses of your speech. With the help of your forensics teacher, you should read these ballots and use the comments to revise and improve your speech.

Seek out patterns and recurring statements in the ballots. If, for example, all the judges commend you for your research, then you know that your evidence is solid. If two of your judges suggest you could use a more energetic delivery, then use your practice sessions to focus on developing a more energetic style.

Your ballots should be of great value to you, but use them with care. Your forensics teacher will help you to discriminate between helpful comments and those that may not be as useful. Because you may have the same judges at the next tournament, you need to read your ballots for insight into the feelings and beliefs of your judges. With their views in mind, work to revise and better adapt your speech to your judges.

Conduct additional research and practice your speech

Your speech should change after every tournament. Some sections of the speech may remain the same; others will need to be slightly altered or completely changed. You should conduct additional research and practice even if you took first place at a tournament. Additional research and practice keep your speech current and your presentation sharp.

Judges give great weight to speakers who use the most recent evidence and sources. The external sources you discover on your topic during your outing to the library may be outdated after the first tournament. Use the most timely and recent information you can find in your speeches. Some speakers read the newspaper every day to find the most recent evidence and proof for their oratories. You might do the same. The libraries you visit should have the most recent periodical literature on your topic. The best orators know they need to conduct research on their topic throughout the forensics season.

You should also continue to practice your speech throughout the forensics season. As you practice, identify specific improvements you wish to make. After delivering the same speech a number of times, some speakers lose interest in the speech. Revising and updating the content of your speech will also help improve the delivery of your speech. Make sure that the delivery of your speech is full of energy and commitment. You can retain the needed energy through your commitment to constantly polishing your speech.

A Model Oratory

You now know the rules of the oratory event and the steps you must take in writing and presenting an oratory. This section examines a model oratory delivered by Betsy Heffernan on the subject of improper sewage disposal. In this speech, Ms. Heffernan uses the problem-solution organizational pattern and provides her judges with strong evidence in support of her central theme.

The guidelines show her organizational pattern. This speech displays all the components of an oratory. As you consider the parts of this speech, think how you might use it as a model.

Guidelines

Organizational Pattern

I.   Introduction
     Presentation of central theme or idea: Improper sewage disposal
     is destroying our environment. Current systems of sewage dis-
     posal can be made more effective and efficient.

II. Review of Body
     A. Damage produced by improper sewage disposal
     B. Why improper sewage disposal occurs
     C. What should be done to improve sewage disposal

III. Transition
     A. The problem: Damage done by improper sewage disposal
     B. The cause: Why improper sewage disposal occurs

IV. Possible Solutions: Solutions to the improper sewage disposal
     problem

V.   Conclusion: Need for action on improper sewage disposal
     A. Review and summary
     B. Call to action

The Introduction

The introduction of an oratory should provide the audience with a good reason
for listening to the speech. An effective introduction should highlight why the
topic is a significant social and political concern. Ideally, the introduction
develops an image that can be used to bind together the introduction, the
body, and the conclusion of the speech. The introduction should also contain
the central thought or theme of the speech. Finally, the introduction should
preview and provide a transition to the body of the speech. As you will see,
the introduction of this speech accomplishes these objectives:

> During our nation's struggle for independence, the citizens of Boston
> were hailed as heroes for dumping tea into Boston Harbor. But not to
> be outdone, many modern day Bostonians are also dumping things into
> the harbor: five-thousand gallons of waste every second. The New En-
> gland Aquarium of Boston states that since 1900, Bostonians have
> dumped enough human sewage into the harbor to cover the entire state
> of Massachusetts chest deep in sludge. Unfortunately, Boston isn't
> alone. All over the country, bays, rivers, and lakes are literally becoming

cesspools. Improper sewage disposal is having widespread effects on our environment, our health, and our quality of life.

Ms. Heffernan gives her audience several reasons to listen: her intriguing reference to the Boston Tea Party, her description of current sewage disposal in Boston harbor, her use of an external source (The New England Aquarium of Boston), and her statement that Boston is not unique in its sewage disposal problem. Because the sewage problem is not limited to Boston, audience members from other parts of the country also should be concerned. Ms. Heffernan previews the body of her speech in the following manner:

> In order to understand how serious these effects are, we'll first look at the damage that improper sewage disposal causes to our environment and to us. [Then we will consider] why this damage is occurring, and finally, [consider] ways that we can improve our efficiency of our sewage treatment facilities. Examination of these areas will reveal the extent of this problem and the urgent need that it be solved.

With this introduction, she establishes a central thought, a clear outline, and a transition to the body of the speech. In the first section of the body, she chronicles the impact of improper sewage disposal on the environment.

The Body

She devotes the body of her speech to three points. First, she documents the destructive impact of improper sewage disposal on the environment. Second, she explains why the problem of improper sewage disposal has not been addressed. Finally, she presents some solutions to the problem.

The Problem: Improper sewage disposal creates environmental disasters

The problem-solution organizational format places the reason for concern at the beginning of the speech. By highlighting and describing a serious and significant problem, the audience of the speech is ready for a solution. In her first point, Ms. Heffernan documents the widespread and detrimental impact of improper sewage disposal. She does a particularly nice job of weaving national statistics together with concrete and local examples:

> Our oceans, lakes, and rivers have incredible cleaning powers. And for centuries, they've been able to withstand the onslaught of billions of gallons of waste. However, according to the Environmental Protection Agency, the total amount of sewage effluent has doubled in the last decade to 7½ million tons per year. The amount of sewage that is dumped into the water is simply too much for aquatic fish and plants to bear. The *New York Times* of September 13, 1988, explains that the

greatest threat posed to water life from sewage is the nutrients found in the sewage, mainly phosphorous and nitrogen. Once introduced into the water, these nutrients fertilize the aquatic plants, creating massive algae blooms. When this algae dies and decomposes, it robs the water of oxygen, suffocating the fish and shellfish. These oxygen-depleted waters are appropriately called "dead zones."

In this segment of her speech, she has clearly and vividly explained the significance of the problem and why sewage leads to the suffocation of fish and shellfish. This passage is particularly strong for several reasons. First, she identifies the source of her information: the Environmental Protection Agency and an article in the September 13, 1988, edition of the *New York Times*. By identifying her sources, she demonstrates to her judges her knowledge of the subject. Second, she provides her judges with specifics. Rather than just suggesting that the amount of sewage in the system has increased, she quantifies the increase for the judge ("total amount of sewage effluent has doubled in the last decade to 7½ million tons per year"). Third, she provides a remarkably vivid account of the chain reaction set off by sewage disposals.

After establishing the significance of the sewage problem and how it creates "dead zones," she continues in this fashion:

> *Newsweek* magazine, August 1, 1988, states that these dead zones can be found in the water off every major city on each coast. And at the south of the Mississippi there is a dead zone measuring 3,000 square miles. The Environmental Protection Agency contends that once a water area becomes oxygen-depleted, at best it can be years before it is able to support life again.

Note, again, how she cites the sources of her information (*Newsweek* and the EPA) and provides a vivid and clear image of a dead zone south of Mississippi. She then moves from dead zones to the impact of sewage on fish:

> Sewage is also thought to contribute to the increasing number of diseased fish. *Time* magazine of August 1, 1988, states that since 1986 New York and New Jersey have dumped ten million tons of sludge in an area known as dump site number six. Located 106 nautical miles from the New York Harbor, this dump site is having wide-reaching effects. Fishermen all the way from South Carolina to New England have begun to catch increasing numbers of hake and kilefish with rotting fins and red lesions on their bellies. Before dumping began, such deformities were rarely seen.

Once again she cites the source of her information (*Time*) and provides concrete and specific details about the effects of sewage.

She continues her description of the problem by connecting the problem of diseased fish with humans: "And the fish are not the only creatures to suffer. Aquatic sewage dumping assaults human sensibilities. And, most importantly, human health."

This is a good transition, for it moves her audience to a problem that should concern everyone:

> William Borden, a resident of a Boston suburb, was jogging along the Boston bayshore when he noticed what appeared to be a beached jelly-fish. Upon closer inspection this jellyfish turned out to be clumps of human fecal matter covered with grease. Up and down the East and West Coast, and along inland shorelines, the story is the same. Scuba divers in the San Francisco area report swimming through clouds of toilet paper and half-dissolved feces. Beaches in Santa Monica, San Jose, and San Diego have all had to be closed several times within the past year due to sewage pollution.

Her use of vivid images is noteworthy. The image of William Borden of Boston makes her description even more concrete. Rather than listing statistics and figures, she gives her audience a graphic picture of the problem. She also is careful to point out specific locations where human sewage has been found (Boston, Santa Monica, San Jose, San Diego). This helps Heffernan establish the problem's national scope.

After describing how sewage "assaults our senses," she itemizes the human health consequences of the sewage threat:

> In addition to this assault on our senses, sewage also threatens our health. According to the United States Department of Health, human sewage is full of pathogens capable of killing us. It is a known carrier of typhoid, cholera, and several strains of harmful bacteria. Sewage's health threat can also be indirect—many of the fish that are caught in areas such as dump site six end up on our dinner tables. *Time* magazine of August 1, 1988, explains that due to a lack of fish inspection, many fishermen sell their diseased fish along with the rest of their catch."

In this segment, she cites her sources (United States Department of Health and *Time*), gives a clear description of the health risks caused by human sewage, and uses an earlier example (dump site six) to connect the segments of her speech. Her first point provides clear and compelling reasons for concern. In her next point, she highlights possible solutions to the problem of improper sewage dumping.

The Cause: Why improper sewage disposal occurs

She devotes the next section of her speech to a careful analysis of why improper sewage disposal is allowed to occur. The problem-solution organizational system leads from a consideration of the problem to an analysis of the cause of the problem. Heffernan explains that the technology is available to solve the problem, but is not being implemented:

> The most frustrating aspect of these problems is that the technology available to us is more than adequate to solve these problems. The *New York Times* of September 18, 1988, states that existing sewage treatment equipment is capable of removing 95 percent of the impurities from our wastewater. Unfortunately, this technology is simply not being implemented. The Environmental Protection Agency claims that 40 percent of our nation's sewage treatment facilities have public health and water quality problems, and 150 communities simply dumped their raw, untreated sewage into the nearest waterway. Furthermore, many older communities, such as New York and Boston, rely on sewage treatment equipment that is more than a hundred years old, and was built for populations half the cities' current size.

In this segment, Ms. Heffernan explains why the problem exists. Again, she uses some excellent external sources to establish her point (*The New York Times* and the EPA), provides specific rather than general pieces of information ("150 communities dump raw sewage" into the nearest waterway rather than "Many communities dump raw sewage"), and uses Boston and New York as concrete examples. Next she points to a second cause: ineffective congressional legislation.

> So far, our government's reaction to our sewage disposal problems has been all show and no go. In 1977, Congress passed the Clean Water Act. One of its functions was to set guidelines for the level of impurities that could be present when water was discharged from a treatment plant. More than a decade later, *Newsweek* of August 1, 1988, reports that more than half the nation disposes of its sewage in an unsafe manner. According to the *Christian Science Monitor* of October 21, 1988, Congress passed a bill stating that anyone dumping sludge in the ocean would be fined. However, as the *Monitor* points out, disposal is much [more expensive] than the cost of the fines. As a result, ocean dumping is still the quickest, and the cheapest, way of disposing waste. Sally Ann Lentz, a lawyer for the Oceanic Society, states the bill will not put an end to ocean dumping, it will merely slightly raise the price tag.

The details she gathers to establish this second claim strengthen the impression that Ms. Heffernan understands her subject. She uses three external sources here: *Newsweek, The Christian Science Monitor,* and lawyer Sally Ann Lentz. With these sources as the foundation of her reasoning, she is able to explain why the government has not reacted to the sewage disposal problem.

At this juncture in her speech, she has recited the problems associated with improper sewage dumping and two causes of these problems. The next segment in her speech features possible solutions to the problems of improper sewage disposal.

Possible Solutions: Solutions to the improper sewage disposal problem

The problem-solution organizational pattern is designed to conclude with a plan for solving the problem that has been identified. She explains how the problem might be addressed by proposing a four-pronged solution. First, she calls for households to take action:

> Clearly, quick and serious action has to be taken to solve our sewage disposal problems. We have to stop burdening Mother Nature with our waste. The best place to begin is right in our homes. Households can dramatically cut the amount of waste they generate by installing low-flow plumbing fixtures. The average toilet flush can be cut by five gallons to two gallons. And low-flow showerheads are also available. These devices are easy to install, and [many cities offer incentive programs] for their use. The logic behind these devices is simple: the less water we get dirty, the less water we have to clean, the less strain on our sewage treatment facilities.

This solution reduces the demand for sewage, and therefore, reduces the problem that is the focus of the speech. Her second proposal moves the audience from individual solutions to community solutions:

> Cities and towns can also contribute by learning to rely less on conventional treatment and more on alternative treatment such as land application. For example, rather than dump its primary treated wastewater into the nearest lake or stream, Plataen County, Georgia, uses it to irrigate forestland. The forest is fertilized by the nutrients it would take treatment facilities millions of dollars to remove, and the soil of the forest serves as a massive filter. . . . In Seattle, Washington, timber companies are lining up to buy city sludge, claiming it makes their trees grow twice as fast. Milwaukee, Wisconsin, sells its sludge under the trade name Millerganite with similar success. The Environmental Protection Agency contends that such land application programs can operate at half the cost of a conventional treatment facility, and in some cases, may even turn a profit.

This proposal is compelling, for it transforms a costly problem into a profitable solution. The proposal is well supported by references to operating programs in Georgia, Wisconsin, and Washington State. She uses for additional proof a conclusion offered by the Environmental Protection Agency.

Next, Ms. Heffernan advocates legislation to mandate regulation of sewage disposal:

As I've mentioned, we do have legislation to help regulate our sewage disposal. It is now a matter of getting this legislation enforced. Citizens can put pressure on their federal, state, and local governments by making phone calls, writing letters, and in some cases, filing lawsuits. William Bordon, the jellyfish jogger, sued the city of Boston on behalf of his community. And as a result of his action and the action by other cities, Boston is slowly being forced to clean up its act.

This solution reminds the judges and the audiences of William Bordon and includes some humor with the use of an alliteration: the jellyfish jogger. Heffernan also calls for new and better treatment facilities:

Finally, new and better treatment facilities have to be built. The Environmental Protection Agency cannot give an exact estimate on how much a national overhaul would cost, only that it would be billions of dollars. However, when we weigh this against the value we put on our health, and quality of life, it becomes a price we must be willing to pay.

Together, these four solutions appear to address and reduce the problem of sewage in America. Now that she has explained the problem and advanced some solutions, she concludes her speech with review and a call for action.

The conclusion

The conclusion of an oratory should review and summarize the speech, call the audience to implement the solution to the problem, and connect the introduction to the summation. Consider how Betsy Heffernan concludes her speech:

In examining our nation's sewage disposal problems, we've learned about the environmental, and the human damage that we're suffering, why this damage is occurring, and finally, ways that we can improve our sewage treatment. Examination of these areas has hopefully made us realize how important it is that we take action on this problem, because for Boston Harbor and the rest of our environment, the party's over.

Ms. Heffernan accomplishes the goals of the conclusion. She returns to the central thought and theme, reminds the judges of the three points in the body of her speech, and ends with a reference to the Boston Tea Party, which she used to begin her speech.

Judges' Reactions

This speaker and speech won the national championship for several good reasons. As you can tell, her speech dealt with an important topic, was well organized and supported, and appears to have been delivered with energy and effective gestures. Let us consider how the judges responded to this speech.

One judge wrote that "Betsy Heffernan's speech on improper sewerage disposal was clearly the most persuasive in the [final] round, for it convinced me that a severe problem does exist." Another judge observed that her arguments were "well supported."

However, some judges felt that the topic of pollution had a "tired ring to it." This judge suggested that her speech needed a "new hook" and asked "Is there new urgency? Has there been some rapid increase in the problem? Is it reaching crisis proportions just now?"

Pollution, gun control, abortion, capital punishment, and a number of other issues are considered "tired" by many judges. Yet, you might choose a familiar topic if you present a novel or an insightful "twist." The judges did find this speech on pollution deserving of a hearing and a national championship.

The judges praised Ms. Heffernan's delivery. One judge wrote that she had a "wonderful command of audience." Another observed that she had a "Nice smooth, pleasant delivery." Still another was specific in her praise: "Betsy employed a crisp, refined delivery complete with persuasive emphasis and effective use of pausing. . . . Her gestures did not appear orchestrated; rather they flowed as natural extensions of the speech. Eye contact was sincere and direct."

The judges did point to some apparent weaknesses in the speech. One judge wanted to know what source she used when she noted that five thousand gallons of human waste flow into Boston Harbor every second. Another judge was not clear on how the low-flowing plumbing device would save water. Still another judge wanted to know how her proposal might be implemented and funded. The judges faulted her speech, as many judges do, for a questionable solution.

Nevertheless, this speech serves as an excellent model of a persuasive speech. The structure, transition, external sources, and the delivery were all first-rate, and you can use this speech as a model for your oratories. When you start to write the first draft of an oratory and need guidance on how to make your points, you can turn to this speech for direction. With this model in mind, the next section provides you with some guidance for practicing your oratory.

Practicing Your Oratory

There are several steps you can take in practicing your oratory. The steps suggested here will be useful after you have followed the suggestions offered earlier in this chapter.

Imagine debating your oratory

As judges hear oratories and other speeches, they often have questions about, or take issue with, the position taken by the speaker. The judges who heard the speech on sewage raised serious questions about the solution Ms. Hefferan offered. If you pretend you are debating your oratory, you may come away with a better sense of the objections or concerns your judges may raise. Debating your oratory will help you discover the weakest part of your speech and develop the best arguments to bolster this section when you rewrite your speech.

Skilled orators anticipate and refute objections in the body of the speech. For example, if you argue that gun control is a good policy option, you should anticipate that many audiences may fear that gun control would leave criminals with guns and honest citizens with no defense. Given this standard and predictable response, the speaker who advocates gun control must address this concern somewhere in his or her speech.

Update your evidence and sources

Some student orators conduct a great deal of excellent research on their topic when they write the first drafts and then never return to the library for more recent evidence. While you may deliver an oratory on the same subject for the entire forensics season, you should continue to conduct research and to search for the most current evidence. Given how quickly things change, you must provide your judges with the best, most recent information on your topic.

In many ways, your speech will never be final or completely finished. As you maintain a research schedule and read new articles and books on your subject, you may need to change the theme of your speech and the quotations and external sources you use. Again, the best orators change their speeches so that they can include the most recent and persuasive information in their orations.

Practice your oratory

As you practice your oratory, you should take the practice sessions seriously. When you are alone, you may wish to tape record your speech. You can then listen to the tape of your speech and think of ways it might be improved. You should also invite your teammates and friends to watch you present your oratory. They can provide you with criticism and advice that you might use to strengthen your speech.

Your forensics teacher also can give you some advice and suggestions for improving your speech. Keep in mind that your forensics teacher understands how your judges think and feel. Your teacher, therefore, is in an ideal position to give you a sense of the preferences and values of your judges. Make sure to use the criticism, advice, and insight your teammates, friends, and forensics teacher offer to you.

Read your ballots and record suggestions for improvement

When the tournament is over, your forensics teacher gives you ballots from your judges. These ballots record the ranking and rating your judges awarded you and written comments on the strengths and weaknesses of your speech.

Judges devote time and energy to writing ballots for you, and you should read them carefully. Read your ballots for both the compliments and the concerns. Your forensics teacher can help you use the comments on the ballots to improve your speech.

You do not need to agree with the judges' comments. However, the comments reveal how your judges reacted to you and your speech. If you wish to persuade judges, you must understand how they view the world and your speech. Among the most valuable lessons forensics can teach you is the need to adapt your speech to the audience, and how to adapt it successfully. Your ballots give you invaluable information on how you can better adapt to your judges.

The following checklist may help you prepare and practice for competition in oratory.

CONCLUSION

Competition in oratory should help you develop the ability to make a persuasive argument in front of judges and other audiences. Oratory is one of the oldest forensics events, and it requires the student to command all the basic theories and skills of public speaking and persuasion. Judges of oratory competition look for well-organized and carefully researched positions on important social issues. Because the oratory event requires such basic but important habits and skills, it is considered by many to be the primary individual event.

Checklist

Checklist for Oratory

Before the Forensic Tournament

1. Know the educational aims of oratory.
2. Know the rules of the oratory.
3. Understand what will happen in the oratory round.
4. Understand what judges expect of oratory speakers.
5. Visualize the steps you should follow in selecting a central thought.
6. Select a central thought and conduct the necessary research.
7. Know how to develop points that support the central thought.
8. Develop introductions, transitions, and conclusions.
9. Consider models of outstanding oratory.
10. Establish practice schedules.

During Practice

11. Practice by yourself.
12. Practice in front of friends.
13. Practice in front of your forensics teacher.

At the Tournament

14. Deliver your speech with energy.
15. Listen to the other speakers and use them as models.
16. Make minor adjustments in your speech if necessary.

After the Tournament

17. After the tournament, read your ballots and use the comments to improve.
18. Conduct more research to broaden and update your knowledge.
19. Practice for the next tournament.

CHAPTER SEVEN

Expository Speaking

The educational aim of expository speaking is to help students develop the habits and skills necessary for explaining an appropriate subject. The rules of this event prohibit speeches with persuasive intent. Judges look for speeches that are developed in a logical manner, are well researched, and are well delivered. Many speakers in this event make use of visual aids. Visual aids help the speaker picture the subject of the speech.

The best informative speeches deal with novel and interesting subjects, or reveal something new about familiar subjects. Speakers who present interesting subjects in a fluent and an engaging manner tend to do well. Finally, the best speakers and speeches teach judges something they did not know and inspire them to learn more about the subject of the speech.

Checklist

Rules of Expository Speaking

Purpose: The primary purpose of expository speaking is for the speaker to explain an interesting topic. The speech must be the original creation of the student. Many tournaments impose a hundred-quoted-word limitation on student expository speaking. In other words, original oratories must not contain over a hundred quoted words.

Length: Most tournaments allow ten (10) minutes with a thirty-second grace period. At the speaker's option, a timekeeper or judge may use cards or hand signals to alert the speaker to the time remaining. For example, the timekeeper may hold up four fingers at four minutes left, three fingers at three minutes left, etc.

Procedures: Many tournaments follow these procedures:

1. A manuscript of the speech must be available to the judge and to other appropriate individuals. A bibliography of the external sources used in the speech should be included.

2. Memorization of the speech is allowed.

3. Visual aids may be used. Most tournaments prohibit use of videos and other similar technology.

4. Other tournament-specific rules may apply.

The rules for expository speaking are easy to follow. Most students have little trouble with the time limits or visual aids. Some have trouble making a clear distinction between expository speaking and oratory speaking. The distinction between the two is one of degree, and can be maintained if you keep your expository speech focused on explaining an interesting subject. The next section explains the event rules for expository speaking.

Rules of Competition and the Original Expository Speaking Round

These rules are enforced by the judges and the tournament director and staff. Competitors who violate the rules risk having their rankings and ratings reduced. Most violations occur because competitors do not know the rules or fail to follow them.

Pay special care to the rules for expository speaking for each tournament you attend, because they may differ. Remember to follow the standard rules: Make sure that you and your forensics teacher have manuscript copies of your expository speech, that your speech does not include more than 100 quoted words, and that your speech is less than ten minutes and thirty seconds in length.

The Expository Speaking Round

The tournament schedule explains when you are to present your expository speech.

According to the schedule, original expository speaking is in the Pattern A events. You will present your oration three times on Friday, at 10:30, 12:30, and 4:30. If you do well in these three rounds, you may present your expository speech at 10:30 (semifinals) and at 1:30 (finals) on Saturday.

As usual, your first order of business when you arrive at the tournament is to find out where the tournament staff is posting. Remember that you will need to know where your rounds are scheduled to take place. Most tournaments post information on each event, including the rooms and judges.

Refer to the checklist on page 136 and assume that you are speaker six in the first round of novice expository speaking.

You need to find Chapman Hall. Your forensics teacher may give you a map of the campus, or you may need to ask for directions. Try to arrive ten to fifteen minutes before the round starts. When the judge and the other competitors have arrived, speaker one (Lee from the Churchill team) is the first to speak. While Lee and the other four competitors speak, be a good audience member. Pay attention to the speaker and the speech, and provide positive and warm reactions whenever possible.

As you listen to your competitors, remember to identify what they do well and learn from their expository speeches. You might ask yourself: How do they introduce their topic? What organizational pattern do they use? What sources of proof do they offer to explain their topic? The answers to these questions may help you understand what distinguishes the strong expository speech from one that needs significant improvement.

Expository speakers use a number of different organizational patterns. The chronological, topical, and cause-effect organizational patterns are among the most popular. The guidelines on page 136 show a model of a chronological organizational pattern.

This organizational pattern is particularly well suited to topics that require a discussion of history. However, the chronological organizational pattern may not be the best organizational pattern for all expository speeches. The organizational pattern you choose depends on your topic and the approach you plan to take. Your organizational pattern and approach should be determined by the judge's expectation of you as an expository speaker.

SAMPLE SPEECH TOURNAMENT SCHEDULE

PATTERN A EVENTS	PATTERN B EVENTS
Extemp	Impromptu
Radio Commentary	Expository Speaking
Expos	Humorous Interp
Serious Interp	ADS

THURSDAY, Feb. 27
11:00 - 12:00 Registration
12:30 - 1:50 SENIOR LD debate, Round I
 2:00 - 3:20 JUNIOR LD and ALL CX debate, Round I
 3:30 - 4:00 ALL DEBATE, Round II
 5:00 - 6:20 ALL DEBATE, Round III
 6:30 - 7:20 Break
 7:30 - 9:00 ALL DEBATE, Round IV

FRIDAY, Feb. 28
 8:00 - 9:30 CX Debate, Round V
 8:30 - 9:30 Registration for schools with IEs only
10:00   EXTEMP DRAW
10:30 - 11:30 Pattern A, Round I
12:00   EXTEMP DRAW
12:30 - 1:30 Pattern A, Round II
 1:30 - 2:30 Pattern B, Round I
 2:45 - 3:30 LD Debate, Round V (both JR & SR)
 4:00   EXTEMP DRAW
4:30 - 5:30 Pattern A, Round III
 5:30 - 6:30 Pattern B, Round II
 6:30 - 7:00 Break
 7:00 - 8:00 Pattern B, Round III
 8:15 - 9:45 ALL DEBATE, Round IV
 9:00   IE Semifinal Postings

SATURDAY, Feb. 29
 7:30   UNIVERSITY CENTER Opens
 7:45   Debate Outrounds Postings
 8:00 - 9:30 ALL DEBATE, Octo-finals
10:00   EXTEMP DRAW
10:30 - 11:30 IE Semifinals, Pattern A & Pattern B
12:00 - 1:00 ALL DEBATE, Quarter-finals
 1:00   EXTEMP DRAW
1:30 - 2:30 IE Finals, Pattern A & Pattern B
 3:00 - 4:30 ALL DEBATE, Semifinals
 5:30 - 7:00 ALL DEBATE, Finals
 8:00   Awards

Checklist

Expository Speaking
Novice Division
Friday, Feb. 28
10:30–11:30
Round One
Judge: R. Smith, Central High
Room: 308 Chapman Hall

Speaker One: Lee, Churchill team
Speaker Two: Gaske, South Albany team
Speaker Three: Hilts, Portland team
Speaker Four: Jason, Madison team
Speaker Five: Trond, Southern team
Speaker Six: YOU, Jefferson team

Guidelines

Using a Chronological Organizational Pattern
Introduction
    Presentation of topic
    Preview of body
   Transition
The history of the topic
    Origins of topic
    Historical significance
Current aspects of the topic
    Meaning of topic in contemporary society
    Use of topic in contemporary society
The future of the topic
Conclusion

Judges' Expectations of the Expository Speaker

Judges of the expository speaking event use relatively similar standards of evaluation. Judges want to learn something new about themselves, society, and the world. They appreciate topics they believe are relevant and important. They also look for well researched, documented, and presented speeches. One judge put it this way: "Informative speaking is a forensic event that incorporates some of the best qualities of a good speech. Not only does this speaking event inform, but a good speaker has the opportunity to entertain, shock, amaze, or offend."

Most judges have at least five questions they consider when evaluating your speech: Did you follow the rules? Did you identify a significant and interesting topic? Did you organize your explanation? Did you provide adequate support for your points? Did you deliver your speech clearly and eloquently? Let us take each of these questions in turn.

Did you follow the rules?

As in any event, judges expect you to know and follow the rules. Depending on the rule violation, judges may penalize you for failing to comply. While some tournaments may have different sets of rules for expository speaking, you must stay within the time limit of ten minutes with thirty seconds grace. Most tournament rules prevent you from quoting more than a hundred words. Many tournament rules require you to have a manuscript of your speech and a bibliography available to the judge and tournament staff.

The rules for district and state tournaments differ from those used by school-sponsored forensics tournaments. For example, the expository speech you present at a district tournament may need to be the same expository speech you present at the state tournament. Check with your forensics teacher for the rules used by individual tournaments.

Did you select a significant and interesting topic?

Judges reward expository speeches that teach them something new. Your topic should be meaningful and pertinent to the judge. Keep in mind that most judges have heard many speeches. The topic you select should arouse their interest and inspire them to listen.

Did you organize your speech?

You need to organize your information for your judges. Judges want to hear speeches that have a clear and purposeful structure. Unlike orators who tend to follow a similar structure, expository speakers use many different organizational patterns. The structure of your speech should highlight the relevant and interesting aspects of your topic.

Did you provide adequate support for your points?

Your judges expect you to be an expert in the subject you address. You will become an expert after you conduct extensive and well-focused library research. Your research should lead you to the best and most recent sources on your subject. By relying on the best and most recent sources of evidence on your topic, you can create a speech that is accurate and insightful.

Judges expect you to clearly document your sources. The articles, books, and other information you use in your speech should be identified and qualified. If you use a statistic or information from an external source, mention the source of this information in your speech. Judges also expect you to qualify your sources. You can meet this expectation by explaining the credentials and the expertise of your sources.

The best expository speeches draw on a number of different sources. You should not rely on one *Discovery* or *Scientific American* article. No one article can possibly capture all there is to know about an issue. Include several different sources in the body of your speech to let your judge know that you have a broad-based understanding of your topic.

Did you deliver your expository speech clearly and eloquently?

Judges reward expository speakers who present their speeches in a clear, conversational mode. Most judges enjoy speakers with an energetic and engaging delivery. You should convey the impression that you are passionately interested in your subject and want to share this interest with your judge. The best expository speakers maintain a balanced delivery and adjust their volume, pace, and tone to the judge, the room, and the situation.

With judges' expectations in mind, let us move to the basic steps of creating and presenting a successful expository speech.

Creating a Successful Expository Speech

These steps or guidelines help you select, develop, and present your expository speech. Each step is important if you are to create a speech that enlightens your audience.

Brainstorm topics and subjects for your expository

You need to find a topic for your expository speech that is interesting and significant, relevant to you and your judges. The topic should inspire you to

---

Guidelines

Steps in the Creation and Presentation of the Expository Speech

Before the Tournament

1. Brainstorm topics and subjects for your expository speech.
2. Conduct research on the topic you have selected.
3. Identify a theme and organize your research into a fitting format.
4. Write and revise your speech.
5. Practice your speech.

During the Tournament

6. Present your speech to your judges.
7. Listen to the other speakers.
8. Modify your speech as necessary.

After the Speech and Tournament

9. After the tournament, read your ballots and use the comments made by your judges to improve.
10. Conduct additional research and practice.

---

conduct the necessary research. It should also intrigue your judges. As you select a topic for your expository speech, try to pick an important issue about which you might say something new.

The process of brainstorming is designed to provoke a wide-ranging discussion between you, your forensics teacher, and teammates on possible topics for expository speeches. During the brainstorming period, search for any topic or subject that sounds at all interesting. At this stage, you should write down every topic that comes to mind.

Let us say the brainstorming session produced the checklist on page 140.

Some of these topics are not appropriate for expository speaking. As you recall, expository speaking should inform and not persuade. The gun control and anorexia nervosa topics most often are the subjects of orations. While you may feature the informative dimensions of these two topics, your judges may think these topics belong in the original oratory event. The other topics appear to be typical and appropriate for the expository category.

Once the group generates a list of topics, you, your teammates, and your

---

Checklist

Results of the Brainstorming Session

Dust	Medical technology	Computers
Earthquakes	New educational technologies	Dinosaurs
Anorexia nervosa	Credit cards	Electric cars
Gun control	National debt	Baseball

---

forensics teacher can select those with the most potential. After the discussion and a brief visit to the library, you may find that dinosaurs and new educational techniques interest you. You need to choose between the two.

Suppose your forensics teacher tells you that the dinosaur topic is overdone; several students delivered expository speeches on dinosaurs the previous year, and judges may be weary of the dinosaur topic. On the other hand, your forensics teacher says that the new educational technologies topic has not been the subject of an expository speech and would be of interest to judges. Given this advice, you would be wise to select the new educational technologies topic, unless you are confident that you can reveal something new and exiting about dinosaurs. Your next step is to conduct extensive research on new educational technologies.

Conduct research on your topic

Once you decide to speak on the new educational technologies topic, you need to find books, articles, and other materials on technological innovations in education. You need to read books and articles from a number of sources that describe new and emerging educational technologies. You should use the source to find statistics, quotations, photographs, and other materials that you might use in your speech.

Quotations are especially useful for explaining your ideas in the body of your speech. Remember to record these quotations on notecards. The sources of these quotations should be recorded on your notecards and in your bibliography. Take care when you record quotations from external sources, for you are responsible for not altering or distorting authors' meanings when you quote them.

You should also look for vivid and appealing visual illustrations of new educational technologies. You might choose to use these illustrations as visual aids for your speech. A visual aid can help your audience envision your topic. For example, you may find illustrations of two or three new educational tools. You might take these illustrations to a photograph shop to have them developed and enlarged. Then you could place them on poster-boards and use them as visual aids. After you have enough evidence and illustrations, you need to organize your information.

Identify a central thought and organize your research into a pattern that highlights what is significant and interesting about your topic

Once you identify a topic and gather enough evidence from external sources to write an informative speech, you will need to identify a central thought or theme and then organize it. This central thought or theme forms the core of the speech. You might suggest that all concerned citizens should know about new educational technologies. You might organize your speech to display the benefits and perils of new educational technologies.

As you organize your speech, plan to present your central thought at the beginning, and then use your organizational pattern to develop the central thought. If you have visual aids that might help communicate your message, decide where they fit in the organizational pattern. The visual aids should contribute to and supplement your explanation.

There are a number of organizational patterns you might use. In writing a speech about new educational technologies, you might want to give a brief history of the role of educational technology in the classroom, describe two or three recent innovations in the field, and provide the judge with a cost-benefit analysis of new educational technologies. (See guidelines on page 142.)

As you organize your speech, give the most time to explanations of interesting and novel topics. In this speech, your judges should be interested in recent advances in educational technologies. Many judges are teachers, and they would have good reason to listen to a speech that addresses their professional concerns. Knowing this, you might devote the greatest proportion of your speech to points two and three (a description of new educational technologies and innovations and an analysis of the costs and benefits of new educational technologies).

Finally, you must decide if you need visual aids and, if so, where they belong in the speech. Because this topic may involve educational technologies unfamiliar to your audience, you might choose to develop two or three visual aids that illustrate innovative educational technologies. When you write your speech, incorporate the visual aids into the structure of your expository.

Write the first draft of your speech

Experienced expository speakers write many drafts of their speeches. The first draft should not be the one you deliver at the tournament. Use an outline to write your speech. Include your central thought and choose an organizational

---

Guidelines

The Benefits-Perils Organizational Pattern

Central Thought: New educational technologies will play an important role in the instruction of students.

1. A history of the subject
   Example: Educational technologies have played and play an important role in the classroom: from chalk to computers.

2. The characteristics of the subject
   Example: A description of new educational technologies and innovations

3. The benefits and the costs of the subject
   Example: An analysis of the costs and benefits of new educational technologies

4. Conclusion
   Example: What we know about new educational technologies

---

pattern that highlights what is significant and interesting about your topic. As with any speech, your expository speech should have an introduction, a body, and a conclusion.

Experienced speech writers keep their audience in mind as they write their speeches. You should do the same. Adapt the introduction, body, and conclusion of your speeches to your audience. Your goal is to inform your audience about a topic they will find significant and interesting. To meet that goal, you must think hard about what will intrigue your audience.

As you write the introduction, do so with your audience in mind. The introduction should give your audience a good reason to listen to the rest of your speech. Most audiences will listen to a speech if the topic is of social and personal importance and interest. Explain the significance of your topic in your introduction. Most important, be sure your introduction contains the central thought or theme of your speech. You want your judges to appreciate the purpose of your speech.

In the body of the speech, you should elaborate on the topic you selected. Remember to devote the greatest amount of time to the topics and subtopics that are of most interest to your audience. Your judge expects you to identify and qualify the external sources you use, and many judges expect expository speakers to use visual aids.

In the conclusion of the speech, you need to summarize and review. Most expository speakers use the conclusions of their speech to underscore the importance of the subject to the audience. For example, in concluding the speech on new educational technologies, you should clarify how your judges might apply what you discussed.

Your first draft should never be your final draft. Good speeches go through many drafts. When you conduct more research and present your speech to a variety of audiences, you will discover that you need to revise the first draft. Your speech should be in a constant state of evolution.

To succeed in expository speaking, you must be willing to modify your speech over the course of the forensics season. Judges provide many good suggestions on how you can improve your speech. Use their ideas to strengthen your performance.

Practice your speech

As in any speaking event, you must establish a practice schedule to discover whether listeners find your speech informative, relevant, and interesting. Take these practice sessions seriously, and, if possible, make them resemble the tournament environment. Practice alone, in front of your friends, and in front of your forensics teacher.

You should use the responses of these and other audiences to improve your speech. Your practice audience can give you important clues about how the judges will react to your speech at the tournament. Your forensics teacher can advise you about how you might better adapt your speech to your audiences. Seek out constructive criticism of your speeches, for it will improve your performance as an expository speaker.

Present your speech to your judges

By the time you arrive at the tournament, your speech should be in good order. You have at least two or three opportunities to present your speech to judges. Remember to deliver your speech each time as if it were the first time. Your scores will be higher if you maintain your enthusiasm and seem interested in your speech.

If you make a mistake, don't be too concerned. Odds are the judge will never know you dropped a sentence or section of your speech unless your face or body reveals your dismay at making the error. Most important, don't stop speaking if you make a mistake. Many beginning and experienced speakers make mistakes. The goal is to continue speaking and to finish making your point.

Before and after you speak, listen carefully to the speeches of your competitors. As you know, you should be a good audience member. This means that treating the other speakers as you would want them to treat you. If you disagree with a speaker, do not give the speaker negative nonverbal reactions. Be a polite audience member.

You can learn much from the speeches delivered by your competitors. Take notes on what they do well and how they organize and present their speeches. Their speeches can provide you clear examples of effective and not-so-effective expository techniques. After the tournament is over, you may wish to use these examples as models for improving your speech.

Modify your speech as necessary

Your speech should be in a constant state of evolution. You may decide after your first round that some minor changes might need to be made. Perhaps you want to change the wording of the introduction or use a different piece of evidence in support of the solution section. Revisions are great, but wait to make major changes in your speech until the tournament is over. You need time to think through any major alterations in your speech. Make sure to talk with your forensics teacher or an experienced team member if you think your expository speech needs significant change.

After the tournament, read your ballots and use the comments made by your judges to improve

When the tournament is over, your forensics teacher will give you the ballots your judges wrote in response to your speech. These ballots explain how your judges ranked and rated you in comparison to your competition, and they record what your judges felt were the strengths and weaknesses of your speech. With the help of your forensics teacher, read these ballots and identify the comments you should use to revise and improve your speech.

Pay special attention to patterns and recurring statements in the ballots. If, for example, all the judges commend you for your research, then you know that your evidence is solid and persuasive. If two of your judges mention that you don't seem comfortable using gestures, make it a goal during your practice sessions to incorporate natural gestures, developing a more energetic style.

Your ballots are a valuable resource, but use them with care. Your forensics teacher can help you discriminate between helpful comments and those that may not be as useful. Remember that you may have the same judges at the next tournament. Reading your ballots can give you insight into the judges' feelings and beliefs, enabling you to adapt your speech to your audience.

Conduct additional research and practice

Your speech should change after every tournament. Some sections will remain the same; yet, other parts will need minor or major alterations. Additional research and practice are essential even if you took first place at a tournament! You must continue to research and practice to keep your speech current and your delivery fresh.

Judges give more weight to speakers whose evidence and sources are current. The external sources you discover on your topic during your early outing to the library may be outdated after the first tournament. A second trip to the library may reveal more recent, timely, and informative books and articles on your topic. Always make sure your resources are up-to-date.

Some speakers read the newspaper every day to find the most recent evidence and proof for their expository speeches. You might do the same. The libraries you visit should have the most recent periodical literature on your topic. The best expository speakers know they need to conduct research on their topic throughout the forensics season.

Continue to practice throughout the forensics season and create a practice session that is as realistic as possible. As you rehearse your speech, focus on the specific improvements you wish to make. After delivering the same speech a number of times, some speakers lose interest in their speeches. You can avoid this pitfall through continued effort to improve the speech. Revisions and improvements benefit the speech and help keep you interested enough to maintain the high level of enthusiasm you will need at the tournament.

A Model Expository Speech

You now know the rules of the expository speaking event and the steps you need to take to write and present a successful expository speech. This section presents a model expository speech for your review. The model speech was delivered by Jay Lane on the subject of dust. He states his central thought clearly: "Dust is more than the mystical substance that makes up daydreams." In this speech, Mr. Lane organizes the subject of dust around three questions: What is dust? Where does dust come from? and How does dust affect us?

On page 146 is an outline of Mr. Lane's expository speech on dust.

This speech contains all the components of a successful expository speech. As you read this speech, consider how you might use it as a model.

The Introduction

The introduction of an expository speech gives the audience a good reason for listening to the speech. An effective introduction highlights why the subject is relevant to the listeners. Ideally, the introduction develops an image that will bind together the body and the conclusion of the speech. The introduction must also contain the central thought or theme of the speech. Finally, a skillful introduction previews and provides a transition to the body of the speech.

This speech is about dust. You might raise an obvious, but very good

---

Guidelines

Organizational Pattern

I.   Introduction

II. Presentation of central theme or idea: Dust is more than the mystical substance that makes up daydreams.

III. Preview of Body
    A. What is dust?
    B. Where does dust come from?
    C. How does dust affect us?
       Transition

IV. What is dust?

V.   Where does dust come from?

VI. How does dust affect us?

VII. Conclusion

---

question: Why would a speech about dust interest the judges? As you read the text of this speech, you will see how Jay Lane presented fascinating information about a common topic. In his introduction, he acknowledges that dust is a topic that we seldom consider, and he gives us reasons why we should:

> Webster says it's fine, dry, and pulverized. We rarely think about it. Strange, really. For there's twice as much in this room as there is anywhere outside. And those who study it tell us that 43 million tons will fall on the United States alone. What is it? In a word, "dust." And I know what you're thinking, but wait. For there is an inspiration in the examination of such a microscopic phenomenon. The November 1986 issue of *Discover* magazine relates the account of author Penny Ward Mosier and the coming of age of dust. In that article, she writes, "I only noticed the dust because my mind was desperately seeking a diversion. That happens during tax time. And so it was one day that I found myself pushing around little clumps of dust, and then it happened, from behind the corner of my desk there appeared a giant dust ball, piloted by my big toe. I picked it up. Intrigued, 'What is this dust ball?' I wondered." The experience of the author is one that is shared by us all at one time or another. How many times have you sat and watched the lazy, floating particles falling slowly in the sunlight. The dust is more than the mystical substance that makes up daydreams. It is also the the-

sis of a speech. One that deals with a subject which "touches us" literally every day of our lives.

This is an outstanding introduction, for it illustrates how a speaker can directly involve the audience. Mr. Lane wrote this speech with his audience in mind. With his first two sentences, he invites his audience to speculate about the topic of his speech. This technique directly involves the audience in the speech because the audience must try to determine what the speech is about. At this point, his audience is intrigued. He then establishes the significance of the topic: 43 million tons of dust fall on the United States. Finally, he asks the audience a rhetorical question (a question to which no direct answer is expected) that helps establish the relevance of dust to his audience: "How many times have you sat and watched the lazy, floating particles falling slowly in the sunlight?"

He devotes the next part of his introduction to an overview of his speech:

And so, with your kind permission, I present dust. What it is, where it comes from, and how on earth it can affect us. Now, I have to admit that until recently, I had never given dust more than a speck of thought. But as my understanding increased, so has my appreciation. You see, what we often think of as, well, dust, blossoms under a microscope, becoming what some might even consider to be exotic. But, I should slow myself down before my story loses its structure. According to the Library of Congress, there are 322 books that have been published on the subject of dust. Let's see what information they can provide.

This is an excellent overview and preview of the speech. At this point in his presentation, the judge has a clear road map of the points Mr. Lane intends to cover ("What it is, where it comes from, and how on earth it can affect us"). You might also note the use of humor in his statement "Now, I have to admit that until recently, I had never given dust more than a speck of thought." Judges enjoy clever puns. Finally, this preview provides an effective transition into the body of the speech.

The Body

This speech is organized around three questions: What is dust?, Where does dust come from?, and how does dust affect us? Mr. Lane provides clear, well documented answers to these questions. In addition, the three questions all point back to the central thought of the speech.

What is dust?

He provides an interesting and well substantiated answer to this question:

In his book entitled *The Secret House,* author David Bodine provides a great deal of information. It seems that the principle element that makes up what we refer to as dust is soil. That is a fancy word for dirt. Followed closely by, of all things, salt. That's right. These tiny crystals dance out of our oceans at a rate of 300 million tons every year. In addition, you will find fabric fibers, fungi, pollens, and a variety of things that, quite frankly, you don't want to hear about. But don't worry, I am merely saving the best part for last. Now, I realize that dust can be a hard sell. Still, I press boldly forward. For dust is becoming serious business. For this reason, the Maryland Medical Laboratories donated several of their shelves, taking them away from growing cultures of new biotechnologies and bacteria in order to grow samples of Mrs. Mosier's dust balls. They immediately blossomed into a collage, warranting closer examination. Of the experience she wrote, "Everyone came by to stare at my dust, oohed and aahed over the slides that we had made. Under a microscope my stained dust was a work of art. I now understand that not only could dust be anything, it could be everything.

In answering the question, "What is dust?" Mr. Lane describes the origins of dust, the composition of dust, and provides a connection to the source (Mrs. Mosier's article in *Discover* magazine) that he put to use in the introduction. His definition of dust is well developed and leads him to the second question: Where does dust come from?

Where does dust come from?

He uses Mrs. Mosier's *Discover* magazine article as a transition between question one and question two. Additionally, he gives his judges a good explanation concerning the origins of dust:

She [Mrs. Mosier] also notes that in addition to being everything, it also comes from everywhere. For example, forest fires. In a good year, for dust, 7 percent of the world's total comes from forest fires. In addition, much of it comes from our oceans, as mentioned earlier. And, of course we can't forget manmade pollutants, industrial dust. But, the single largest contributors to the world supply of dust are volcanoes. In fact, the infamous eruption of Krakatoa in 1883 was the dust event of recorded history. But, you know that happened a long time ago . . . . *Nature* magazine in November of 1986 notes that the winds that blow across the African deserts carry with them so much dust that at times it falls as a light pink rain on Miami. But is it possible that dust carries all the way across the country, that the dust here in San Diego is from Africa, that the dust in your home has an international flavor. . . . What's more, much of it comes from outer space. Extraterrestrial dust. Coming principally from comets and disintegrating meteorites, at a rate of 10,000 tons every year. Well, with so many things coming from so many places, it's not surprising that everything you own is covered by that fine thin layer, and you don't know half the story yet. Again, according to *Discover* magazine, the average six-room city or urban dwelling takes in forty pounds of dust every year, forty pounds. And a single cubic inch of air space can contain 1,600,000 tiny particles (Cough). Sorry, it got just a little difficult to breathe.

There are four particularly strong points about this answer. First, his explanation of the origins of dust is well developed. The judges know, at the end of this section, that dust has origins in Africa and outer space. Second, he relates this explanation directly to the judge; he makes dust relevant to his audience ("But is it possible that dust carries all the way across the country, that the dust here in San Diego is from Africa, that the dust in your home has an international flavor. . . .") The tournament took place in San Diego, so his reference to San Diego was particularly relevant. Additionally, he invited his judges to think about dust in their homes. This invitation made the speech even more pertinent to the judges. Third, he cites his sources (*Discover* and *Nature* magazines). Fourth, his use of humor at the end of the section is effective.

How does dust affect us?

Mr. Lane's third question, about the effect of dust, is the true center of his speech. As you know, the most important task of the expository speaker is to explain why the judge should consider the topic interesting and of importance. Mr. Lane fulfills this task in his third answer by associating dust with his audience's pillows, mattresses, skin, and water:

> With so much dust in the air, it seems like it should have some kind of impact on your life, shouldn't it? Good point. Let's see. Now you've already heard about dust and how it affects us through hay fever. Of course, that's pollen, a significant source of dust. And I know you've seen a cobweb at one time or another. But there was something else that I wanted to share. Now, I don't want to be the cause of anyone's nightmares, and I don't want to keep you awake tonight, but this is the point where I recreate all of your childhood fears. You know, as kids it's fairly easy for us to handle dirt. We roll around with the fungi and the fabric fibers and never really give it a second thought, but it's the monsters, do you remember, the ones under your bed. Well, I'm here today to tell you that those childhood memories are very real in a sense.

By relating dust to monsters and nightmares, he has made dust a graphic and remarkable substance. Consider how he transforms dust into monsters:

> For this was discovered by the Maryland Medical Laboratories in the research they did for Mrs. Mosier. Dr. and scientist Charles McCloud discovered under the microscope something he said that he had never seen

before. He said it had mouth parts on its legs, and described it as an angry rhinoceros with crustacean appendages. In short, he said it is the ugliest thing you have ever seen. So go ahead. Even that tough group of scientists uttered their share of . . . ughs when they saw this little guy. He is a member of a family of house mites. The scientific name is, ahem, uh-huh, I wrote it down. Dermitoffaginouossparine, I think. Personally, I just write dust. There are fifteen species of these little guys that live in various parts around the world. They live in your pillows, in your mattresses, in your sheets, and in your dust balls. Don't worry, they can't eat anything if it's still attached. Although they will chew on your toenail dirt if you give them half a chance.

As you read this part of his speech, notice that he presented a visual aid to help his audience picture a Dermitoffaginouossparine. He makes reference one more time to Mrs. Mosier, the author of the *Discover* magazine article, and the Maryland Medical Laboratories. And, he gives a vivid, graphic, and startling description of house mites that made his presentation directly relevant to all the listeners in the room.

He continues to develop an answer to the third question:

But now I don't want you to leave with the idea that this isn't really a significant problem. According to Ian Fielding in his book entitled *Dust,* there are about two million of these dust mites in every twin sized bed. Kind of makes you want to wrap your body in Saran Wrap, doesn't it? Well that was the response of Mrs. Mosier, but don't worry, even after finding all this out, she, her husband, and their two million tiny pets have learned to share the bed just fine. Of course, that was before she found out her air conditioner had gangrene. Yet another element [of] that simple term that we call dust.

This is another graphic illustration of the role played by dust in human society. The now familiar Mrs. Mosier makes another appearance and provides Mr. Lane with one more link to his audience. He concludes his speech by highlighting the benefits of dust:

But I don't want to leave you with a negative impression. Like everything that has to do with dust is bad. For there are many benefits from dust as well. Consider . . . a *Forbes* magazine article of August 12, 1985, entitled "A Handful of Dust." The article relates a revolution in scientific research. It seems that Dr. Von Bryant, a pollentologist, that is a term for someone [who] studies dust, at Texas A&M University is conducting a group of experiments that they call "chomap." The purpose of this project is to recreate the environmental conditions over the past ten thousand years by using dust. According to Dr. Von Bryant, they have already discovered some pollen samples as old as 2.5 billion years. Talk about a direct link to your past, AT&T has nothing on these guys in terms of long distance communication.

Here, Mr. Lane establishes the basic description of Dr. Von Bryant's research. Once again, he uses humor to maintain the attention of his audience. He concludes this section as follows:

> But, seriously, Dr. Bryant notes that there is some information that we get from dust we simply cannot get anywhere else. There are also some implications and impacts of dust closer to home. It seems that dust has an interesting effect on light waves. It breaks up the blues and purples at the short end of the spectrum, but leaves the reds and oranges untouched. The result, beautiful red, orange, yellow in the sunset you saw last night. Oh yes, there was one more thing. According to the *American Academic Encyclopedia* of 1983, dust serves as an . . . essential foundation. It seems that as dust floats around in the atmosphere it allows water molecules to bond, the result, condensation and precipitation. In case you're wondering if dust has any social significance, try getting a drink of water without it.

In wrapping up this answer to the third question, Mr. Lane has explained why dust is relevant and interesting to his audience. He has transformed dust into monsters and the things of nightmares, revealed dust as our bedmate, and unveiled the social benefits of dust as it tells us about our history and provokes our rain. At this point, he has answered the three questions set forth in the introduction, and he turns to his conclusion.

Conclusion

The conclusion of an expository speech should provide the judges with a brief summary of what they have learned. Mr. Lane's conclusion attains these goals:

> Dust, what a simple term. But it is anything and everything. It is a glass of water, a sunset, a very ugly bug. But whatever dust may be, the dust ball discovered by Mrs. Mosier was more than just a word, rather an entire world of fascination.

This is an unusually short conclusion, but in four sentences he accomplishes a great deal. In his first sentence, he reminds his judges of his introduction in which he states: "What is it, in a word, dust." He then reviews the answer by recalling three vivid images he developed in the body of the speech: a glass of water, a sunset, and an ugly bug. His last sentence returns us to the durable Mrs. Mosier and her dust ball.

Judges' Reactions

This speech, on the topic of dust, won the national championship in expository speaking. The speaker took something in our common environment and taught the judges something new. One judge wrote that "Anyone who can speak about dust and keep my attention deserves a high ranking." Another judge wrote "Lane took an aspect of our everyday life with which we believe we are familiar, household dust, and made it interesting, informative, and significant." The judges had mostly positive comments for the structure, content, and the style of the speech.

One judge commented that the "introduction to this speech was very good. A sense of suspense was created and the preview statement was specific. The uniqueness of the topic (dust) provided an additional interest factor." Recall that Mr. Lane did not specify the subject of his speech until the fifth sentence. He kept his audience in suspense, which was a good artistic choice. In addition, he did provide the judges with a clear overview of the three questions he addressed.

The same judge observed that the judges learned about the origins of dust and that the "significance of the topic was best developed in explanations of how dust affects us." She also commended Mr. Lane for his conclusion: "The conclusion was very strong. That dust can be anything and everything from a sunset, to a glass of water, to an ugly bug, served to provide a strong sense of finality to the speech."

This judge wanted Mr. Lane to make his points on house mites more meaningful to his audience:

> Initially, the subpoint on house mites was related to the audience's childhood fears. Although such statements served to relate the information to audience experiences, I believe Mr. Lane could have worked to make the ensuing information on these mites more meaningful for the audience. I know, for instance, that two million mites can be found in a single twin bed. Yet, I am not sure what else I should do with this information. I would have liked to have heard it developed in such a way that this information becomes "important" for the audience to know.

The judges also commented on his use of humor and his delivery. In commenting on the use of humor in an expository speech, one judge concluded that Lane and Ehling [another speaker in the final round] both made exceptional use of humor:

> A witty and urbane style can arouse, sustain, and heighten an audience's interest in the speaker and subject. We enjoy laughing, consequently, we attend more closely to those who successfully utilize humor. The ap-

propriate use of humor also provides a release between more serious elements of a speech.

A fellow judge agreed: "Jay added humor to his speech to spark the interest in his audience."

As a cautionary note, speakers can go overboard in the use of humor. This comment, made by one of the judges, is instructive on the use of humor. "Finally, although I want to compliment Mr. Lane on his use of humor, I do want to stress that he may have over-relied on it at the expense of working to make the information more meaningful for the audience."

The judges applauded Lane's delivery. One judge wrote that "Mr. Lane did a fantastic job of engaging the audience in this particular speech." Another noted: "I felt that Jay Lane excelled in two areas: style and delivery. His presence before an audience was animated and well controlled (with the exception of a somewhat distracting shaking leg. I was particularly pleased to listen to someone who could project adequately in a room with poor acoustics." At the same time, one judge did feel that his delivery lacked spontaneity: "I had the sense that at times, the delivery was forced (especially when such phrases as 'a speck of thought' and 'I should slow myself down' were delivered). Although I realize that this speech has been delivered numerous times, the sense of spontaneity needed to be consistent throughout the speech."

One judge had a concern about the citation of external sources in Lane's speech. As you know, most judges want to know the sources of the information you use in your speech. One judge faulted Lane for failing to cite his sources:

Mr. Lane, for instance, has a fair amount of "half sourcing." He told us who said something, but not where we could find it or when it was said. A fair number of key facts are entirely unsourced.

Despite these flaws, Mr. Lane's speech is an excellent example of an expository speech. He took a common topic and revealed much that was significant, relevant, and interesting to his audience. You can use the introduction, body, and conclusion of his speech as models for your own expository speech. Finally, you can learn from his use of humor and his ability to deliver his ideas to his audience. With the rules and theories and a good model of expository speaking in mind, the next step is for you to develop a system for practicing your own expository speech.

Practicing Your Expository Speech

There are several steps you can take in practicing your expository speaking. The steps suggested here are useful after you have followed the suggestions offered earlier in this chapter.

Listen to your speech from the perspective of a judge

As judges hear expository speeches, they often have questions about points raised by the speaker. One judge who heard the speech on dust wanted to know how she might use the information on house mites. If you take the perspective of the judge, you may come away with a better sense of the concerns your judges may raise about your speech. If you have not delivered the speech in competition, pretend that you are hearing your speech for the first time. As you listen to your speech, ask yourself if your ideas are well organized, explained, and documented. As you revise and rewrite your speech, work to better organize, explain, document, and deliver your ideas.

Remember that judges want to hear expository speeches that are significant, relevant, and interesting. As you take the perspective of a judge, ask if the parts and the whole of your speech are significant. Does your topic deal with an issue of social and public importance? Is your speech relevant to the values and concerns of most audiences? Is your speech of interest or does it reveal something new?

Update your evidence and sources

Some student expository speakers conduct a great deal of excellent research on their topic when they write the first drafts and then never return to the library for more recent evidence and sources. While you may deliver an expository speech on the same subject for the entire forensics season, you should continue your research and search for the most current sources. Given how quickly things change, you must provide your judges with the best, most recent information on your topic.

In many ways, your speech is never completely finished. As you maintain a research schedule and read new articles and books on your subject, you may need to change the theme of your speech and the quotations and external sources upon which you rely. Again, the best expository speakers take time to change their speeches so that they can include the most recent and relevant information.

Practice your expository speaking

As you practice your expository speaking, take the practice sessions seriously. When you are alone, you may wish to tape record your speech. You can then listen to the tape and think of ways to improve your speech. You should also invite your teammates and friends to watch you present your expository speech. They can provide you with constructive criticism and advice on how to strengthen your speech.

Your forensics teacher can also give you suggestions on how to improve your speech. Keep in mind that your forensics teacher understands how your judges think and feel. This puts your forensics teacher in an ideal position to give you a sense of the preferences and values of your judges. Make sure to use the criticism, advice, and insight your teammates, friends, and forensics teacher offer you.

Their advice should lead you to make the necessary revisions to your expository speech. Each time you make a needed change, your speech becomes stronger. Writing teachers suggest you go through many drafts before you hand in a paper. Historians, novelists, and poets rewrite their works many times before they are published. In the same way, you should constantly revise and improve your speeches.

Read your ballots and record suggestions for improvement

When the tournament is over, your forensics teacher will give you ballots from your judges. These ballots record the ranking and rating your judge awarded you and written comments on the strengths of your speech and areas that need improvement. Judges devote time and energy to writing ballots for you, and you should read them with care. Everyone enjoys praise, but read your ballots for both the compliments and the concerns expressed by the judges. Your forensics teacher can help you use the comments on the ballots to improve your speech.

You may not always agree with the judges' comments. However, the comments reveal how your judges reacted to you and your speech. If you wish to inform and explain your topic to the judges, you need to understand how they view the world and your speech. Among the most valuable lessons forensics can teach you is the need to adapt each speech for your audience. Your ballots give you invaluable information on how you can better adapt to your judges.

On page 156 is a checklist to help you prepare and practice for competition in expository speaking.

CONCLUSION

Competition in expository speaking should help you develop the ability to explain and describe significant and interesting topics. Along with original oratory, expository speaking is one of the oldest and most basic forensics events. It requires the student to understand and apply all the basic theories and skills of public speaking. The judges of expository speeches look for well organized and researched positions on significant and relevant subjects. Because the expository speaking event requires such basic but important habits and skills, it is considered by many to be an essential forensics event.

Guidelines

Checklist for Expository Speaking

Before the Forensic Tournament

1. Know the educational aims of expository speaking.
2. Know the rules of expository speaking.
3. Understand what will happen in the expository speaking round.
4. Understand what judges expect of expository speakers.
5. Visualize the steps you should follow in selecting a central thought.
6. Select a central thought and conduct the necessary research.
7. Know how to develop points that support the central thought.
8. Develop introductions, transitions, and conclusions.
9. Consider models of outstanding expository speaking.
10. Consider use of visual aids, checking tournament rules.

During Practice

11. Follow established practice schedules.
12. Practice by yourself and in front of friends or relatives.
13. Practice in front of your forensics teacher or coach.

At the Tournament

14. Deliver your speech with energy.
15. Listen to the other speakers and use them as models.
16. Make minor adjustments in your speech if necessary.

After the Tournament

17. After the tournament, read your ballots and use the comments to improve.
18. Conduct more research to broaden and update your knowledge.
19. Practice for the next tournament.

CHAPTER EIGHT

Radio Commentary

The educational aim of the radio commentary event is to provide students with an opportunity to present an original critical analysis of current events. In most cases, radio commentaries are opinion pieces in which the commentator offers his or her views on socially significant issues and current events. The radio commentary event is not designed for students to summarize events or read the news; rather, judges expect the competitor to present a well-reasoned position to a radio audience.

Because the event is intended to simulate actual radio commentaries, time limitations are strictly enforced, and many tournaments require competitors to speak into a microphone and out of eye contact with the judge. Most tournaments

---

Guidelines

Rules of Radio Commentary

Purpose: The primary purpose of radio commentary is for the speaker to present an analysis of a topic dealing with current events. The speech must be the original creation of the student and be read from a script Many tournaments will impose a limit of seventy-five quoted words on the student radio commentary. At most tournaments, the contestant stands out of sight of the judge.

Length: Most tournaments require the commentary to end between 4:45 and 5:15 minutes. Speakers ending before 4:45 and after 5:15 will be disqualified. A timekeeper or judge will use cards or hand signals to alert the speaker to the time remaining. For example, the timekeeper may hold up four fingers at four minutes left, three fingers at three minutes left.

Procedures: Many tournaments follow following procedures

1. A manuscript of the speech must be available to the judge and to other appropriate individuals. A bibliography of the external sources used in the speech should be included.

2. Memorization of the speech is not allowed.

3. Tournament-specific rules may apply.

---

require competitors to read from a manuscript and use no more than seventy-five quoted words in the commentary. Because the tournament is designed to replicate an actual radio studio, judges are encouraged to be particularly vigilant in enforcing the rules of the event.

The best radio commentaries offer the listener an original, intelligent, and well-delivered analysis of a current event. Because time is limited, championship caliber radio commentaries are tightly written. Speakers who do well in this event attempt to provide commentaries that are pointed but not divisive. That is, these speakers take positions that are acceptable to a reasonable audience.

You must know and follow the rules of this event. Speakers who end before 4:45 and after 5:15 are disqualified by the judges. On occasion, students with the best written radio commentaries are disqualified because they exceed the time limits. Pay close attention to the time signals, and make sure that you finish your speech in time. The next section explains the event rules for radio commentary.

Rules of Competition and the Radio Commentary Round

The rules on page 158 are enforced by the judges and the tournament director and staff. Competitors who violate these rules risk disqualification and having their rankings and ratings reduced. The most frequently violated rule, as you might guess, is the rule on time limits. You must work hard to keep your speech within the time boundaries.

The Radio Commentary Round

The tournament schedule lists the times you are to present your radio commentary.

According to the schedule on page 160, radio commentary is in the pattern A events. You will present your radio commentary three times on Friday, at 10:30, 12:30, and 4:30. If you do well in these three rounds, you may present your radio commentary at 10:30 (semifinals) and at 1:30 (finals) on Saturday.

When you arrive at the tournament, find out where the tournament staff is posting. You need to know where your rounds are scheduled to take place. Most tournaments post the panels in each event, listing the rooms and judges.

Referring to the postings on page 161, let us assume that you are speaker three in the first round of novice radio commentary.

You will need to find room one in Bond Hall. Your forensics teacher may give you a map of the campus, or you may need to ask for directions. Try to arrive ten to fifteen minutes before the round starts. When the judge and the other competitors have arrived, speaker one (Stolp from the Roseburg team) will be the first to speak. While Stolp and the other four competitors speak, your job is to be a good audience member. You should pay attention to the speaker and the speech and provide positive reactions whenever possible.

As you listen to your competitors, try to identify what they do well so you can learn from their radio commentaries. You might ask yourself: How do they introduce their topic? What organizational pattern do they use? What sources of proof do they offer? The answers to these questions may help you to understand what distinguishes the strong radio commentary from one that needs significant improvement.

When it is your turn to speak, you will walk to a table or podium, with your manuscript, and present your radio commentary. At most tournaments, the rules require you to be out of sight of the judge. This may seem awkward at first, but you will become accustomed to the radio commentary scene.

As you speak, you will use an appropriate organizational pattern. A number of organizational patterns are in use by radio commentary speakers. The chronological, topical, and cause-effect organizational patterns are among the most

SAMPLE SPEECH TOURNAMENT SCHEDULE

PATTERN A EVENTS
Extemp
Radio Commentary
Expos
Serious Interp

PATTERN B EVENTS
Impromptu
Expository speaking
Humorous Interp
ADS

THURSDAY, Feb. 27
   11:00 - 12:00 Registration
   12:30 - 1:50 SENIOR LD debate, Round I
   2:00 - 3:20 JUNIOR LD and ALL CX debate, Round I
   3:30 - 4:00 ALL DEBATE, Round II
   5:00 - 6:20 ALL DEBATE, Round III
   6:30 - 7:20 Break
   7:30 - 9:00 ALL DEBATE, Round IV

FRIDAY, Feb. 28
   8:00 - 9:30 CX Debate, Round V
   8:30 - 9:30 Registration for schools with IEs only
   10:00   EXTEMP DRAW
   10:30 - 11:30 Pattern A, Round I
   12:00   EXTEMP DRAW
   12:30 - 1:30 Pattern A, Round II
   1:30 - 2:30 Pattern B, Round I
   2:45 - 3:30 LD Debate, Round V (both JR & SR)
   4:00   EXTEMP DRAW
   4:30 - 5:30 Pattern A, Round III
   5:30 - 6:30 Pattern B, Round II
   6:30 - 7:00 Break
   7:00 - 8:00 Pattern B, Round III
   8:15 - 9:45 ALL DEBATE, Round IV
   9:00   IE Semifinal Postings

SATURDAY, Feb. 29
   7:30   UNIVERSITY CENTER Opens
   7:45   Debate Outrounds Postings
   8:00 - 9:30 ALL DEBATE, Octo-finals
   10:00   EXTEMP DRAW
   10:30 - 11:30 IE Semifinals, Pattern A & Pattern B
   12:00 - 1:00 ALL DEBATE, Quarter-finals
   1:00   EXTEMP DRAW
   1:30 - 2:30 IE Finals, Pattern A & Pattern B
   3:00 - 4:30 ALL DEBATE, Semifinals
   5:30 - 7:00 ALL DEBATE, Finals
   8:00   Awards

```
┌─ Checklist ──────┐──────────────────────────────────┐
│  └──────────────┘                                    │
│                                                      │
│  Radio Commentary                                    │
│  Novice Division                                     │
│  Round One                                           │
│  Judge: J. Robyns                                    │
│  Room: Bond Hall, Room 1                             │
│                                                      │
│  Speaker One: Stolp, Roseburg team                   │
│  Speaker Two: Wu, Lake Oswego team                   │
│  Speaker Three: YOU, Jefferson team                  │
│  Speaker Four: Garcia, Sheldon team                  │
│  Speaker Five: Lee , David Douglas team              │
│  Speaker Six: Wayne, Barlow team                     │
│                                                      │
└──────────────────────────────────────────────────────┘
```

popular. For purposes of explanation, the outline below uses the chronological organizational pattern. The outline shows how most radio commentaries are organized to develop a central theme idea with supporting points and proof.

Let us say your commentary is on the need to reduce the deficit and that you believe defense spending is the major cause of the deficit:

```
┌─ Checklist ──────┐──────────────────────────────────┐
│  └──────────────┘                                    │
│                                                      │
│  Organizational Pattern Using a                      │
│  Cause-Effect-Organizational Pattern                 │
│  I.    Introduction                                  │
│        A.  Presentation of central idea: Defense spending creates the │
│            national deficit and should be reduced    │
│        B.  Preview of Body                           │
│            Transition                                │
│  II.   Cause of Problem: Defense spending creates the national deficit. │
│  III.  Effects of Problem: The national deficit destroys the national │
│        economy.                                      │
│  IV.   Suggested solution or perspective on cause and effects: Defense │
│        spending should be cut.                       │
│  V.    Conclusion                                    │
│                                                      │
└──────────────────────────────────────────────────────┘
```

This organizational pattern is particularly well suited for topics that call for an analysis of both the causes and the consequences of major social problems. Your choice of an organizational pattern depends on the topic you choose and the approach you plan to take. As you decide how to organize and approach the topic, keep in mind the expectations judges have about what students should do in the radio commentary event.

Judges' Expectations of the Radio Commentary Speaker

Judges of the radio commentary event expect speakers to present a well-organized, analyzed, and presented opinion on current events. In many ways, the radio commentary is a mini-oratory. However, as a radio commentator you are not required or expected to offer solutions to the problems you address. Judges do look for reasoning and proof. They also expect you to have done some research and reading on the subject of your commentary.

Most judges have at least six questions they ask themselves when they evaluate your radio commentary: Did you follow the rules? Did you identify a significant and interesting current event? Did you present an insightful opinion? Did you organize your analysis? Did you provide adequate support for your points? Did you deliver your speech clearly and eloquently? Let us take each of these questions in turn.

Did you follow the rules?

Judges expect you to know and follow the rules of radio commentary. Depending on the rule violation, judges may penalize you for failing to comply with the rules. While some tournaments have different sets of rules for expository speaking, your speech must not end before the 4:45 mark and must not go beyond 5:15. Unlike the other events, your judge will not give you a thirty-second grace period. Most tournament rules prevent you from quoting more than seventy-five words. Many tournaments require you to have a manuscript of your speech and a bibliography available to the judge and tournament staff.

The rules for district and state tournaments differ from those used in school-hosted forensics tournaments. For example, the radio commentary you present at a district tournament may need to be the same radio commentary you present at the state tournament. Check with your forensics teacher for the rules used by individual tournaments.

Did you identify a significant and interesting current event?

Judges expect you to provide them with a well-analyzed opinion on current events. The topic you select should be meaningful to the judge. Keep in mind that most of your judges have heard many speeches: the topic you select should arouse their interest and inspire them to listen.

Did you present an insightful analysis or opinion?

You should, if possible, develop innovative analysis that will leave the judge with a new insight or two. Your analysis should reflect some real thought. Many judges do not see this as a "gripe" speech. Judges will be on the lookout for fresh, intelligent, and revealing perspectives on current events.

Did you organize your analysis and opinions?

You will need to organize your information for your judges. Judges want to hear speeches that have a clear and purposeful structure. The pattern you use should highlight the relevant and interesting aspects of the topic you address.

Did you provide adequate support for your points?

Your judges expect you to be an expert on the subject and you select. You become an expert after you conduct extensive, well-focused library research. Your research should lead you to the best, most recent sources on your subject. By relying on these recent sources of evidence, you can create a speech that reflects the most accurate and insightful information on your topic.

In addition to having recent sources, you must clearly document your sources. The articles, books, and other sources you use in your speech should be identified and qualified. If you use a statistic or information from an external source, include the source of the statistic or information in your speech. Judges also expect you to qualify your sources; you need to tell the judge why the external source you use is credible. This expectation can be met if you explain to the judge the credentials and expertise possessed by your sources.

The best radio commentaries draw on a number of different sources. Do not rely on one *New York Times* or *Christian Science Monitor* article for your commentary. No one article can possibly capture all there is to know about a subject. While you will not have time to cite every external source you use to build your opinion, you should list every one in your written bibliography.

Did you deliver your radio commentary clearly and eloquently?

Judges expect radio commentators to present their speeches in a clear, conversational manner. To impress the judges, your delivery should be energetic and engaging. You want to convey your intense interest in your subject and your desire to share this interest with your judge. The best radio commentators maintain a balanced delivery and adjust their volume, pace, and tone to the judge, the room, and the situation.

Creating a Successful Radio Commentary

With judges' expectations in mind, let us move to the steps you need to take to create and present a successful radio commentary.

Guidelines

Steps in the Creation and Presentation of the Radio Commentary

Before the Tournament

1. Brainstorm topics for your radio commentary.
2. Conduct research on the topic you select.
3. Identify a theme and organize your research into a fitting format.
4. Write the first draft of your speech.
5. Practice your speech.

During the Tournament

6. Present your speech to your judges.
7. Listen to the other speakers.
8. Modify your speech as necessary.

After the Speech and Tournament

9. After the tournament, read your ballots and use the comments made by your judges to improve.
10. Conduct additional research and practice.

The steps above should help you select, develop, and present your radio commentary. Each step is important if you are to create a speech that enlightens your audience.

Brainstorm topics and subjects for your radio commentary

You need to find a topic for your radio commentary that is interesting and relevant to you and your judges. The topic you select should inspire you to conduct the necessary research and inspire your audience to listen closely to your speech. As you select a topic for your radio commentary, try to pick one that will sustain your interest and allow you to enlighten and entertain your audience.

The purpose of brainstorming is to provoke a wide-ranging discussion between you, your forensics teacher, and teammates on possible topics for radio commentary. During the brainstorming period, search for any topic or subject that even remotely sounds interesting. At this stage, you should write down all the topics that come to mind.

Checklist

Results of the Brainstorming Session

Foreign policy	Higher education	Foreign trade
The energy crisis	The Middle East	The deficit
Gang violence	Drugs	Trade wars
Welfare	The environment	Medical care

Let us say your brainstorming session produced the above topics.
These are all worthy topics for a radio commentary. You would want to pick one that sparks your interest and gives you the opportunity to tell your judges something novel. As you continue to brainstorm about potential topics, you should eventually narrow your choices. You may find after the brainstorming session and a visit to the library that the national deficit and medical care are two interesting topics about which you have some opinions. You need to choose between the two.

Suppose your forensics teacher tells you that the medical care topic is overdone. She says many competitors in radio commentary have delivered speeches on medical care in the last several years. She also says that she has not heard a good speech or radio commentary on the deficit. Given this advice, you should select the deficit topic, unless you are confident you can reveal something new and exiting about medical care. Your next step is to conduct thorough research on the deficit.

Research your topic

Once you decide to speak on the deficit, you need to find books, articles, and other materials on the issue. Select books and articles from a number of authors and sources that describe the causes, consequences, and potential solutions to the deficit. These authors and sources will provide you with statistics, quotations, and other materials you might use in your speech.

Guidelines

Outline of a Radio Commentary on the Deficit

Central thought: We should not be too concerned about the deficit because it does no long-term damage to the economy.

1. History
   Example: Past deficits have not damaged the economy.

2. Present
   Example: The current deficit is not damaging the economy.

3. Future
   Example: The deficit will not damage the economy in the future.

4. Conclusion: We should not be alarmed about deficits.

As you read books and articles on your topic, look for quotations you might use in the body of your radio commentary. You may use these quotations to explain your ideas. Don't forget to record these quotations on notecards. The sources of these quotations should be recorded on your notecards and in your bibliography. Take care when you record quotations from external sources, for you must preserve the author's meaning.

Identify a central thought and organize your research and analysis into a logical pattern

Once you identify a topic and gather enough evidence from external sources to write a radio commentary, you will need to pinpoint a central thought or theme and then select an orgnizational pattern to develop the thought. You might choose to identify two or three points in support of your central thought. The body of the speech could be devoted to the development of these points.

A number of organizational patterns are possible. You might develop three points in support of the central thought that the deficit does no long-term damage to the economy as shown above. First, you review deficits in American history, then discuss the current deficit, and the implications of the future deficit. In developing the central thought and these three points, you need to provide your judge with proof that the deficit has not been, is not, and will not be a threat to our economic health. As with an original oratory, you would need to offer expert sources who agree with your opinion.

As you organize your speech, plan to devote the most time to interesting and novel points of analysis. In this speech, your judges will be interested in your counter-intuitive (against common sense) approach to the deficit topic.

Many people believe the deficit is a major threat to our economic well-being, so you need to work hard to convey a different opinion.

Write the first draft of your speech

Experienced radio commentary speakers write many drafts of their speeches. The first draft is not the one to use at the tournament. The outline, with a central thought and an organizational pattern that highlights what is significant and interesting about your topic, should be used to write your speech. As with any speech, your radio commentary should have an introduction, a body, and a conclusion.

Experienced speech writers keep their audience in mind as they write their speeches. You should do the same. Adapt the introduction, body, and conclusion of your speech to suit your audience. Your goal is to present your audience with an opinion on a current event that your audience will find relevant and interesting. To do this, you must think hard about what will intrigue your audience.

As you write the introduction, keep your audience in mind. The introduction should give your audience a good reason to listen to the rest of your speech. Explain to the audience why your topic is of social and personal importance to them. Most important, the introduction should contain the central thought or theme of the speech so that the judges clearly understand your purpose.

In the body of the speech, you should clarify your topic and your opinion about it. Remember to devote the greatest amount of time to the topics and subtopics that will most interest your audience. Also keep in mind that your judge expects you to identify and qualify the external sources that you use.

In the conclusion of the speech, you need to summarize your major points and underscore your perspective for the audience. For example, at the end of the radio commentary on the deficit, you want to make your stance on the issue clear.

To achieve these goals, you must write many drafts of your radio commentary. As you conduct continuing research and present your speech to a variety of audiences, you will find you need to modify sections and sentences of your first draft. Remember that your speech should be in a constant state of evolution. Your research, the reactions of your audience, and the comments you receive from judges on your ballots may all prompt changes that will make your radio commentary more successful the next time you deliver it.

Practice your speech

You must establish a practice schedule so that you can hear from others whether they find your radio commentary persuasive. Take these practice sessions seriously and make them resemble the tournament environment as closely as possible. Take time to practice by yourself, in front of your friends, and in front of your forensics teacher. Don't forget that your practice sessions should resemble the tournament setting. Your audience should be out of sight, and you should read your speech from a manuscript. Most important, your speech should be timed to end between 4:45 and 5:15 minutes.

Use the responses of your practice audiences to improve your speech. These responses give you important clues about how judges will respond to your speech at the tournament. Your forensics teacher can help you adapt your speech to your audiences. Seek out constructive criticism of your radio commentary; your speech will benefit from it.

Present your speech to your judges

By the time you arrive at the tournament, your radio commentary should be in good order. You have at least two or three opportunities to present it to the judges. While you may have practiced your commentary many times, make sure that you deliver it with the same energy you did the first time. Judges will give you higher scores if you appear to be sincerely interested in your speech.

Don't be too concerned about mistakes you might make. Above all, don't stop speaking if you make a mistake. It is upsetting to make a mistake, but remember that the judges will probably be unaware of the error unless you reveal it through your delivery. Many beginning and experienced speakers make mistakes. The goal is to continue speaking and to finish making your point.

Listen to the other speakers

Before and after you speak, listen carefully to the speeches of your competitors. As you know, part of your responsibility at a speech tournament is to be a good audience member. This means treating the other speakers as you would want them to treat you. If you hear a speaker present an idea you disagree with, do not give the speaker negative nonverbal reactions. Remain a civil and attentive audience member.

You can learn much from the commentaries delivered by your competitors. You should take notes on what they do well and how they organize and present their radio commentaries. Their speeches can provide you clear examples of effective and not-so-effective radio commentaries. After the tournament is over, you may wish to use these examples as models for improving your commentary.

Modify your radio commentary as necessary

Your radio commentary should be in a constant state of change. You may decide after your first round that some minor modifications need to be made.

For example, you may decide to change the wording of your speech or use a different piece of proof for one of your points. You should, however, wait until the tournament is over to make major changes in your radio commentary. You need time to think through any major alterations in your speech. Make sure to talk with your forensics teacher or an experienced team member if you think your radio commentary needs significant change.

After the tournament, read your ballots and use the comments made by your judges to improve

When the tournament is over, your forensics teacher will give you the ballots your judges wrote in reaction to your radio commentary. These ballots tell you how your judges ranked and rated you in comparison to your competition, and they record what your judge felt were the strengths and weaknesses of your speech. With the help of your forensics teacher, identify the comments made by your judges that you should use to revise and improve your speech.

Seek out patterns and recurring statements in the ballots. If, for example, all the judges commend you for your research, then you know that your evidence is solid. If two of your judges suggest you could use a more energetic delivery, then you should focus during your practice sessions on developing a more energetic style.

Your ballots should be of great use to you, but you should use them with care. Your forensics teacher can help you discriminate between helpful comments and those that are not as useful. Because you may have the same judges at the next tournament, reading your ballots for insight into their feelings and beliefs may improve your scores. Keep your judges' opinions in mind as your speech evolves.

Conduct additional research and practice

Your speech should change after every tournament. Some sections of the speech may remain the same; others may need minor or major alterations. You need to conduct additional research and practice even if you took first place at a tournament! Additional research and practice keeps your information up-to-date and your delivery sharp.

Judges give great weight to speakers who use the most recent evidence. The external sources you discover on your topic during your early outing to the library may be outdated after the first tournament. Continue to check the library for timely and informative articles on your topic. Some speakers also read the newspaper every day to find the most recent evidence for their radio commentaries. You might do the same.

In addition to continuing your research, you should continue to practice your speech throughout the forensics season. Your practice sessions should resemble the tournament environment. Identify specific improvements you wish to work on during your practice sessions. After delivering the same commentary a number of times, some speakers lose interest in it.

Concentrate on making specific improvements in the content and delivery of your commentary. Your commitment to constantly improving your radio commentary can help you maintain your interest in the commentary. This interest will show in your delivery and your scores at the speech tournament.

A Model Radio Commentary

You now know the rules of the radio commentary event and the steps you need to take in writing and delivering a successful radio commentary. This section presents a model radio commentary delivered by the well-known journalist Daniel Schorr. Mr. Schorr, in a commentary for National Public Radio's "All Things Considered," focused on Hillary Rodham Clinton's call for a "politics of meaning," which she borrowed from the writings of Michael Lerner. In his commentary, Schorr notes that Mrs. Clinton's call has been ridiculed by the *New Republic*, the *New York Times Magazine*, and other popular media. His commentary is a description and explanation of Clinton and Lerner's politics of meaning.

Following is an outline of Mr. Schorr's radio commentary on the politics of Hillary Rodham Clinton, Michael Lerner, and the politics of meaning. This speech displays the characteristics of a successful radio commentary.

Guidelines

Organizational Pattern of Daniel Schorr Radio Commentary

I. Introduction: Hillary Rodham Clinton's Speech in Austin
    Presentation of central theme or idea: The Clintons should be
    allowed their more progressive version of spiritual values and
    Lerner should know that his ideas will be subjected to critical
    scrutiny.

II. Hillary Rodham Clinton and the politics of meaning

III. The Clintons, Michael Lerner, and the politics of meaning

IV. Criticism of the politics of meaning

V. Justification of politics of meaning and support of the Clintons
    and Lerner

The Introduction

The introduction of a radio commentary should provide the audience of the speech with a good reason for listening. An effective introduction should highlight why the subject of the speech is significant and relevant to judges. Ideally, the introduction develops an image that can be used to bind together the body and the conclusion of the speech. The introduction should also contain the central thought or theme of the speech. Finally, the introduction previews and provides a transition to the body of the speech.

Hillary Rodham Clinton and the politics of meaning

Daniel Schorr's radio commentary is about Hillary Rodham Clinton's use of Michael Lerner's "politics of meaning" approach. Consider his introduction:

> This would not be much of a story were it not for the intriguing involvement of President and Mrs. Clinton and what this may say about them. On April 6th in Austin, Texas, Hillary Rodham Clinton delivered what some are already calling 'The Speech.' It was a passionate appeal for Americans to develop a sense of community. She spoke of 'cities that are filled with hopeless girls with babies and angry boys with guns.' She spoke of a 'crisis of meaning' and urged a remolding of society by defining what it means to be a human being in the twentieth century moving into the new millennium. "What is needed," she said, "is a new kind of politics—the politics of meaning."

Schorr immediately establishes the significance of his commentary; he is talking about an important philosophical idea that First Lady Hillary Rodham Clinton used in a speech. He also gives his listeners a brief synopsis or overview of this speech. He then develops the connection between the Clintons, Lerner, and the politics of meaning.

The Clintons, Michael Lerner, and the politics of meaning

At this point in the speech, the listener may be wondering about the history of the politics of meaning. In the next part of the commentary, Mr. Schorr explains the history of the concept:

> The Politics of Meaning is a concept of Michael Lerner, the editor of *Tikkun,* a liberal Jewish monthly. Had she gotten the phrase from him? He himself was not clear, but at a subsequent White House reception, she made clear that she had. She said to him, "Am I your mouthpiece or what?" and "It's amazing how we seem to be on the same wavelength." In a later meeting in her office, she told Lerner that she and her husband had been reading him since 1988. In fact, Governor Clinton had once written him, "You have helped me clarify my thinking."

Here, he establishes the connection between the Clintons, Lerner, and the politics of meaning. In the next section of his commentary, Mr. Schorr reports on the controversy provoked by the politics of meaning.

Criticism of the politics of meaning

At this point in the speech, the listener may wish to know what issues have been raised by the politics of meaning speech and by Michael Lerner. Mr. Schorr portrays the controversy in this manner:

> Michael Lerner, an observant Jew with a strong sense of ethics, has become a celebrity as the Clintons' spiritual adviser. He called the other day to say that he was not enjoying his celebrityhood very much. For reasons he found puzzling and distressing, the media—not quite knowing what to make of him and his influence on the first couple—were treating him with something close to hostility. *The New Republic* spoke of psychobabble, and the *New York Times* magazine made him the centerpiece of an article sarcastically presenting Mrs. Clinton as "Saint Hillary." I've heard references to Lerner as Rasputin, and one civil libertarian friend raised the question of whether such spiritual guidance might have implications for the separation of church and state.

Schorr describes this controversy in an interesting, informative manner. The listener is drawn into the controversy and may want some answers. In the last nine sentences of the commentary, Schorr provides some answers.

Justification of politics of meaning and the resulting criticism

Schorr offers an even-handed critique and an analysis of the controversy:

> What makes people so jittery about ideas of mutual responsibility and caring for one another that seem no more threatening than the golden rule? If presidents Reagan and Bush could embrace a conservative Christian ethic, well why should the Clintons not be allowed their more progressive version of spiritual values?

This is his first opinion on the controversy, and he makes this point by reminding the listeners that previous presidents have adopted spiritual ethics. If this is so, then, to be fair, the Clintons should have the same option. Schorr then turns his attention to those who have criticized Lerner and the Clintons:

> Journalists tend to be made uncomfortable by the very abstractness of the ideas, by an inability to reduce them to concrete proposals and programs which are the stuff of journalism. Although most presidents and first ladies have their own friends and advisers—even astrologers—still, advice from an unconventional source not spelled out in the Constitution seems unsettling.

Here, he explains why journalists are suspicious of the politics of meaning. With the reference to astrologers (to whom Nancy Reagan purportedly turned for counsel), Schorr again reminds his audiences that other presidents and first ladies have relied on extra-constitutional sources of advice.

Schorr then offers a description of Lerner's social programs:

> In fact, Lerner does have some concrete suggestions that he spelled out in a memo to the president. Budget requests from departments should include statements about how the programs foster caring concern. The Labor Department should send teams into the workplace to develop a spirit of mutual cooperation. . . . .

The Conclusion

Finally, Schorr concludes by placing the criticism of Lerner's politics of meaning in its context:

> I can understand why Michael Lerner is troubled about being met with something between bafflement and hostility in the news media, but the White House is, for most Americans, a crucial arena and who sets foot in that arena to influence the course of national events will, however benevolent the intention, be subjected to critical scrutiny.

In the first section of the commentary, Schorr sets up the controversy and in the second section, he offers four opinions on the controversy. His opinions are well reasoned and presented. He provides reasons for his opinions and gives his listeners a balanced and well-developed perspective on the politics of meaning controversy.

Critique of Schorr's Radio Commentary

Obviously, Daniel Schorr was not required to follow the rules of competitive forensics; he is not a student. His commentary does provide an excellent model for students competing in radio commentary. First, he identifies a relevant and interesting current event. The people and ideas that affect the American presidency are worthy topics for commentaries. Second, he presents an insightful analysis and four well-stated opinions. His analysis of the controversy is enlightening, and his four-point conclusion is revealing.

Third, his analysis and opinions were organized. However, unlike many beginning forensics speakers, he does not explicitly identify his organizational pattern. Less experienced commentators are wise to clearly state the organizational pattern they will use. Fourth, Mr. Schorr provides adequate support and reasoning for his opinions. Because he is a well-known and highly respected news personality, he did not need to cite his sources. You, however, will not command the same credibility, and you will need to cite and qualify your sources. Finally, the spoken and written versions of this commentary are clear, if not eloquent. His word choice and the structure of the commentary enhance the effectiveness of the speech.

This speech is an excellent model of a radio commentary. The structure, transitions, proof, and delivery were all first-rate, and you can use this speech as a model for your radio commentary. When you start to write the first draft of a radio commentary and you need guidance and examples, you can turn to this speech.

With this model in mind, review the next section for guidance on practicing your radio commentary.

Practicing Your Radio Commentary

Here are several steps you can take in practicing your radio commentary. The steps suggested here are useful after you have followed the suggestions offered earlier in this chapter.

Imagine debating your radio commentary

As judges hear radio commentary and other speeches, they often question the position taken by the speaker. The listeners who heard Schorr's speech on the politics of meaning may have resisted his conclusions. To anticipate and counter these possible objections, it helps to imagine debating your radio commentary. By doing so, you may come away with a better sense of the concerns your judges may raise. As you debate your radio commentary, you should find the weakest part of your speech and develop the strongest possible arguments to bolster it. For example, the speaker who argues that the deficit does no harm to the economy must address the common sense observation that it is not good to be in debt.

Update your sources

Some student radio commentators conduct a great deal of excellent research on their topic when they write their first drafts and then never return to the library for more recent evidence. While you may deliver a radio commentary on the same subject for the entire forensics season, you should continue to conduct research and to search for the most current sources. Given how quickly things change, you must provide your judges with the best, most recent information on your topic.

In many ways, your speech is never completely finished. As you maintain a research schedule and read new articles and books on your subject, you may need to change the theme of your speech and the quotations and external sources upon which you rely. Again, the best radio commentators change their speeches frequently so that they can include the most recent and persuasive information in their orations.

Practice and Revise Your Radio Commentary

As you rehearse your radio commentary, take the practice sessions seriously. When you are alone, you may wish to tape record your speech. You can then listen to the tape and think of ways your commentary might be improved. You should also invite your teammates and friends to watch you present your radio commentary. They can provide you with criticism and advice on how to strengthen your speech.

Your forensics teacher can also provide excellent suggestions for improving your radio commentary. Keep in mind that your forensics teacher understands how your judges think and feel. Therefore, your forensics teacher is in an ideal position to give you a sense of the preferences and values of your judges. Make sure to use the criticism, advice, and insight your teammates, friends, and forensics teacher offer to you.

Read your ballots and record suggestions for improvement

When the tournament is over, your forensics teacher will give you ballots from your judges. These ballots record the ranking and rating your judge awarded you and written comments on the strengths of your speech and areas that need improvement. Judges devote time and energy writing ballots for you, and you should read them carefully, noting both the judges' compliments and their concerns. Your forensics teacher will help you to use the comments on the ballots to improve your radio commentary.

You do not need to agree with the comments made by your judges. However, the comments reveal how your judges reacted to you and your speech. If you wish to persuade judges, you must understand how they view the world and your speech.

Among the most valuable lessons of forensics is why and how you should adapt your comments to your audience. Your ballots give you invaluable information about your judges.

Use the checklist on page 176 as you prepare and practice for competition in radio commentary.

CONCLUSION

Competition in radio commentary should help you develop the ability to present an original analysis of current events in a situation that resembles a

Guidelines

Checklist for Radio Commentary

Before the Forensics Tournament

1. Know the educational aims of radio commentary.
2. Know the rules of the radio commentary.
3. Understand what will happen in the radio commentary round.
4. Understand what judges expect of radio commentary speakers.
5. Visualize the steps you should follow in selecting a central thought.
6. Select a central thought and conduct the necessary research.
7. Know how to develop points that support the central thought.
8. Develop introductions, transitions, and conclusions.
9. Consider models of outstanding radio commentary.
10. Establish practice schedules.

During Practice

11. Practice by yourself.
12. Practice in front of friends.
13. Practice in front of your forensics teacher.

At the Tournament

14. Deliver your speech with energy.
15. Listen to the other speakers and use them as models.
16. Make minor adjustments in your speech if necessary.

After the Tournament

17. After the tournament, read your ballots and use the comments to improve.
18. Conduct more research to broaden and update your knowledge.
19. Practice for the next tournament.

radio studio. You will select a topic, conduct research, and write a manuscript in which you present your opinions. While you may rarely find yourself in a radio studio, the skills you learn in the radio commentary event are of great use. For example, the skills you develop in the radio commentary will enable you to write better position papers and essay examinations. In addition, radio commentary gives you an opportunity to sharpen your opinions on important current events. Finally, this event is enjoyable, for it gives you a chance to exchange ideas and opinions with your fellow competitors.

CHAPTER NINE

After-dinner Speaking

The educational aim of after-dinner speaking, also known as special event or special occasion speaking, is to help students develop the habits and the skills necessary to entertain and inform an audience. While the rules of the event call for the after-dinner speech to have a serious undertone, the best after-dinner speakers approach their subject with good humor. The rules of the event also require the competitor to develop original material—that is, the speech must not be copied and translated from CDs, movies, or published materials. The after-dinner speaking event should encourage witty speeches on important topics. After-dinner or special occasion speeches are prepared in advance for a real-life situation; the speaker should always have a specific audience in mind.

Guidelines

Rules of After-dinner Speaking

Purpose: The primary purpose of after-dinner speaking is for the speaker to entertain the audience. The speech should, however, have a serious undertone. The speech should have a thematic connection. The speech should not be a skit or a vaudeville performance. Many tournaments prohibit after-dinner speeches that depend upon impersonations or are "acted out."

Length: Most tournaments allow eight (8) minutes with a thirty-second grace period. At the speaker's option, a timekeeper or judge may use cards or hand signals to alert the speaker to the time remaining. For example, the timekeeper may hold up four fingers at four minutes left, three fingers at three minutes left.

Procedures: Many tournaments apply the following procedures:

1. A manuscript of the speech must be available to the judge and to other appropriate individuals.
2. No notes are permitted; the speech must be memorized.
3. Other tournament-specific rules may apply.

The best after-dinner speeches are entertaining, thematically connected, and well presented. They are also in good taste. In fact, the rules of the event prohibit offensive humor. Skilled after-dinner speakers are flexible and can adjust to the moods and the reactions of their audiences. Championship after-dinner speakers entertain and educate their audiences.

The rules of the after-dinner speaking event require the speaker to stay within an eight-minute maximum time limit, with the usual thirty-second grace period. Most competitors have little trouble with the time limit or the requirement that the speech have a socially significant message. Some competitors do cross the line that separates appropriate from inappropriate and hurtful humor. Keep in mind that what might be funny to you and to certain audiences may be disagreeable and offensive to your judge and to other audiences. In addition, some competitors borrow too freely from other sources. The after-dinner speech must be the original work of the speaker. The next section presents the event rules for after-dinner speaking.

Rules of Competition for the After-dinner Speaking (Special Occasion) Round

These rules are enforced by the judges and the tournament director and staff. Competitors who violate these rules risk having their rankings and ratings reduced. Among the most frequently violated rules is the one that requires students to write an original speech. On occasion, some after-dinner speakers transcribe comedy routines off CDs or other sources. Make sure to understand and to follow the rules of the event.

The After-dinner Speaking Round

The following tournament schedule lists the times you will present your after-dinner speech. ADS stands for after-dinner speaking.

According to the schedule, after-dinner speaking is in pattern B. You will present your after-dinner speech three times on Friday, at 1:30, 5:30, and 7:00. If you do well in these three rounds, you may present your after-dinner speech at 10:30 (semifinals) and at 1:30 (finals) on Saturday.

When you arrive at the tournament, you need to find out where the tournament staff is posting. Find out as soon as possible where your rounds are scheduled to take place. Most tournaments post the panels in each event, listing the rooms and judges.

Referring to the checklist on page 182, let us assume that you are speaker six in the second round of novice after-dinner speaking.

You will need to find Villard Hall. Your forensics teacher may give you a map of the campus, or you may need to ask for directions. You should try to arrive ten to fifteen minutes before the round starts. When the judge and the other competitors have arrived, speaker one (LaRusso from the Florence team) will be the first to speak. While LaRusso and the other four competitors speak, you should be a good audience member. Pay attention to the speaker and the speech, and provide positive reactions whenever possible. Remember that all the speakers are trying to entertain and be funny. As a good audience member, you should help the speakers by laughing (even if the jokes aren't terrific).

As you listen to your competitors, try to identify what they do well and what you can learn from their after-dinner speeches. You might ask yourself: How do they introduce their theme? What organizational pattern do they use? What stories and jokes do they tell? The answers to these questions may help you understand what distinguishes the strong after-dinner speech from one that needs significant improvement.

A number of organizational patterns are possible in after-dinner speaking. Speakers may use chronological, topical, or cause-effect organizational patterns. For purposes of explanation, the outline on page 182 uses the topical organizational pattern. This pattern allows the speaker to divide a topic into themes.

Your choice of an organizational pattern depends on your topic and your approach. In choosing your structure and your topic, you should be guided by the expectations judges hold for the after-dinner speaker. Judges expect you to entertain them with a speech that has a serious message.

SAMPLE SPEECH TOURNAMENT SCHEDULE

PATTERN A EVENTS
Extemp
Radio Commentary
Expos
Serious Interp

PATTERN B EVENTS
Impromptu
Expository speaking
Humorous Interp
ADS

THURSDAY, Feb. 27
    11:00 - 12:00 Registration
    12:30 - 1:50 SENIOR LD debate, Round I
     2:00 - 3:20 JUNIOR LD and ALL CX debate, Round I
     3:30 - 4:00 ALL DEBATE, Round II
     5:00 - 6:20 ALL DEBATE, Round III
     6:30 - 7:20 Break
     7:30 - 9:00 ALL DEBATE, Round IV

FRIDAY, Feb. 28
     8:00 - 9:30 CX Debate, Round V
     8:30 - 9:30 Registration for schools with IEs only
    10:00   EXTEMP DRAW
    10:30 - 11:30 Pattern A, Round I
    12:00   EXTEMP DRAW
    12:30 - 1:30 Pattern A, Round II
     1:30 - 2:30 **Pattern B, Round I**
     2:45 - 3:30 LD Debate, Round V (both JR & SR)
     4:00   EXTEMP DRAW
    4:30 - 5:30 Pattern A, Round III
    5:30 - 6:30 **Pattern B, Round II**
     6:30 - 7:00 Break
    7:00 - 8:00 **Pattern B, Round III**
     8:15 - 9:45 ALL DEBATE, Round IV
     9:00   IE Semifinal Postings

SATURDAY, Feb. 29
     7:30   UNIVERSITY CENTER Opens
     7:45   Debate Outrounds Postings
     8:00 - 9:30 ALL DEBATE, Octo-finals
    10:00   EXTEMP DRAW
    10:30 - 11:30 IE Semifinals, Pattern A & Pattern B
    12:00 - 1:00 ALL DEBATE, Quarter-finals
     1:00   EXTEMP DRAW
    1:30 - 2:30 IE Finals, Pattern A & Pattern B
     3:00 - 4:30 ALL DEBATE, Semifinals
     5:30 - 7:00 ALL DEBATE, Finals
    8:00   Awards

Checklist

After-dinner speaking
Novice Division
Round One
Judge: R. Withycombe
Room: 211 Villard Hall

Speaker One: LaRusso, Florence team
Speaker Two: Gottesman, South Planes team
Speaker Three: Nutz, Walsenburg team
Speaker Four: Pearson, Madison team
Speaker Five: Griffey, Mariner team
Speaker Six: YOU, Jefferson team

Guidelines

Topical or Thematic Organizational Pattern
I.   Introduction
    A. Presentation of topic
    B. Preview of body
        Transition
II. Theme One: How topic is used in America
III. Theme Two: How topic is used in the Middle East
IV. Theme Three: How topic is used in China
V.   Conclusion

Judges' Expectations of the After-dinner Speaker

The purpose of the after-dinner or special occasion speech is to entertain the audience with a message that has a serious undertone. Judges appreciate after-dinner speakers who have an interesting and important topic, a coherent and well-developed theme, an appropriate style of humor, strong audience analysis, and an effective delivery. Most judges ask themselves at least five questions as they evaluate your speech: Did you follow the rules? Did you identify a relevant and serious theme? Did you organize your after-dinner speech? Did you develop your points with humor and insight? Did you deliver your speech clearly and eloquently? Let us take each of these questions in turn.

Did you follow the rules?

Judges expect you to know and follow the rules of this event. Depending on the rule violation, judges may penalize you for failing to comply with the rules. While some tournaments may have their own rules for after-dinner speaking, you must stay within the time limit of eight minutes with thirty seconds grace. Tournament rules may require you to have a manuscript of your speech available to the judge and tournament staff.

The rules for district and state tournaments may differ from those used by school-sponsored forensics tournaments. For example, the after-dinner speech you present at a district tournament may need to be the same after-dinner speech you present at the state tournament. Make sure to check with your forensics teacher for the rules used by individual tournaments.

Did you identify an important, relevant theme?

Judges expect after-dinner speeches to focus on a topic of some consequence. The topic you select should be meaningful and pertinent to the judge. Keep in mind that most of your judges have heard many speeches; your topic must arouse their interest and inspire them to listen.

Did you organize your after-dinner speech?

You need to organize your ideas for your judges. Judges want to hear speeches that have a clear and purposeful structure. Many organizational patterns are appropriate for after-dinner speaking. The pattern you use should highlight the humor and insight in your speech.

Did you develop your points with insight and humor?

Judges expect an entertaining but intelligent speech on a significant topic. Successful after-dinner speakers conduct library research on their topic. This research should help you develop the insightful analysis you wish to share with your judge. Rely on the best, most recent sources of evidence on your topic when you conduct research for your speech.

You should present your analysis with many forms of humor. Stories, jokes, irony, and plays-on-words can all help you convey your message and provoke laughter from the audience at the same time. As you write your after-dinner speech, search for entertaining and humorous means of communicating your ideas.

The humor you use should be directly connected to your central theme and amusing to your audience. What is funny to you and your friends may not amuse your audience. As you search for humorous ways of expressing your central theme, keep your audience in mind and adjust your sense of humor to the values of your audience.

Did you deliver your after-dinner speech clearly and eloquently?

Judges reward after-dinner speakers who present their speech in a clear, conversational mode. Most judges appreciate an energetic, engaging, and humorous delivery. You should convey the impression that you find your subject interesting and entertaining, and that you want to entertain your audience. The best after-dinner speakers maintain a balanced delivery and adjust their volume, pace, and tone to the judge, the room, and the situation. They also integrate the humor they offer with their analysis of the topic.

With the judges' expectations in mind, let us move to the steps you must take to create and present a successful after-dinner speech.

Creating a Successful After-dinner Speech

The following guidelines are designed to help you select, develop, and present your after-dinner speeches. Each step is important if you are to create a speech that entertains and enlightens.

Brainstorm topics for your after-dinner speech

You need to find a topic for your after-dinner or special ocassion speech that is interesting, relevant, and potentially humorous to you and your judges. The topic you select should inspire you to conduct the necessary research, and it should inspire your audience to listen to what you have to say. As you select a topic for your after-dinner speech, try to pick a subject that is important and one about which you might say something novel and humorous.

The process of brainstorming is designed to provoke a wide-ranging discussion between you, your forensics teacher, and teammates on possible topics for after-dinner speeches. During the brainstorming period, search for any topic that even remotely sounds interesting. At this stage, you should write down all the topics that come to mind.

Let us say the brainstorming session produced the topics on page 185.

Guidelines

Steps in the Creation and Presentation of an After-dinner Speech

Before the Tournament

1. Brainstorm topics and subjects for your after-dinner speech.
2. Conduct research on the topic you select.
3. Identify a theme and organize your research into a format that puts your ideas into a meaningful order.
4. Write the first draft of your speech.
5. Practice your speech.

During the Tournament

6. Present your speech to your judges.
7. Listen to the other speakers.
8. Modify your speech as necessary.

After the Speech and Tournament

9. After the tournament, read your ballots and use the comments made by your judges to improve.
10. Conduct additional research and practice.

Checklist

Results of the Brainstorming Session

First day of school	Clothes	Muzak	Drugs
Daytime talk shows	Diets	Beer	Bad dates
Diamonds	Brothers	Braces	New jobs
Bad movies	Cars	1-900 numbers	Dogs

You should keep in mind that treatments of some of these topics might offend certain judges. For example, the beer and drugs topics may not be suitable for some judges. However, if you do choose these topics and develop a tasteful and an intelligent speech, these judges might respond favorably. Your forensics teacher can help you make the right artistic choice once you have generated topics during the brainstorming session.

You, your teammates, and forensics teacher can determine which topics have the most potential. You may find after the discussion and after a brief visit to the library that you find daytime talk shows and diets to be topics with potential humor and significance. You will need to choose between the two.

Your forensics teacher may tell you that dieting has been the topic of several after-dinner speeches in the past few years. She may worry that the topic has been overdone. On the other hand, your forensics teacher may tell you that daytime talk shows have not been the subject of an after-dinner speech for some time and that this topic has potential. Unless you are confident you can write a novel after-dinner speech on diets, you should choose talk shows as your topic. Your next step is to do some library research on talk shows.

Research your topic

Once you have decided to speak about daytime talk shows, you need to find books, articles, and other sources that address this topic. You should read books and articles by a number of authors describing the role talk shows play in our society. These sources can provide you with statistics, quotations, photographs, and other materials that you might use in your speech.

As you conduct your research, look for useful quotations for the body of your speech. You may use these quotations to explain your ideas. You should record these quotations on notecards. The sources of these quotations should be recorded on your notecards and in your bibliography. Take care when you record quotations from external sources, for you are responsible for not distorting the meaning of those who authored the quotations.

You should also look for vivid and appealing visual illustrations that you can use as visual aids (if the rules permit) during your after-dinner speech. A visual aid can help your audience envision your topic. For example, you may find photographs of two daytime talk show hosts. You might take these illustrations to a photograph shop to have them enlarged. Once you enlarge them, you could place them on posterboards and use them as visual aids. After you have done enough reading on talk shows to develop an after-dinner speech, you need identify a theme to organize your ideas.

Identify a theme and organize your research into a meaningful format

The theme of your after-dinner speech should be the center of your speech. You should capture the theme in two or three sentences. The theme of a speech on talk shows might be that "Talk shows tell us who we are and who we aren't. Talk shows define America." From this theme, you could draw several points

---

Guidelines

Outline of an After-dinner Speech

Central Thought: "Talk shows tell us who we are and who we aren't. Talk shows define America."

1. A history of the subject
   Example: A brief history of the talk show

2. The speaker's favorite talk show
   Example: A description of the talk show, its host, guests, and common topics

3. The speaker's least favorite talk show
   Example: A description of the talk show, its host, guests, and common topics

4. Conclusion: In praise of the talk show; the good, bad, and ugly

---

to build your speech. You could, for example, expand the topic to include specific talk show hosts, talk show stories, or talk show guests.

A number of organizational patterns are possible. In writing this speech, you might want to give a brief history of the talk show in the American culture and then describe your two or three favorite (or not-so-favorite) talk shows. As you describe and celebrate your favorite talk shows, you might joke about talk show hosts, their guests, and the conversations that occur on these shows. The outline above displays a possible after-dinner speech on talk shows.

The serious undertone of a speech on talk shows might be the significant influence such shows have on the American culture. This insight could be bridged to a humorous characterization of your favorite and not-so-favorite daytime talk show. You would need to develop a clever and witty portrayal of these talk shows. Such a portrayal should be fun for you and your judge.

You might decide that your speech needs visual aids (if the tournament rules permit). These visual aids should complement the central theme you wish to develop and should contribute to the humor of your commentary. The visual aids you use should be incorporated into the organization and the flow of the speech. Your goal is to weave your central thought throughout the points you present, and the visual aids should help you enhance the central thought and the humor of the speech.

Write the first draft of your speech

Experienced after-dinner speakers write many drafts of their speeches. Your first draft should not be the one you use at the tournament. Use your outline as you write your speech, incorporating your central thought and using a structure that highlights what is serious and entertaining about your topic. As with any speech, your after-dinner speech should have an introduction, a body, and a conclusion.

Experienced speech writers keep their audience in mind as they write their speeches. You should do the same. Adapt the introduction, body, and conclusion of your speech to your audience. Your goal is to entertain your audience on a topic that has a serious undertone. The best after-dinner speakers attempt to determine what topics their audiences believe to be important and open to humorous interpretations.

As you write the introduction, keep your audience in mind. The introduction should give your audience a good reason to listen to the rest of your speech. The after-dinner speech should begin with a catchy introduction. Since your judges are looking for entertainment, that should be the goal of the introduction. At the same time, the introduction should provide the audience with good reasons why the topic of your speech is of social and personal concern. Most important, the introduction should contain the central thought or theme of the speech.

In the body of the speech, you should develop themes and ideas that illustrate, in a humorous and entertaining manner, the central theme of your speech. You should devote the greatest amount of time to topics and subtopics that will lend themselves to humorous applications. The central theme, which should reflect a serious undertone, ought to connect all the topics and subtopics into a coherent whole.

In the conclusion of the speech, you must create a sense of completion for the judges. Many after-dinner speakers use the conclusions of their speech to underscore the importance of the subject to the audience. In concluding an after-dinner speech, many speakers rephrase the central thought, usually in the form of a joke.

Your audience's reaction to your speech and your continuing research on the subject should prompt you to modify sections and sentences in the first draft. Your speech should be in a constant state of evolution over the course of the forensics season. Always take time to make the necessary revisions, and your speech will be more successful as a result.

Practice your speech

You must establish a practice schedule so that you can hear from others whether they find your speech entertaining, humorous, and significant. Take these practice sessions seriously. They should, if possible, resemble the tournament environment. You should practice alone, in front of your friends, and in front of your forensics teacher.

Use the responses of these practice audiences to improve your speech. Your friends and teacher can give you important clues about how the judges will respond to your speech at the tournament. Your forensics teacher can advise you on how to adapt your speech so that it better suits your audience. Seek out constructive criticism and advice that can improve your after-dinner speech.

Present your speech to your judges

By the time you arrive at the tournament, your speech should be in good order. You have at least two or three opportunities to present your speech to judges. While you may have practiced your speech many times, make sure you deliver it with the energy of your first performance. Judges give speakers higher scores if they appear to be sincerely interested in the speech. This is particularly true for the after-dinner speaker. Judges reward speakers who deliver their speeches with vigor. Judges expect after-dinner speakers to connect with the audience and bring the subject of the speech to life.

Don't be too concerned about mistakes you might make. Often, the judge will not know if you forgot a sentence or a paragraph of your speech unless you let on through your facial expression or delivery. If you do make a mistake, don't stop speaking. Many beginning and experienced speakers make mistakes. The goal is to continue speaking and to finish making your point.

Listen to the other speakers

Before and after you speak, you should listen carefully to the speeches of your competitors. As you know, you should be a good audience member. This means that you should treat the other speakers as you would want them to treat you. If you hear a speaker present a perspective with which you do not agree, do not let your disagreement show. Be a good listener and a civil audience member.

You can learn much from the speeches of your competitors. Take notes on what they do well and how they organize and present their speeches. Their speeches can provide you clear examples of effective and not-so-effective techniques. After the tournament is over, you may wish to use these examples as models for improving your speech.

Modify your speech as necessary

Your speech should be in a constant state of evolution. You may decide after your first round that some minor changes need to be made. For example, you may decide to change the wording of the introduction or use a different joke in the body of the speech. You should, however, wait to make major changes in your speech until the tournament is over. You should take time to think through any major alterations in your speech. Make sure to talk with your forensics teacher or an experienced team member if you think your after-dinner speech needs significant change.

After the tournament, read your ballots and use the comments made by your judges to improve

When the tournament is over, your forensics teacher will give you the ballots your judges wrote in reaction to your speech. These ballots tell you how your judges ranked and rated you in comparison to your competition, and they record what your judge felt were the strengths and weaknesses of your speech. With the help of your forensics teacher, read these ballots and identify the comments you should use to revise and improve your speech.

Seek out recurring statements in the ballots. If, for example, all the judges commend you for the topic you have selected and the organization of the speech, then you know you don't need major changes. If two of your judges suggest that your delivery needs more pep and that the conclusion is weak, then during your practice sessions you should focus on developing a more energetic style and a stronger conclusion.

Your ballots should be of great use to you, but use them carefully. Your forensics teacher can help you to discriminate between helpful comments and those that may not be as useful. Because you may have the same judges at the next tournament, you will need to read your ballots for insight into their feelings and beliefs. This insight will help you adapt your speech to your judges.

Conduct additional research and practice

Your speech should change after every tournament. Some parts of the speech may remain the same; others will need to be modified, slightly or drastically. Your research and practice sessions should be ongoing, even if you took first place at a tournament! Additional research and practice are always necessary to keep your information up-to-date and your delivery sharp.

Judges give great weight to after-dinner speakers who incorporate current events into their speeches. This means that you should keep up on the latest news about your subject. For example, if you plan to speak about talk shows, keep up on the latest developments on this topic by reading *T. V. Guide* and other sources. The external sources you discover on your topic during your early outing to the library may be outdated after the first tournament. You must incorporate the most timely and recent information into your speeches.

Some speakers read the newspaper every day to find the most current news on the topic of their after-dinner speech. You might do the same. The libraries you visit should have the most recent periodical literature on your topic. The best after-dinner speakers keep current on their topic throughout the forensics season.

You should also continue to practice your speech throughout the forensics season. Your practice sessions should resemble the tournament environment. As you practice, identify specific improvements you wish to make. Your on-going commitment to improving your speech will help you retain the energy you need to be a successful after-dinner speaker.

A Model After-dinner Speech

You now know the rules of the after-dinner speaking event and the steps you need to take to write and present an after-dinner or special occasion speech. This section presents a model after-dinner speech delivered by Chris O'Keefe on the subject of Shakespeare. He states his central thought clearly: "O, I come not to bury Shakespeare, but to praise him." In this speech, Mr. O'Keefe presents two major topics. First, he examines the major problems people have in understanding Shakespeare. Second, he argues that despite Shakespeare's talent, he probably would not be very successful if he were writing today.

On page 191 is an outline of Chris O'Keefe's after-dinner speech about Shakespeare.

This speech displays all the components of a successful after-dinner speech. As you consider the parts of this speech, think how you might use this speech as a model.

The Introduction

The introduction of an after-dinner speech should provide the audience with a good reason for listening. An effective introduction should highlight why the subject of the speech should amuse and interest the judge. Ideally, the introduction develops an image that can be used to bind together the body and the conclusion of the speech. The introduction should also contain the central thought or theme of the speech. Finally, the introduction should preview and provide a transition to the body of the speech.

The introduction of Mr. O'Keefe's speech provides a clever overview of his central thought and of the two points that form the body of his speech. The introduction provides the judges with a clear topic, a developed organizational pattern, a sense of coherence, and a series of clever statements and antics:

> At a certain point in my life, I came to the realization that I wanted to spend my life's effort to become a great playwright. (Looks at watch) It has been about an hour and a half now and the feeling is still growing strong. As a matter of fact, I have already written my first play. I wrote

---

Guidelines

Organizational Pattern of Chris O'Keefe's After-dinner Speech on Shakespeare

I.   Introduction
     Presentation of central theme or idea: "O, I come not to bury Shakespeare, but to praise him."
     Preview of Body
     A. The major problems people have in understanding Shakespeare.
     B. Despite Shakespeare's talent, he probably would not be very successful if he were writing today.
         Transition
         Body
II. The major problems people have in understanding Shakespeare.
III. Despite Shakespeare's talent, he probably would not be very successful if he were writing today.
IV. Conclusion

---

it out in the hall, or really wherever I could find a place to sit down. (Pulls out toilet paper). I hope that a hundred years from now that people still admire, appreciate, and respect my work. It is that reason that I stand here today to praise a sixteenth-century playwright whose works are still with us. O, I come not to bury Shakespeare, but to praise him. In order to better understand Shakespeare, let's look first at major problems people have in understanding Shakespeare. And second, and this is more of a statement on today's society, why despite Shakespeare's talent he probably would not have been very successful if he were writing today.

As you read this introduction, you will observe that he begins with two puns, a clear statement of his central thought, and an overview of his two major points. This introduction entertains his judges and establishes that the topic has a serious undertone.

Modern people have major problems understanding Shakespeare

As you read his explanation on the next page, notice that O'Keefe identifies reasons why people do not understand Shakespeare:

Now many people have problems understanding Bill's work, and understandably so. Many state that when they hear Shakespeare for the first time, it is literally like listening to a foreign language.

"Hung be the heavens of Mantou. Forborne, gaudy and remorseful. Made felony to drink of such large style. He who dies has not o'ergrown the honor, garden or injustice"

* * * * * * * *

"What?

What did he say?

The guy in the leotards up there, what did he just say?"

In this sequence, he reads a section from Shakespeare's work to illustrate his first point. The humor is also evident in the follow-up. He continues to develop his first point in this manner:

Many people would like to read Shakespeare, but they are put off by his intricate and his complicated story lines. But, Shakespeare only does this for the sake of drama. The more complexity, the more human conflict. And the greater the human conflict, the greater the scene:

"Give me the money."

"By my family name I shall not."

"Then fight to the death!"

"To the death."

And this is *brilliant* play writing, because we want to know what happens next. But take away the conflict, and everything changes:

"Give me the money."

"Okay, here you go, here's the money."

"Uh, give me . . . *more* money!"

"Look, that's all I got. How about a back rub?"

Something gets lost in the translation, hum?

Again, he demonstrates, through humorous juxtaposition, the truth of his first point: that many people in today's society do not understand Shakespeare. He brings this home by performing an updated version of the famous Shakespearean play *Romeo and Juliet:*

Now that we can understand Shakespeare, let's see one of Shakespeare's plays. It can't be done, you say. It would take three hours you say! Well, you obviously never heard of O'Keefe's theater for Shakespearean drama! Today's production the one-minute version of *Romeo and Juliet.* Music please. (He hums the theme from *Romeo and Juliet.*) Our story begins in the small town of Verona.

"All Montagues unite and kill the Capulets! Ugh! Ugh! Ugh!"

"All Capulets unite and kill the Montagues! Ugh! Ugh! Ugh!"

"Hello, my name is Romeo and I'm a Montague."

"Hello, my name is Juliet and I'm a Capulet."

"I think I'll go to the Capulet dance tonight and shake my booty."

"I can hardly wait for the dance tonight!"

"Maybe I'll meet someone and fall in love at first sight."

"Hello there young lady. What a wonderful dance. My name is Romeo."

"My name is Juliet."

"May I have this dance? May I fall in love with you?"

"Would you like to get married?"

"Yes. Yes. Yes. But I am a Capulet."

". . . And I'm a Montague, and our families hate each other."

"Oh, oh, oh, oh, oh, oh."

"Well, let's get married anyway. Shall we?"

"Oh yes, let's do. Oh, Friar Lawrence!"

"Yes, that's me."

"Uh, where are you Friar Lawrence?"

"Right here. In the middle focal point."

"Friar Lawrence. Friar Lawrence. Juliet and I want to get married."

"Will you do it? Huh? Huh? Huh?"

"All right, I'll do it. Do you solemnly swear . . . ?

"Do you solemnly swear . . . ?

"I now pronounce you man and wife." (Big kiss)

"But Juliet, what will your mother say? What will your father say?"

"Oh, they'll probably want to kill you."

"Oh, oh, oh, oh, oh. Well, I'd better run away."

"Goodbye for now, my love!"

"Juliet, it's me Friar Lawrence. Drink this! It will make it seem as if you're dead for 48 hours."

"Oh, just what I always wanted. Thank you (gulp)."

"Juliet, I'm back! Oh my goodness, it looks like you're dead.

"I think I'll kill myself! Ugh! Ugh! Ugh! Ugh! Egh!"

"Oh, my goodness, I just awoke. But my Romeo is dead. I think I'll kill myself too! Ugh! Ugh! Ugh! Ugh! Egh!"

"For never was a story of more woe
Than this of Juliet and Her Romeo."

God, Shakespeare was the greatest! Unfortunately, Shakespeare probably wouldn't have been very successful if he were writing today. If Juliet committed suicide in a [modern] setting, audience members would be too distracted to appreciate the scene: "Hey, Marge, you think her insurance policy is going to cover that?"

While we do not have the benefit of hearing his performance of this one-minute version of *Romeo and Juliet,* you can tell that he had great fun putting together and presenting this humorous interpretation. His characterizations of the three principals in the play (Romeo, Juliet, and Friar Lawrence) were a humorous parody of the original play. At the end of this parody of *Romeo and Juliet,* he returns to the point he has developed by bringing the audience back to the present.

He develops a second reason why modern people fail to understand and appreciate Shakespeare:

> Another reason [why moderns fail to understand Shakespeare] is that Shakespeare was lousy with titles. They lacked a certain pizzazz needed for today's commercialized culture. For example, Shakespeare's first play was written about the War of Roses, and he called it "Henry the VI, Part I." Shakespeare's second play was entitled "Henry the VI, Part II," and the creative title for the third play was "Henry the VI, Part III." Brilliant plays, each and every one. However, if he tried to pull that number today, no one would even read his work. Unless, he agreed to certain improvements in the packaging. Hut-t-t-t-t-t-t-t- 20th Century Fox presents a Billy the Bard trilogy, "Henry VI, Part I: Rose Wars!", "Henry VI, Part II: Cardinal Beaufort and the Temple of Doom!" and "Henry VI, Part III: Petruchio Lives." Eee. Eee. Eee. Now those are interesting titles.

The humor of this section is striking. He takes the titles Shakespeare gave to his plays and gives them to Hollywood. The modernized titles "Henry VI, Part I: Rose Wars!" and "Henry VI, Part II: Cardinal Beaufort and the Temple of Doom!" remind us of the "Star Wars" trilogy and the "Raiders of the Lost Ark" series of movies. In yet another way, Mr. O'Keefe gives his audience reason to agree with the central theme of the speech. With this reason he concludes his first point and turns to his second point.

Despite Shakespeare's talent, he probably would not have been very successful if he were writing today

In this section of the speech, he pictures Shakespeare writing greeting cards for Hallmark, working as a math teacher and a stand-up comedian, and applying for a job with the *National Enquirer:*

> Now, I suggest that Shakespeare's inability to play Hollywood's game would force him to seek another form of employment. For example, writing the cheerful fillers for Hallmark greeting cards: "Life is a tale told by an idiot! Happy Birthday, Dad!" With failure here, we might see William Shakespeare, math teacher, "2b or maybe 3d, perhaps 2c, that is the question." And of course, William Shakespeare, stand-up comedian:

"Hello, I'd like to talk to you today about the lunatic, the lover, and the poet, and then we'll talk about relatives on my father's side."

"Sometimes, I call my friends together: Horatio, Mercutio, [Phebe], Troilus, [Iago], gather here. I want you all to go out and get *real* names. Please laugh."

Oh, but Shakespeare would not perish. No. For the Bard had a unique gift in his ability to write about relationships. Especially the relationships of influential, famous people.

"Have a seat, Mr. Shakespeare. You know, we usually don't have need of any playwrights here at the *National Enquirer,* but since your work is only loosely based on the truth, we are going to give you a chance."

The four scenarios he sets are humorous and firmly establish the second point of his speech. The way he weaves these scenarios together is an excellent example for you when you begin writing your after-dinner speech. After completing his second point, he moves to his conclusion.

Conclusion: Read Shakespeare!

In his conclusion, he makes sure that his judges are aware of the serious point and message at the center of his after-dinner speech:

So, what's the point? Well, actually, there's two. The first is: Go home and read a Shakespeare play. The second: Go home and read a Shakespeare play or else! No, ah . . . I guess the reasons I am up here are really very selfish ones; you see, I am in love. I am in love with the thirty-eight plays of William Shakespeare. And, I've had a fling or two on the side with a poem, but it didn't amount to anything. For all the reasons I have mentioned, I don't think people read Shakespeare enough. So what if he is difficult to understand. That can be learned. So what if he's not commercial enough. You try to be commercial 400 years after you've been dead. It's tough! So go home, read, and enjoy.

You know if Shakespeare were sitting in this room—alive and well— sitting right here in this chair, he would be 412 years old. That's Lorne Greene's age in dog years. And I would approach this great man, and I might say, "Mr. Shakespeare, perhaps you would like to see the way it's supposed to be done." Ah No. Or—or—, I might say, "Willy, baby, I've read all of your plays. Thanks!"

This conclusion is a clear statement of the central theme of his speech. Recall one of the statements from the introduction: "O, I come not to bury Shakespeare, but to praise him." With this conclusion Mr. O'Keefe crystallizes the serious undertone of his speech: People should read Shakespeare!

Judges' Reactions

Mr. O'Keefe became the national champion in after dinner-speaking with this speech. However, four of the six speakers in the final round received first place ranks from the judges, making this a close decision. The judges were consistent in their praise for Mr. O'Keefe's topic selection, introduction, use of humor, and delivery. As you read the comments made by these judges, think how you might adapt your after-dinner speech to their values and stated preferences.

One judge commented that the "topic [O'Keefe] chose lent itself very well to [after-dinner speaking]. I believe that topics should be fresh and novel, and his Shakespearean theme did this. He took a topic common to all of us and presented a wide range of humor, which was effective." Another judge agreed and wrote that O'Keefe's topic choice was "exceptionally apt. It allowed him to comment on Shakespeare and his writings, but also served as a vehicle for comments on other related subjects."

The judges commended him for his introduction and use of humor: "His catchy introduction and one-minute version of *Romeo and Juliet* were delightful." A second judge wrote: "The introductory gimmicks worked well; so did the humor adapted to his forensics audience (always a risk, unless it is fresh and exceptionally clever)." A third judge observed: "While the other speakers obviously used unique humor, their themes have all been done before." Perhaps the most revealing comment came from a fourth judge who ranked O'Keefe's speech second out of six:

> All the speeches were entertaining, but in the less successful speeches, although I laughed, I found myself asking what that funny story or example had to do with the topic of the speech. In the more successful speeches, every time I laughed I found myself reinforcing the thesis of the speaker. I ranked Doyle #1 and O'Keefe #2 and gave them equal speaker points because they both had selected manageable subjects, used an appealing style of humor, analyzed their audience well, and developed a coherent point of view through their use of humor.

Most judges prefer that speakers use humor to reinforce the central thesis of their after-dinner speech. O'Keefe's central point was well developed and coherent in the judges' opinions. One judge wrote that: "Perhaps the most outstanding feature of O'Keefe's speech was his use of a serious point. To his credit, it was carefully woven throughout the speech, instead of being tacked on the end. His plea to read a Shakespeare play was very realistic."

Finally, the judges applauded Mr. O'Keefe's delivery. One of his judges commented:

> Chris was outstanding in his delivery. He demonstrated versatility (as could be assumed from the success of his impersonations) and an excellent sense of timing. Never did he push humor too much. The stage

area proved an impediment for some speakers whose speeches required them to move into the audience. This led one speaker to avoid the stage totally (a poor choice, since she was not visible to her audience) and another leapt from stage floor and back again. Chris lost nothing from the stage setting; instead, he demonstrated command of the speaking area.

Another judge agreed:

Finally, O'Keefe's delivery was excellent. He was conversational in his style which added a naturalness to his humor which is important in this event. Too often, ADS speakers must try too hard to make an audience laugh and their style becomes affected. Fortunately, this did not happen to O'Keefe as he gave a very professional performance, one which befits a national champion!

Not all of the judge's reactions were positive. One judge did not like the *Romeo and Juliet* rendition: "My only complaint is that the 'one-minute version' of *Romeo and Juliet* is a convention that has been used very often in ADS speeches, and has appeared in many previous final rounds. ADS contestants should always be striving to use new conventions which add originality to their speeches."

One judge criticized O'Keefe's conclusion: "There was no need for Chris to tack on a serious point at the end of his speech (in fact, I think he erred by 'hitting us over the head' with a statement of the serious point), because he had integrated substantive material throughout the entire speech." Finally, another judge faulted O'Keefe for failing to project his voice.

No speech is perfect, but this one does serve as an excellent model of an after-dinner speech. The theme and structure, the humor and delivery were all first-rate. When you start to write the first draft of an after-dinner speech, and you need guidance and some examples of how you might make your points, turn to this speech for direction.

The next section will provide you with some guidance on how to practice your after-dinner speech.

Practicing Your After-dinner Speech

There are several steps you can take in practicing your after-dinner speech. The steps suggested here are useful after you have followed the suggestions offered earlier in this chapter.

Imagine how your judges will respond to your after-dinner speech

As you know, your after-dinner speech should entertain your judges and possess a serious undertone. A primary instrument used by after-dinner speakers to entertain the audience is humor. As you create and discover humorous techniques (jokes, puns) to use in your after-dinner speech, try to use humor that will entertain a broad spectrum of people. One of Mr. O'Keefe's judges put it this way:

> For an ADS to be successful there must be a universal understanding of the humor employed by the speaker. That is where audience analysis comes to the forefront. I felt that both Doyle and O'Keefe employed humor that was entertaining to a broad spectrum of people that could be expected to be in an audience at a forensics contest.

One way to check the universal appeal of the humor you use is to imagine how your judges will react when they hear your after-dinner speech. Many judges do not enjoy humor that insults or demeans; nor do they like humor that is silly or shallow. As you write your after-dinner speech, keep your judges in mind. Write your jokes for a broad spectrum of people rather than for one generation or group of people.

Revise and Refine Your After-dinner Speech

In many ways, your after-dinner speech will never be completely finished. You should look for ways to improve and to strengthen your speech. As the forensics season progresses, your after-dinner speech should also progress and evolve. You should add new jokes, stories, and puns to your speech.

Practice Your After-dinner Speech

As you practice your after-dinner speech, you should take the practice sessions seriously. When you are alone, you may wish to tape record your speech. You can then listen to the tape and think of ways to improve your speech. You should also invite your teammates and friends to watch you present your after-dinner speech. They can provide you with criticism and advice on how to strengthen your speech.

Your forensics teacher can also counsel you about how to improve the speech. Keep in mind that your forensics teacher understands how your judges think and feel, and can help you understand the preferences and values of your judges. Make sure to use the criticism, advice, and insight your teammates, friends, and forensics teacher offer to you.

Read your ballots and record suggestions for improvement

When the tournament is over, your forensics teacher will give you ballots from your judges. These ballots record the ranking and rating your judge awarded you and written comments on the strengths of your speech and areas that need improvement. Judges devote time and energy to writing ballots for you, and you should read them with care, noting both the compliments and the concerns of the judges. Your forensics teacher will help you to use the comments on the ballots to improve your speech.

You do not need to agree with the comments made by your judges. However, the comments reveal how your judges reacted to you and your speech. If you wish to persuade judges, you need to understand how they view the world and your speech. Among the most valuable lessons forensics can teach you is why and how you must adapt every speech to your audience.

Make use of the checklist on page 201 as you practice for competition in after-dinner speaking.

CONCLUSION

Competition in after-dinner, or special occasion, speaking should help you develop the ability to entertain audiences with a humorous speech that has a serious undertone. Judges expect to be both entertained and enlightened by an after-dinner speech. As you write your after-dinner speech, use humor that appeals to a universal audience and deliver your speech with energy and pizzazz. After-dinner speaking is and should be an event that celebrates tasteful humor.

Checklist

Checklist for the After-dinner Speech

Before the Forensics Tournament

1. Know the educational aims of after-dinner speaking.
2. Know the rules of the after-dinner speech.
3. Understand what will happen in the after-dinner speaking round.
4. Understand what judges expect of after-dinner speakers.
5. Visualize the steps you should follow in selecting a central thought.
6. Select a central thought and conduct the necessary research.
7. Know how to develop points that support the central thought.
8. Develop introductions, transitions, and conclusions.
9. Consider models of outstanding after-dinner speeches.
10. Establish practice schedules.

During Practice

11. Practice by yourself.
12. Practice in front of friends.
13. Practice in front of your forensics teacher.

At the Tournament

14. Deliver your speech with energy.
15. Listen to the other speakers and use them as models.
16. Make minor adjustments in your speech if necessary.

After the Tournament

17. After the tournament, read your ballots and use the comments to improve.
18. Work to revise, update, and strengthen your after-dinner speech.
19. Practice for the next tournament.

SECTION FOUR

The Principles and Practices of Oral Interpretation: The Literary Study and Performance of Prose, Dramatic, and Poetic Literature

Forensics provides you with a variety of events that can help you develop stronger habits and skills of communication. Many tournaments offer competitors the opportunity to present oral interpretations of prose, drama, and poetry. Participation in the oral interpretation should help competitors accomplish two primary educational objectives. First, speakers should come to fully understand and appreciate the literary selections they present and perform. Such an understanding and appreciation results from careful research, thoughtful analysis, and a search for authentic meanings. Second, speakers master the habits and skills necessary for effective oral performance of literature.

The successful student of oral interpretation understands that these two objectives work together. Charlotte I. Lee and Timothy Gura in their book *Oral Interpretation* combined these two objectives when they defined oral interpretation as "the art of communicating to an audience a work of literary art in its intellectual, emotional, and aesthetic entirety." According to Lee and Gura, the interpreter must recreate the intent and the vision of the author of the work being performed. At the same time, the interpreter becomes a creative artist by making choices about the arrangement, presentation, and performance of a literary work. In short, oral interpretation involves, in the words of Lee and Gura, "sharing an experience, first with the writer or the speaker of a selection, and then with an audience."

There are several events in the interpretative category. Many tournaments offer forensics students opportunities to compete in serious reading, memorized serious, humorous reading, memorized humorous, poetry readings, and reader's theatre. All events in the interpretative category rely on some basic principles. Chapter 10 is devoted to an explanation of the principles that should guide the student in the oral interpretation of prose, drama, and poetry. Chapter 11 explains how prose and dramatic literature can be subjects of oral interpretation. Poetry is the subject of chapter 12. Reader's theatre is covered in the appendix of this book.

CHAPTER TEN

The Principles of Oral Interpretation

Competitors in serious, humorous, and poetry events select and perform cuttings from published novels, short stories, plays, or poetry in front of other competitors and judges. In all the interpretative events, you will create a theme and find novels, short stories, plays, and poems to develop and present the theme to your judge. In serious interpretation, for instance, you might cut selections from the novels of Saul Bellow, the writings of K. Kam, and the plays of August Wilson to illustrate the theme of family love and conflict. The selection of these authors would demonstrate the multicultural theme of family love and conflict, for many of Saul Bellow's novels deal with Jewish-American families, K. Kam's fiction features Chinese-American families, and August Wilson's plays are about African-American families.

In the humorous interpretation event, you might wish to make fun of stuffy professors and teachers. You could use Aristophanes' play *The Clouds,* David Lodge's novel *Small World,* and the poetry of W. H. Auden to create your interpretation. All three works portray professors and teachers in a humorous light.

You might create a poetry reading on poems read at presidential inaugurals. Robert Frost was invited by John F. Kennedy to read a poem at Kennedy's inaugural. Maya Angelou was invited by Bill Clinton to read a poem at Clinton's inaugural. A wonderful poetry reading might consist of the inaugural poems of Frost and Angelou.

With the assistance of your forensics teacher, choose the category of interpretation that best fits the theme and the type of literature you selected, and the mood it produces for your audience. You also need to select the division of competition that will inspire you to do your best.

You might ask why oral interpretation is a forensics event and not an activity sponsored by the theater department. This is a good question. Unlike theater, the specific goal of forensics is to teach competitors how to make strong and ethical arguments. Most forensics teachers believe forensics should provide speakers with opportunities to learn good habits and skills of argumentation. When you identify a theme and supporting materials for an oral interpretation, you do so to persuade and move your judge. Your humorous reading should produce laughter, smiles, and a light mood that is consistent with the theme; your serious reading should arouse anger, pity, or other similar emotions that relate to a central point, and your poetry reading should produce feelings and thoughts that flow from the sound and the content of the poems you select.

In all three events, you identify a theme and an argument you wish advance. You then present selections designed to persuade your judges that this theme and argument are important. Your theme becomes the claim of your speech, and your selections become the proof. As such, your oral interpretation is an argument designed to persuade your judge to feel and think in a certain manner.

The rules of these events are designed, in part, to focus your attention on the materials and texts you use in your oral interpretation. Theater students have a stage, costumes, props, and casts. Forensics students have their text, their voice, and their bodies. Forensics teachers do not intend to be drama coaches or to compete with theater instructors. While acting and oral interpretation have much in common, there are some differences between the two that result from the different educational goals of forensics and educational theater. The rules of the events, as you will see in chapters 11 and 12, guarantee that the text and the competitor's voice and body—not full-scale acting—are the primary components of oral interpretation. At least four differences exist between oral interpretation and acting.

The Differences Between Interpretation and Acting

A fine line separates acting from interpretation. However, some distinctions exist according to forensics teachers and oral interpretation experts. Many forensics teachers would describe the major difference this way: The actor represents and is the character or characters; the interpreter presents and suggests the character or characters. This distinction produces four differences between acting and interpretation. First, the tournament rules for almost all interpretive events prohibit the use of costumes, props, and other accessories commonly associated with the stage and acting. Without the accessories available to the theater actor, the oral interpreter is restricted to the text, voice, and body. Second, judges expect you to use gestures and body movement with restraint. Your voice, not your gestures and body movement, should be the primary means of communication.

A third difference between oral interpretation and acting is that in serious reading, humorous reading, and poetry, the emphasis is on the text. In fact, the rules of this event may call for contestants to "keep both hands on the manuscript and stand in one place when the text is presented." Because the rules may restrict hand and body movement, competitors in these categories of interpretation must communicate primarily through voice, facial gestures, and body posture.

Fourth, the actor has a broader frame than the interpreter. That is, the actor has a costume, backdrops, makeup, and performs on a stage between the curtain and the orchestra. The interpreter's body, voice, and text are the frames of the interpretation. That is why your text, voice, and body are the essence of your interpretation.

You now know why oral interpretation is a forensics event and how it differs from acting. In order to create a persuasive oral interpretation, you need to know the guidelines for choosing, interpreting, and presenting your selection. These principles explain what makes up a persuasive oral interpretation and how you can create a powerful theme and select literature that effectively illuminates the theme.

The Principles of Oral Interpretation

The oral interpreter should make an argument to an audience about the intellectual, emotional, and the artistic meanings of literature

The message of your oral interpretation is an argument that you want to adapt to the feelings and beliefs of your audience. An argument in oral interpretation consists of the theme and the supporting materials. This does not mean you will argue with your judge. Rather, your oral interpretation program should give your judges reasons for thinking and feeling in a manner consistent with the theme of your program.

For example, if your interpretative cuttings are designed to develop the theme that racism is evil, or that love is tragic, your goal is to persuade the judge that racism is evil or love is tragic. You want the theme, cuttings, and the performance to appeal to the judges' intellect and emotions; the judges should feel an urge to fight racism, or appreciate the tragedy of love after listening to your interpretation. As with the creation of any other speech, you should adapt your oral interpretation to your judges. Your oral interpretation is an argument made for an audience.

While the kind of argument you present may not belong in a debate, it should include appeals to the logic, emotions, and the artistic sensibilities of the judges. Another way of putting this is that your oral interpretation should achieve a balance among logic, emotion, and art.

Most respected works of literature sound more than one note. The best works of literature challenge your intellect, make you angry or sad, and impress you with their eloquence and artistry. Choose sources of material from the best and most respected writers, and take care to fully and fairly represent their work to your judges. A full and fair representation requires you to cull and to cut scenes and poems that reflect the intellectual, emotional, and the artistic impulses of the authors and the literature you perform.

Some oral interpretations are imbalanced. They tend to overemphasize the emotional components of the selections. For example, some competitors take a 200-page novel and present the most graphic and dramatic scene for the purposes of their oral interpretation program. The interpreter has an obligation to present an author's work in a manner that represents the full meaning of the work. To take one scene and present it as representative of the entire play may violate the integrity of the playwright's work.

Whenever possible, provide your judges with a fair representation of the authors' work that you use in your oral interpretations. A fair representation explains to the judge why a character speaks as she does and what the intellectual grounds are for the character's action. Again, oral interpretation should be more than a compilation of emotion-provoking settings, scenes, characters.

At the same time, you should select scenes that do have a dramatic flair and still provide the judge with an intellectual framework. Certainly oral interpretation should be an event with passion. However, the passion should be integrated with the other aspects of the cuttings.

Oral Interpretation is an argument . . . made to an audience

Because you present your oral interpretations to forensics judges, you should be aware of their values and preferences concerning interpretation. Once you are aware of these values and preferences, you can better adapt your oral interpretation. What do judges want? Based on the comments judges write on ballots, judges pay great attention to the competitor's understanding of the literature, development of mood and character, and delivery.

Competitors should demonstrate an understanding of the material they present

Some forensics coaches worry that speakers spend more time on presentation techniques than on the literary study of their selections. The literary study of your materials, as the next principle outlines, is essential in order for you to understand the context in which the author wrote, the author's intentions, and the meaning of the entire work and of the cutting you select. Judges can tell when oral interpreters do not understand the literature they present.

In making such determinations, judges check to see if you have maintained the integrity of your materials and sources. Some competitors alter plots and make other significant changes in their materials to achieve dramatic impact. As you will see later in this chapter, maintaining the integrity of the materials is an important principle of oral interpretation.

Competitors should develop characters and images that are consistent with the theme and intent of the material

Judges wish to hear oral interpretations in which the competitor's interpretation reveals an understanding of the thoughts and emotions of the characters. Again, this requires a careful literary study of the material. In addition, judges pay close attention to matters of technique.

Judges often comment in their ballots about distinctions between characters, the interaction between characters, the nonverbal messages sent by the characters, and the focus of the characters. Judges give the best scores to interpreters who present well-developed characters who engage in believable dialogue. Again, judges expect you to master the techniques necessary to establish believable characters and convey your understanding of the material.

Judges look for well-delivered and well-performed oral interpretations

The vocal variety, volume, and gestures you use should fit the tone of the material and the immediate speaking situation. Judges reward oral interpreters whose skillful delivery enhances the effectiveness of their selections. Additionally, you should adjust your delivery to the room and the situation in which you present your selections.

The best oral interpreters understand and adjust to their audiences and to the speaking situations in which they perform. Because you will present your oral interpretation to many different judges in many different rooms at many different times, you must be sensitive to the volume of your voice, your body posture, and so on. On occasion, oral interpreters forget that the room in which they perform may be too small for a loud voice. If, for example, you are scheduled to present your interpretative selections in a small room, you may need to reduce your volume. The need to adjust to your judges should be in the forefront of your mind from the time you select your theme to the moment you pick up your trophy! In summary, the material, characterizations, and delivery are the three key categories used by judges to evaluate oral interpretations.

Given the need to adjust your theme and materials to your judge, how should you choose the prose, poetry, and short stories for your oral interpretations? With your judges in mind, use these three guidelines for selecting the best material.

Guidelines for Selecting Literature

The oral interpreter should select good literature, themes that embody experiences with broad appeal, and selections that can be performed in a fresh and revealing style that invites audience participation.

The oral interpreter should select good literature and themes

Begin your search for a theme and material by casting a wide net. There are many poems, plays, short stories, and novels from which you can draw your selections. The first step you can take is to think of the novels, short stories, plays, and poems you have read that caused you to think and feel deeply. Make a list of the literature you know and appreciate that you would like to share with others.

The second step you can take to identify an effective theme and appropriate materials is to talk to your forensics teacher, your English teacher, your drama teacher, and other people who appreciate literature. They may give you useful suggestions. Add these suggestions to your list.

Third, you should consult anthologies of literary pieces for suitable materials. The editors of these anthologies include poems, stories, and other literature that eloquently portray important ideas and emotions. Your teachers may have good anthologies, or you might consult your librarian.

How are you to choose selections for your oral interpretation program? You may want to begin by identifying a theme for your program. You need to find a theme that is interesting and significant to you and your judges; it should also have humorous or dramatic potential. Select a theme that inspires you to discover literary selections to interpret. Because you will deliver your oral interpretation to diverse audiences, the theme you select should be potentially entertaining and interesting to a broad spectrum of people. As you select a theme for your oral interpretation, try to pick a theme that is important and find literature that expresses the theme with energy and animation.

You might also start in the opposite direction and think about the novels, short stories, and plays that you have read. Perhaps a common theme will emerge that connects this literature. Once you identify a theme, you can begin the process of selecting material that helps you illustrate it.

Broad appeal
As you search for a theme and literature, use three touchstones in making your decisions. First, the theme and material you select should have a broad-based appeal and a universal impulse. Some literature is restricted in its meaning and focus. Other literature, like the *Diary of Anne Frank,* touches upon more general emotions and thoughts. This touchstone is particularly helpful, for you will present your oral interpretation to a number of judges and audience members who may see the world in many different ways.

Individuality
The second touchstone you can use to select a theme and material is the individuality expressed by the theme and the authors of the materials you choose. While you want to select material that has universal appeal, you want that appeal expressed in an innovative way. Again, *The Diary of Anne Frank* represents writing that expresses universal feelings and thoughts in a personal and intimate fashion.

Audience participation
You should also use a third touchstone: select literature that is rich, moderately subtle, and open to suggestion. Such literature encourages your audience to play an active role in your performance. How can your judges play an active role when you are the one who performs the oral interpretation? If your materials are rich, subtle, and open to suggestion, then your judges can use their experiences, background, and feelings in responding to your oral interpretation. Your goal is to present a theme and material that your judges can fully appreciate given their life experience.

After you select a theme and the literature you want to use to develop it, you still need to cut sections from that literature to create your program. You must study the literature carefully, for you are responsible for a fair and authentic interpretation of the authors' work. The next principle gives you some guidelines for creating a fair and an authentic interpretation.

Analyzing literature selected for the oral interpretation program
Forensics is an activity designed to encourage knowledgeable speaking. Some judges of oral interpretation are concerned that speakers spend too much time practicing and perfecting their performances and not enough time becoming knowledgeable about their selections. Beyond the skills of performance you

learn when competing in oral interpretation, you should also learn how to study and appreciate good literature. Research and study literature so that you understand how literature works and why it moves the reader and, ultimately, the listener.

You can take many approaches to gain an understanding of the literature you wish to present. For the beginning interpretation competitor, teachers of interpretation suggest two types of literary analysis: internal and external.

Internal analysis of the literature

An internal analysis involves a careful reading of the entire text from which you take cuttings. To achieve an understanding of the text, you need to look at the author's story. Any piece of material you elect to interpret tells a story about something. Even poems tell stories. Taking this perspective, the first question to ask is: What story or argument is the author trying to present?

To understand the author's story or argument, you must read the entire text, not just the selections you make from the text. You gain a much better sense of the selections if you have read and thought about them as they relate to the entire work. If you read only the selections, you cannot appreciate how they relate to the whole. If you fail to see how the totality of the text defines the meaning of your selections, you risk violating the integrity of the interpretative process.

Judy Yordon, author of *Roles in Interpretation* (Wm. C. Brown, 1982) suggests you ask the following questions to achieve an understanding of the literature you select:

Who is speaking?
To whom is the persona (the character) speaking?
Where is the persona speaking?
When is the persona speaking?
About what is the persona speaking?
How is the persona speaking?
Why is the persona speaking?

Answers to these questions reveal the shape and purpose of the materials you selected. These answers help you understand the author's original intent and communicate it through your oral interpretation. These answers also help you identify the argument the author is attempting to make. Remember, literature makes arguments about the world. You have a responsibility to accurately represent the authors' meaning through your oral interpretation of their work.

After you determine the answer to these questions, you need to classify the literary form used by the author to present the story and argument. Essentially, three forms of literature are available to you: prose, drama, and poetry. Prose literature involves ordinary speech or writing as distinguished from verse. Dramatic literature is usually written for actors who perform on a stage. Dramatic literature may involve prose and verse. Poetry is writing arranged to feature patterns of timing, rhythm, rhyme, syntax, and condensed language not usually seen according to a metrical pattern.

Once you classify your literary selection, you must acquire an understanding of why the author chose the story, argument, and the literary form you will perform. The text may reveal some partial answers to these questions, but you will need to go beyond the text to gain more complete answers. An external analysis of the literature can provide the necessary information needed to complement a thorough textual analysis.

External analysis of literature

As Lee and Gura note, novels, short stories, plays, and poems should be understood in their "intellectual, emotional, and aesthetic entirety." You can gain a partial understanding of the material by analyzing the story and the complete text. Such an analysis is a necessary beginning. Once you have analyzed the text, you need to consider a host of other factors.

Context and culture. First, you must discover the context and cultural problems that shaped the literature you have selected. Some writings are responses to a universal human condition. For example, many of the passages in the Torah, the Christian Bible, the Koran, and other sacred texts speak to problems all humans face. Other writings may address universal problems in culturally specific ways. Shakespeare's plays often revolve around universal problems, but an understanding of Elizabethan England and the problems faced by the English in the sixteenth century clarifies and explains Shakespearean dramatic literature. Once you identify the context and cultural problems faced by the authors of your selections, you gain a better understanding of your selections.

You need to conduct some library research to complete an external analysis of your literary selections. At this stage, you want to know how the outside world influenced the creation of the literature and how the author wished to influence the outside world in return. If you only read the text, the full meaning of the literature will elude you. For example, if you found your father's high school diary (and if you had his permission to read it!), he would need to explain what he meant by certain passages in the diary, and why he wrote certain sentences.

In the same manner, you need to read about the historical and cultural background that influenced the authors whose material you plan to use. For example, the poem "Ringing the Bells" by Anne Sexton tells a story about a woman who is institutionalized in a mental hospital. The text of the poem does not reveal the fact that Anne Sexton was hospitalized for mental illness and that she chose to take her life. Before you can gain an authentic understanding of "Ringing the Bells," you must know something about Anne Sexton's background, how her culture and society treated mental illness, the status of the mental institution, and the philosophical and moral implications of suicide.

Author's intent. Once you have a good idea about how outside forces influenced the creation of the literature, you need to determine how the author's literature was a response to these forces. That is, all prose, drama, and poetry is a response by an author to societal pressures and problems. The poem Maya Angelou ("On the Pulse of Morning') delivered at Bill Clinton's inauguration celebrated the multicultural make-up of the American people. The poem was her response to attacks on multiculturalism and was a strong argument justifying diversity. You must identify the author's intent in writing the prose, drama, and poetry you present.

Another way of conducting your literary analysis is to read the writings of critics who analyze and respond to literature. These critics offer their opinions about the quality and meaning of prose, drama, and poetry you might select for your programs. They offer you reasoned and documented explanations and evaluations of literature.

In many ways, you have to develop the skill of a literary critic as you prepare for your oral interpretation. You must select poems, plays, short stories, and novels; your choices depend on your evaluation of this literature. By reading literary critics, you can learn how to create and apply standards to literary works.

Lee and Gura, in their book *Oral Interpretation,* illustrate the value of good criticism. They take two poems about death; one by Helen Hoyt and the other by Emily Dickinson. They analyze the structure, content, and tone of the two poems and conclude that Emily Dickinson's poem better meets the standards of universality, individuality, and suggestion. Other critics apply different standards and may offer readers competing judgments concerning the worth of literary works. As you prepare for oral interpretation, read the criticism of those who are experts in the area.

In summary, before you can put together and perform a successful oral interpretation you must conduct an internal and an external analysis of your literary selections. An internal analysis is an evaluation of the selection and the entire text. An analysis of the cultural forces at work on the author and the author's reaction to these forces constitutes an external analysis of the text. Finally, the literary criticism offered by scholars and professional critics should play a role in any literary study.

All of this is much to ask of you as an oral interpreter. However, if you are to truly understand the literature you present, then such research is essential. Forensics judges often complain that competitors are good performers, but frequently fail to reflect a good understanding of the material they perform. You can emerge as an outstanding oral interpreter if you spend the time necessary to gain an understanding and an appreciation of the work you present. After you complete a thorough literary study of the novels, short stories, plays, and poems that you find compelling and thematically connected, you need to excerpt selections from these materials. The next principle provides you with the guidelines necessary for making proper cuttings.

When excerpting texts, the oral interpreter should preserve the essence of the literature

Obviously, the time limits of the interpretative events prevent your reading an entire novel, short story, or play. The time limit of humorous and dramatic reading is ten minutes. Prose and poetry performances are limited to five minutes. You need to find a representative passage from a thirty-five-page novel or a scene that displays the central idea of a play. Therefore, you need to excerpt, or cut for performance, representative scenes and passages from the texts you have selected.

When you excerpt you take representative passages from a novel, short story, play, or poem. You face great danger in cutting texts when you alter or delete characters, lines, and scenes to meet the time limit. Teachers of oral interpretation recognize the need for cutting but recommend, whenever possible, that you excerpt and not cut. In their book *Oral Interpretation,* Lee and Gura write: "Since virtually any limitation can be accommodated by excerpting, try to solve your dilemma by selecting segments to perform that are entire in and of themselves, thereby avoiding any internal cutting. Most works can be excerpted; few do not suffer seriously when they are cut internally."

Use the following guidelines in excerpting and cutting your texts.

When excerpting and cutting texts, you must maintain the essence of the literature

How do you determine what makes up the essence of the literature you have selected? Your careful literary study of the texts should reveal the intellectual, emotional, and aesthetic goals of the literature. An effective literary study also reveals the author's story and argument; it helps you understand the soul of the literature and the author's central point.

When you excerpt or cut a text, ask yourself if the author of the text would agree with your choices. Your literary study should give you insight into the author's values and the purpose of the literature. Keep these values in mind when you cut the author's literary creation. If, by deleting or altering a line or adding words or characters, you create a new message or change the mood intended by the author, you have failed to present the essence of the literature.

When cutting literature, do not alter the argument or the mood intended by the author

Experts on oral interpretation agree that cutting literature should be a last resort. In fact, teachers of oral interpretation encourage beginning students to avoid cutting altogether. If, however, you need to cut literature to meet the time limits, do so with care. Here are some suggestions you can use to maintain the essence of the literature:

—You can cut passages that describe the scene or provide information that can be put into the introduction. For example, if one of the characters gives the details of the scene, these details might be cut from the dialogue and made part of the introduction.

—You can cut complete episodes and characters if the story, argument, and the essence of the literature is intact.

—It is fine to cut tag lines and stage directions if you can communicate the intended message without them. If the author writes "And then Herzog said: 'My letters express my feelings and thoughts, but should not be read.' He then left the room and closed the door." You can cut the tag line "And then Herzog said" without violating the essence or the integrity of the work. You could also cut the stage direction "He then left the room and closed the door" if you convey this action with your performance.

—Poems should not be cut, unless you work closely with your forensics teacher. Experts in oral interpretation recommend use of poems that fit the time limit.

Once you have selected the literature and made appropriate excerpts and cuts, you need to mold your selections into a coherent, thematically connected program. To create such a program, you must carefully craft your introduction and transition. The next principle highlights the importance of your organization, introduction, and transitions in competitive oral interpretation.

Introduction, Transitions, and Organization

The oral interpreter should provide an introduction, transitions, and an organizational pattern that justify and advance the argument of the literature to be performed. Once again we return to the notion that an oral interpretation is an argument. This should be evident in the introduction, transitions, and organization of your program. Each component should feature the central theme and the argument of your program.

The introduction

At a minimum, the introduction should provide the judges with the author and the titles of the selections, the argument and theme connecting the selections, and the reasons why the judges should listen. Providing the judges with the authors and the titles of your selections is easy; explaining the argument and the theme of the literature and inspiring them to listen is more complicated.

Your introduction should accomplish three specific goals. First, you should give the judges enough information so they can understand and appreciate the literature. Often, information about the author and title may not be enough.

Your literary study may reveal some biographical information on your author that would help your judge understand the meaning of the literature. For example, if you chose to read Anne Sexton's poem on mental illness, you might tell your judges about her experiences with mental illness.

A second goal of the introduction is to specify the theme and the argument of the program and to justify your selection of literature. This is a critically important element of the introduction, for your judges need to know what intellectual, emotional, and artistic claims you plan to make and how the literature you have selected supports these claims.

A third goal of the introduction is to inspire an interest in your audience about the argument and the literature that make up your program. Consider how you can use appealing, vivid, and enticing stories, jokes, or illustrations to capture your judges' attention. Analyze how the following introductory remarks from an award-winning interpretation of *The Children's Story* achieve these three goals:

> When confronted with a threat of physical harm, we generally respond quickly and directly. But what about the unseen threat—one that seeks to control the mind and the heart? In order for a short story author to convey this vulnerability effectively, he or she must create a situation and characters that are characterized by strong subtlety and innuendo, yet cast sufficient doubt and suspicion to alert the reader to important clues that will eventually lead to a clear understanding of the events and characters involved. Author James Clavell achieves these goals in his chilling tale, *The Children's Story.*

This introduction accomplishes the objectives outlined above. First, the judges know that the text is James Clavell's *The Children's Story.* Second, the introduction identifies the argument of the program: that there may be an "unseen threat—one that seeks to control the mind and the heart." Further, the introduction justifies the selection of James Clavell's short story by setting up the goals that a short story must meet. The author of a short story must create situations and characters that are suggestive and are developed with subtlety and innuendo. The speaker justifies the selection of James Clavell's short story by suggesting that it "achieves these goals." The introduction provides the argumentation of the program, the central theme, and it invites the judges to actively participate in the interpretation.

Transitions

If your program includes more than one selection, you will need a series of powerful transitions in addition to a strong introduction. These powerful transitions remind the judge of the program's argument and connect the selections.

Assume you are presenting a poetry program on the pain suffered by those who encounter mental illness, and the first poem you read is Anne Sexton's

"Ringing the Bells." You might read a second poem, by another poet, and provide the judge with the following transition: "Anne Sexton's poem tells us of the pain suffered by those who are institutionalized because of their mental illness." In the next poem, entitled [insert name] the poet [insert name] expresses the grief of one who has lost a loved one to mental illness." With these transitions, you remind the judge of the argument and the theme of your program as you provide a bridge between poems.

Organization

Regardless of the literature you select for your program, you must write an introduction and transitions, and create a fitting organizational pattern. Most interpretative literature shares some basic characteristics. Drama, prose, and poetry all tend to reach stages of *climax,* or moments of crisis and resolution. Teachers of oral interpretation encourage their students to organize their selections and their programs around these moments of crisis and resolution.

In dramatic and prose readings, the movement to and from the climax reflects the organizational sense of the playwright. While the resolution or the "answer" may be part of the introduction, the problems that the answer addresses may make up a majority of the program. In poetry readings, an important turning point may exist within each poem. This turning point is called a *fulcrum.* Fulcrums are significant changes and shifts in the rhythm, language, or pitch and intonation of a poem.

The moments of crisis and resolution that make up the logical and emotional high points of drama, prose, and poetry exist within the context of a story and an argument. In drama and prose, the story and argument is organized by a plot. A plot provides an introduction, a body, and a conclusion to the story. In a poetry reading, the introduction should provide the judge with a coherent theme, and the poems should structure images and sounds around this theme and story line.

After you select your literature, make the appropriate excerpts and cuts, and write the introduction, you can then select the best organizational pattern. The organizational format you choose should fit the kind of literature you selected. Be sensitive to the differences between various types of literature.

Organizational patterns of dramatic literature. Typically, plot structures of drama move in this sequence: an initial exposition of the plot, scene, and characters; development of a conflict; a crisis and climax; and the outcome.

The exposition should provide additional introductory information on the plot, characters, scenes, and sets without repeating the introduction. You may choose to use the exposition to identify the problems and issues addressed in the play. You will base this decision on the nature of the play, for some plays give the audience the resolution at the beginning; others give the resolution in the body; finally, others place the resolution in the conclusion.

Checklist

Traditional Organizational Pattern for Dramatic Literature
1. Introduction and Exposition
2. Conflict
3. Crisis and Climax
4. Outcome

The development of the conflict takes place after the exposition. The conflict of the play identifies an issue, a problem, or a clash between characters that should capture the attention of the audience. The conflict reveals the theme and argument of the play.

The crisis and climax stage occurs when the conflict produces a turning point in the play that will eventually bring a sense of resolution. In the crisis state, the characters make, or are forced to make, choices that bring the literature to its highest point. When the action of the play reaches its highest point, or its climax, the issues and conflicts between the characters are fully realized.

The last stage of many dramatic plots provides the play with a conclusion that offers some solutions. The outcome may not solve the issues identified during the conflict stage. This final stage should make clear to the judges the meaning of the literature.

The plot structure of dramatic literature is often the organizational format used by authors of prose literature as well. Even though authors of dramatic and prose literature may use the same plot sequences, some clear differences exist between plays, prose, and poetry. Scripts written for the theater are written in the present tense; they de-emphasize the role of the narrator and place more emphasis on the scenes in which stories are told. These differences affect the choices you make in organizing your dramatic readings.

Organizational patterns for prose. In most prose readings, the narrator is the essential speaker and reports the feelings and actions of the major characters. In most dramatic readings, you become the major characters, conveying their feelings and actions through your interpretation. Prose literature is usually written in ordinary speech rather than in verse, which is a key characteristic of poetry. Dramatic literature can be written in both prose and poetry. Prose literature does not adopt the conventions and rituals of theater, which is a key characteristic of drama. The predominant form of prose literature is the story.

The prose you select for your program will be made up of stories. In your introduction, you set up the stories. If you present more than one story, you need to write transitions linking the stories together and back to the argument

---

Checklist

Traditional Organizational Pattern for Prose Literature
1. Introduction
2. Exposition of Story
3. Conflict
4. Crisis and Climax
5. Outcome

---

of the program. You must organize the stories you select around a central theme and argument. The plot of a story is the sequence of actions and events that occur in the story.

Stories have their own plots, so excerpt or cut prose literature in a way that maintains the integrity of the original plot. The organizational structure of the typical dramatic reading is similar to the plots found in prose literature. Most plots for prose literature build toward a climax. The climax reveals the meaning of the story. The arguments found in prose literature are often found in the climax of the story.

The plots used by authors of prose literature vary. Some authors begin with the climax of the story; others build toward the climax. Some authors tell their stories in chronological order; others move from one time period to another. Some authors use a tight logical ordering of events, while others use a looser, more associative structure. As you excerpt and cut your literature, maintain the integrity of the author's plot. Determine the sequence of your performance according to the plot of the story.

Organizational patterns for poetry. Judges do not expect you to adopt the organizational patterns used for drama and prose to organize your poetry readings. Poems do make arguments and tell stories, however, and you may organize them in sequences similar to those used for oral interpretation of drama and prose. You should organize the stories that make up your poetry reading to reveal the arguments advanced by your poems.

If, for example, your poetry reading consists of three poems, each poem should advance an argument in support of the theme of the program. Identify the fulcrum within each poem. The fulcrum marks the change that takes place in the attitude, thought, direction, emphasis, and mood of a poem. As with the crisis and climax stages in drama and prose, the fulcrum of a poem best reveals the argument made by a poem.

In summary, the organizational structure you use in your interpretative

---

Checklist

Traditional Organizational Pattern for Poetry
1. Introduction
2. Poem #1
3. Poem #2
4. Poem #3

---

performance should be drawn from the literature you select. Dramatists, prose writers, and poets use an organizational pattern designed to develop a powerful theme and a compelling argument. As you organize your interpretative programs for performance, identify and use the arrangement that is the foundation of the literature you have selected.

The oral interpreter should purposefully use nonverbal and verbal messages to perform the literature

As you remember from chapter 1, the purpose of forensics is to help students connect knowledge with eloquence. Once you complete a thorough study of the literature you intend to interpret, you should have a good understanding of the text and of the author's intent. Then you are ready to perform and share this understanding with your audience. You can do so through verbal and nonverbal communication and with the audience.

While the principles of persuasion discussed in chapter 2 should guide your delivery of forensics speeches, specialized standards exist for delivering a successful oral interpretation. The delivery of an oral interpretation must be tied to the meaning, intent, and the essence of the literature you interpret. Again, the meaning, intent, and the essence of the literature should be discovered through careful literary study *before* you deliver your interpretation.

The delivery of an oral interpretation must be true to the meaning of the literature. Yet, the presentation of an interpretation is also a creative act. You add to and provide your own insights on the literature you present. The choices you make when you move, gesture, and speak influence how your audience understands your interpretation and the literature. The best oral interpreters are careful to communicate their interpretations in a way that preserves the essence of the literature and helps the audience appreciate the work on emotional, intellectual, and aesthetic levels.

Scholars of communication and of oral interpretation believe nonverbal and verbal communication are keys to human understanding. You may have a deep understanding of the literature you have selected, but if you are unable to communicate this understanding, then it is meaningless to others. A strong command of nonverbal and verbal communication is necessary if you are to convey your understanding of the literature to your audience.

The rules of oral interpretation limit the range of nonverbal and verbal messages available to you. These rules prohibit the use of broad ranges of movement, sets, costumes, and props that stage actors use. As a result, your action and voice are your primary vehicles of communicating the meaning of your selections. While these rules do restrict your options, skillful use of your voice and gestures allow you to communicate a wide range of ideas and emotions.

Your literary study of the literature you intend to interpret will help you practice your nonverbal and verbal communication. An important result of this literary study will be a series of insights into how you should interpret the narrator, characters, and lines. Your literary study will help you communicate with your body and your voice the intellectual, emotional, and artistic meanings of the literature you have selected.

Nonverbal messages

Nonverbal communication is the foundation of all human communication. Even before audiences listen to and evaluate the verbal messages of public speakers, they attend to the nonverbal messages speakers send. A speaker's posture, gestures, and dress may strengthen or undermine an audience's perception of a speaker's message. The oral interpreter should use these nonverbal means to communicate the essence of the literature.

Remember that your body, the text, and your voice make up the stage, backdrop, and framework of your interpretation. Unlike the actor on stage, you do not have costumes or props to help you create the scene. However, you can use your posture, gestures, movements, space, and all possible nonverbal means to portray characters and interpret the intellectual, emotional, and aesthetic meanings of your literature. For our purposes, let us focus on posture, gesture, movements, and the script.

Posture. As you recall from chapter 2, your posture sends a message to your audience about you and your speech. You should stand in a central location so that all members of your audience can see and hear your interpretation. Whenever possible, use a posture that feels and looks comfortable. Assume a posture that allows you to move and gesture. Above all, your posture should be balanced; you should not stand too erect or too relaxed. The weight of your body should be evenly distributed, although some speakers may prefer to place more weight on one leg than the other. Your posture should enhance the message you are sending to your audience.

Unlike the public speaking events in which competitors represent their own ideas, in oral interpretation you will play the roles and speak the words of other people. When you interpret and perform characters found in prose or dramatic literature, your posture reflects your portrayal of these characters. For example, if you are interpreting a character known for her pride, you should stand tall and exude confidence and strength.

The posture you use to interpret a character should fit the character's age, mood, temperament, and the message the author wishes to communicate through the character. For example, a very old character has a different posture than a very young character. An angry character calls for a different posture than one who is happy. As you can tell, the posture you use in your interpretation helps communicate the essence of the literature.

Gestures. Gestures are the purposeful movements you make with your hands, arms, shoulder, head, and body. We all use hand and other gestures when we talk. Most of the time we are unaware of our gestures. In oral interpretations, posture and gestures must be considered and intentional. Your literary study will help you select gestures that suit each character.

The gestures you select should convey the personal mannerisms of the characters. If the character you are portraying is angry, a clenched fist might be a fitting gesture. If the character is amazed, then gestures indicating surprise would be appropriate. As you conduct your research, mark statements you believe should be accompanied by gestures.

The rules of this event may require you to keep both hands on the manuscript and stand in one place when you present the text. The rules do allow you to make appropriate physical movements when the text is not the focus You need to think carefully about the timing and form of your gestures.

Bodily movements. The nonverbal messages you use in your oral interpretation should communicate the emotional, intellectual, and aesthetic meanings of the literature. Since your body is the stage and the frame for the interpretation, you need to use your body as an essential part of your performance. Movement can be used to convey the tone of the literature.

As with posture and gesture, your bodily movements should fit the literature. Your muscles and body movement should correspond to and communicate the feelings of the characters and the tone of the piece. For example, if a character is weary, you can communicate that exhaustion through your movements.

The script. In serious, humorous, and poetry reading, your script should play a major part in the nonverbal performance of your literature. First, it is an important nonverbal sign that reminds all the participants that literature is at the center of the competitive activity. Judges expect you to have completed a careful literary study of the texts you will perform.

The script is more than a prop. Judges and audiences should feel that you are attempting to communicate the meanings the author of the literature intended. The script is the guiding physical symbol of interpretation, and you should be careful to share the text with your audience. In sharing the text with your audience, you should not memorize your text. Rather, you should use the script and achieve eye contact with your judges. You should interpret from the script for your judges.

Many oral interpreters type their selections onto letter-sized pages, and then place these pages into black, three-ring notebooks. Teachers of oral interpretation encourage competitors to double-space when they type their selections to make reading the script easier. Hold your notebook near the center of your chest. The audience should see your face and hear your voice.

Some oral interpreters mark their scripts with reminders to emphasize a certain word or to move in a certain direction. You might want to use similar reminders after you have analyzed your selections for performance. Finally, turn the pages of your script with care. If the scene involves rapid movement, you may need to turn the pages quickly. All of the important nonverbal messages you present should help the judge understand the argument and the mood of the literature.

Your literary analysis of the literature will suggest the nonverbal messages you should choose to interpret your selections. Ideally, these nonverbal messages will combine with your verbal messages to produce the desired effect. The literary analysis you conduct should help you to coordinate your use of movements with effective vocal techniques.

Verbal messages

Your voice will be of great importance in your interpretation. Your voice brings to life the characters you perform and brings interpretive life to the poetry you read. The best oral interpreters work to control the volume, pitch, stress, and rate of their voices. Such control gives speakers the power to fit their voices to the literature and the literature to their voice.

Giving your literature voice is a complicated matter. Most teachers of oral interpretation stress the need for vocal qualities that suit the literature. The qualities of voice that are most important for oral interpretation are volume, clarity, pitch, and rate. Competition in oral interpretation will help you to develop these qualities of voice.

Volume. Your judge should hear your interpretation. You are responsible for adjusting the volume of your performance to your literature, your judges, and the situation. The literature you select may call for some scenes in which the characters are loud and intense, others in which the characters speak at a normal volume, and others in which characters speak softly. While your first obligation is to the literature you have selected, you also need to adjust the volume to the judge, the room in which the interpretation is held, and other situational factors.

If, for example, your judge is sitting in the back of a very large room, you should increase the volume of your speech. In a smaller room, you might need to moderate and decrease the volume of your interpretation. All public speakers and oral interpreters must be sensitive to their audiences and the situations in which they speak.

Clarity. Your judges should hear you and understand what you are saying. All speakers must strive for vocal clarity. The sentences and words you speak should be clear and distinct. You should not pronounce words indistinctly or slur them. To achieve clarity in speech, you must work on your articulation and pronunciation of words.

Articulated language is speech in which the words are clear and distinct and the language is clear and expressive. Casual speaking is often sloppy speaking. You must achieve a higher level of clarity in oral interpretation. When you interpret the literature you have selected, make sure that you read the author's language distinctly and expressively.

Having clear pronunciation means using accepted accents, sounds, and vocal patterns in delivering sentences and words. Judges expect you to use proper English. When in doubt, consult a dictionary.

You may choose literature that calls for a specialized accent or dialect. Many of William Faulkner's works, for example, are set in the south. The characters in his novels and short stories would speak with a southern accent. If you were capable of speaking in a southern accent, doing so would improve your interpretation of Faulkner; however, there is no rule mandating use of a particular accent. Regardless, you should either use standard English pronunciation (as defined in popular dictionaries) or use the dialect used by the author.

Pitch. As you recall from chapter 2, to be an effective speaker, you should vary the pitch of your voice. Pitch refers to the musical range of the human voice. Teachers of speech recommend that you vary the tones and the pitches of your voice to suit the topic, the audience, and the situation. During your oral interpretation, the pitch of your voice should fit the character, mood, argument, and theme of the literature you are presenting.

Pitch determines vocal variety. Vocal variety gives lines of poetry and characters in prose their individuality. You should develop your ability to vary the tone you use to perform literature.

Rate. Rate was also discussed in chapter 2. To review, most conversations occur at a rate of 150–185 words per minute. Speakers who talk at rates exceeding 185 words per minute tend to irritate and confuse most audiences. However, speakers who talk at rates below 150 words per minute also risk irritating or boring the audience. As with the other aspects of good speaking, you should strive for balance.

As with the other vocal qualities, the rate at which you speak when you interpret literature should be determined by your literary analysis of your selection. Different characters should speak at different rates. The mood of the selection also determines the rate at which you speak.

Checklist

Principles of Oral Interpretation

1. The oral interpreter should make an argument to an audience about the intellectual, emotional, and the artistic meanings of literature.

2. The oral interpreter should select good literature and themes that embody ideas and experiences with broad appeal, and present them in a fresh and revealing style that invites audience participation.

3. When cutting and excerpting texts, the oral interpreter should preserve the essence of the literature.

4. The oral interpreter should provide an introduction, transitions, and an organizational pattern that justifies and advances the argument of the literature performed.

5. The oral interpreter should purposefully use nonverbal and verbal messages to perform the literature.

Scholars and teachers of oral interpretation offer to students these and many other suggestions regarding the nonverbal and verbal messages needed to interpret literature. First master the techniques described in this chapter, then feel free to experiment with nonverbal and verbal messages in your oral interpretation.

CONCLUSION

In this chapter, you surveyed the five fundamental principles, as shown above, that guide the creation of the interpretative performance. Regardless of the literature you prepare and present, you can use the five principles discussed in this chapter to make wise choices in the analysis and presentation of prose, drama, and poetry.

CHAPTER ELEVEN

Interpretation of Prose and Dramatic Literature

The educational aim of oral interpretation is for the speaker to gain an understanding of good literature through a careful literary analysis done in preparation for the oral interpretation. Judges expect competitors to understand the intellectual, emotional, and aesthetic meanings of the literature they select. The competitor's program should also entertain the audience. This chapter focuses on the interpretation of prose and dramatic literature. Poetry, which can also be included in oral interpretations, is the subject of the next chapter.

The best oral interpretations of prose and drama demonstrate the competitor's understanding of the intellectual, emotional, and aesthetic meanings of the literature through a fitting and moving oral interpretation of these meanings. In short, the best oral interpretations are a result of a careful study and guided performance of the literature. You need to gain an understanding of the specific steps you need to take in selecting good literature, constructing a program, and performing the literature you select.

Most tournaments allow competitors to use published novels, short stories, plays, and poetry in their oral interpretations. Many tournaments sponsor serious and humorous divisions of oral interpretation. Oral interpretations of serious literature tend to develop themes and arguments of grave importance. Death, divorce, disease, and the like are often topics in this division. Oral interpretation of humorous literature tends to develop themes and arguments that make light of the human condition.

Two categories of oral interpretation exist: reading and memorized. The reading division requires competitors to read from a printed text. Frequent references are to be made to the text during the performance. The memorized division requires competitors to learn the literature by heart. The standards used in judging the two divisions are similar and differ only when questions of memorization or textual focus are raised.

On the next two pages are the rules commonly used for each literary classification and style of presentation.

With the rules of serious and humorous interpretation in mind, we can now turn to the interpretative round. You need to know how to read the tournament schedule and to find out where your competitions will take place.

The Oral Interpretation Round

The tournament schedule lists the times you will present your interpretation. As you can tell (and if the tournament permits), you may choose to compete in more than one interpretative event. For example, you might compete in serious interpretation in pattern A and in humorous interpretation in pattern B. At some tournaments you might do two events in the same pattern. This is called "double entering." For example, the sample tournament schedule on page 230 might allow a student to compete in both humorous and poetry. If you competed in both events, you would present your humorous interpretation and your poetry reading in the same hour. Let us assume you have entered the humorous interpretation competition. As you can tell from the schedule, humorous interpretation is in pattern B.

You will present your humorous interpretation three times on Friday at 1:30, 5:30, and 7:00. If you do well in these three rounds, you may present your humorous interpretation at 10:30 (semifinals) and at 1:30 (finals) on Saturday.

When you arrive at the tournament, you need to find out where the tournament staff is posting so that you know where your rounds are scheduled to take place. Most tournaments post panels in each event that list the rooms and judges.

Referring to the postings on page 231, let us assume that you are speaker two in the first round of novice humorous reading.

You need to find Friendly Hall. Your forensics teacher may give you a map of the campus, or you may need to ask for directions. Try, if possible, to arrive ten to fifteen minutes before the round starts. When the judge and the other

Rules for Memorized Serious and Serious Reading

Purpose: The primary purpose of memorized serious and serious reading is for the speaker to communicate the intellectual, emotional, and aesthetic meanings of good literature. The speaker's program should also entertain the audience. This event prohibits acting.

Length:

Serious Reading: Contestants will speak no more than eight (8) minutes. Many tournaments allow a thirty-second grace period. Many tournament rules call for the disqualification of competitors who violate the time limit.

Memorized Serious: Contestants will speak no more than ten (10) minutes. Many tournaments do not provide a grace period.

Procedures
For Serious Reading and Memorized Serious

1. The texts and materials used shall come from cuttings of materials that can be discovered in the public realm. Published and printed novels, short stories, plays, or poetry are appropriate.

2. Acting and materials associated with acting are not allowed.

3. No speaker is allowed to use materials performed by the speaker in forensics competition during previous years.

4. Students are not to use the same materials in other events.

5. Competitors will identify the title(s) and the author(s) of their selection(s).

Procedures Used Only in Serious Reading:

1. The interpretation is to be read from a printed text. Frequent references are to be made to the text during the performance.

2. Contestants will keep both hands on the manuscript and stand in one place when presenting the text. Appropriate physical movements and gestures can be made during introductions, transitions, and moments when the text is not the focus.

3. Contestants can use facial, verbal, and vocal modes of communication.

4. Materials drawn from recordings are allowed.

C. Procedures Used Only in Memorized Serious

1. All materials are to be memorized.

2. Materials drawn from recordings are often prohibited by tournament rules.

Rules for Memorized Humorous and Humorous Reading

Purpose: The primary purpose of memorized humorous and humorous reading is for the speaker to communicate the intellectual, emotional, and aesthetic meanings of good literature. The speaker's program should also entertain the audience. This event prohibits acting.

Length:

Humorous Reading: Contestants will speak no more than eight (8) minutes. Many tournaments allow a thirty-second grace period. Many tournament rules call for the disqualification of competitors who violate the time limit.

Memorized Humorous: Contestants will speak no more than ten (10) minutes. Many tournaments do not provide a grace period.

Procedures
For Humorous Reading and Memorized Humorous

1. The texts and materials used shall come from cuttings of materials that can be discovered in the public realm. Published and printed novels, short stories, plays, or poetry are appropriate.

2. Acting and materials associated with acting are not allowed.

3. No speaker is allowed to use materials performed by the speaker in forensic competition during previous years.

4. Students are not to use the same materials in other events.

5. Competitors will identify the title(s) and the author(s) of their selection(s).

Procedures Used Only in Humorous Reading:

1. The interpretation is to be read from a printed text. Frequent references are to be made to the text during the performance.

2. Contestants will keep both hands on the manuscript and stand in one place when the text is presented. Appropriate physical movements and gestures can be made during introductions, transitions, and moments when the text is not the focus.

3. Contestants can use facial, verbal, and vocal modes of communication.

4. Materials drawn from recordings are allowed.

Procedures Used Only in Memorized Humorous

1. All materials are to be memorized.

2. Materials drawn from recordings are often prohibited by tournament rules.

SAMPLE SPEECH TOURNAMENT SCHEDULE

PATTERN A EVENTS PATTERN B EVENTS
Extemp   Impromptu
Radio Commentary   Expository speaking
Expos   **Humorous Interp**
Serious Interp   ADS

THURSDAY, Feb. 27
   11:00 - 12:00 Registration
   12:30 - 1:50 SENIOR LD debate, Round I
    2:00 - 3:20 JUNIOR LD and ALL CX debate, Round I
    3:30 - 4:00 ALL DEBATE, Round II
    5:00 - 6:20 ALL DEBATE, Round III
    6:30 - 7:20 Break
    7:30 - 9:00 ALL DEBATE, Round IV

FRIDAY, Feb. 28
    8:00 - 9:30 CX Debate, Round V
    8:30 - 9:30 Registration for schools with IEs only
   10:00   EXTEMP DRAW
   10:30 - 11:30 Pattern A, Round I
   12:00   EXTEMP DRAW
   12:30 - 1:30 Pattern A, Round II
   1:30 - 2:30 Pattern B, Round I
    2:45 - 3:30 LD Debate, Round V (both JR & SR)
    4:00   EXTEMP DRAW
    4:30 - 5:30 Pattern A, Round III
   5:30 - 6:30 Pattern B, Round II
    6:30 - 7:00 Break
   7:00 - 8:00 Pattern B, Round III
    8:15 - 9:45 ALL DEBATE, Round IV
    9:00   IE Semifinal Postings

SATURDAY, Feb. 29
    7:30   UNIVERSITY CENTER Opens
    7:45   Debate Outrounds Postings
    8:00 - 9:30 ALL DEBATE, Octo-finals
   10:00   EXTEMP DRAW
   10:30 - 11:30 IE Semifinals, Pattern A & Pattern B
   12:00 - 1:00 ALL DEBATE, Quarter-finals
    1:00   EXTEMP DRAW
   1:30 - 2:30 IE Finals, Pattern A & Pattern B
    3:00 - 4:30 ALL DEBATE, Semifinals
    5:30 - 7:00 ALL DEBATE, Finals
   8:00   Awards

```
┌─────────────────────────────────────────────────────────────┐
│  ┌──────────────────┐                                        │
│  │   Checklist      │                                        │
│  └──────────────────┘                                        │
│                                                              │
│  Humorous reading                                            │
│  Novice Division                                             │
│  Round One                                                   │
│  Judge: J. Musato, Centennial High                           │
│  Room: 124 Friendly Hall                                     │
│                                                              │
│  Speaker One: Wong, Northfield team                          │
│  Speaker Two: YOU, Jefferson team                            │
│  Speaker Three: O' Rourke, Twinfalls team                    │
│  Speaker Four: Larson, Humbolt team                          │
│  Speaker Five: Wade, Grants Pass team                        │
│  Speaker Six: Gottesman, Hilo team                           │
│                                                              │
└─────────────────────────────────────────────────────────────┘
```

competitors have arrived, speaker one (Wong from Northfield) will be the first to speak. When Wong and the other four competitors speak, you should be a good audience member. You should pay attention to the oral interpretations of your competitors and provide positive reactions whenever possible. Remember that all the speakers are trying hard to interpret literature that means much to them.

As you listen to your competitors, try to identify what they do well and what you can learn from their interpretive programs. You might ask yourself: What literature did they pick? Why did they pick those particular selections for interpretation? How did they introduce their program? What organizational pattern did they use? What transitions did they use? How did they perform the characters in their selections? The answers to these questions may help you to understand what distinguishes the strong interpretative program from one that needs significant improvements.

The heart of an interpretative performance is the literature. In organizing poetry readings, serious, and humorous interpretations, you need to create an introduction that provides the judge with the title(s) and the author(s) of your cuttings. Judges also expect clear and strong transitions between your selections. (See page 232 for a traditional pattern.)

In most cases, your interpretative selections should be connected by a unifying theme. This theme can help you decide how to organize your selections. The transitions you use are of great importance, for they help remind your judges how the selections are connected by the theme.

When it is your turn to perform your oral interpretation, walk from your seat to the front of the room with confidence, and position yourself so that

---

Guidelines

A Traditional Organizational Pattern Used in Interpretative Events

I. Introduction: Argument, Author[s], Title[s], and Justification.
    Transition and introduction of title and author of first selection

II. Selection One
    Transition and introduction of title and author of second selection

III. Selection Two
    Transition and introduction of title and author of third selection

IV. Selection Three

V. Conclusion

---

all the members of your audience can see you. If you are in the reading division, you should pause and open your text. Most competitors place their text in a black notebook and open the notebook before they begin.

Judges' Expectations

Judges look for student interpreters to select high-quality literature and to have important themes, coherent and well-connected cuttings, and an effective style and delivery. Most judges would agree with Lee and Gura when they write:

It is the perfect tribute when members of the audience are captured so thoroughly by the experience of the material that they cannot immediately break the spell to applaud. If an audience says "What a beautiful voice!" or "What graceful gestures!," the interpreter has failed. When the audience's attention is held by the effect of the material presented, the interpreter has succeeded. But this unobtrusiveness on your part does not result from casual preparation or from a feeling that since the literature is the important thing, you need do no more than face the audience, open the book, and open your mouth. On the contrary, your effectiveness is the result of a preparation so thorough and a technique so perfectly coordinated that the audience cannot see the wheels go around.

Lee and Gura emphasize the need to prepare and to develop technique. Preparation and the development of performance technique are of equal importance. Most judges have at least five questions they ask themselves when evaluating your speech: Did you follow the rules? Did you identify an important, relevant, and consequential theme? Did you organize and provide transitions for your selections? Did your interpretations reveal an understanding of the literature you selected? Did your delivery enhance the effect of the literature? Let us take each of these questions in turn.

Did you follow the rules?

Judges expect you to know and follow the rules of this event. Depending on the rule violation, judges may penalize you for failing to comply with the rules. For example, you may be disqualified if your performance is overtime. Also, keep in mind the distinctions between acting and interpretation. Some judges will rank you down if they see evidence of acting.

The rules for district and state tournaments differ from those used by school-sponsored forensics tournaments. For example, the humorous reading you present at a district tournament may need to contain the same selections as the one you present at the state tournament. Make sure to check with your forensics teacher for the rules used by individual tournaments.

Pay close attention to the difference between the memorized and reading divisions. The reading division requires you to read the texts from a printed script. The rules of the reading division may require you to make many references to the text during the performance, to keep both hands on the manuscript, and to stand in one place when you present the text. The rules of memorized serious and humorous interpretation require you to memorize all selections. Scripts and notes are not allowed.

Did you identify a relevant and serious theme?

Judges reward interpretations that center on a topic of some consequence. The theme you select should be meaningful and pertinent to the judge. Many of your judges will have heard many oral interpretations: The theme you develop should arouse their interest and inspire them to listen.

How do you know if you have selected a consequential theme? Your judges consider your theme important if it reveals and develops a broad and basic truth and experience; if it speaks to this truth and experience in a unique manner; and if the materials you select are rich, profound, and of the highest quality.

Did you organize and provide transitions for your selections?

You need to organize your theme and cuttings for your judge. Judges want to hear oral interpretations that have clear and fitting patterns. The words you use to introduce your theme and the sentences you use to create transitions between your cuttings are key to helping your judge understand your oral interpretation. In addition, the order of your selections should reflect a purpose. You may wish to begin with a powerful cutting and end with a soothing piece. The choices you make in organizing and ordering your materials should depend on the theme and the mood you wish to develop.

Did your interpretations reveal an understanding of the literature you selected?

Your judges expect you to exhibit an understanding of the materials you present. You must understand the backgrounds, the cultures, and the impulses of the novelists, playwrights, poets, and the other creative artists whose work you interpret. Your library research and literary analysis should help you gain a thorough appreciation of the materials you perform.

Did your performance enhance the effect of the literature?

Most judges look for a delivery style that fits the material. Because your goal is to share meaning and the experience of your material with your judge, your delivery should reflect the tone and the spirit of the selections. For example, if you select a cutting in which a character expresses anger, you need to convey this anger with your body and your voice. The best oral interpreters adjust the volume, pace, and the tone of their delivery to their theme, materials, judge, room, and the situation.

Creating and Presenting Your Oral Interpretation

With the judges' expectations in mind, let us move to the steps you must take to create a successful oral interpretation

These guidelines are designed to help you select, develop, and present your oral interpretation. Each step is important if, to quote Lee and Gura, you are to create an oral interpretation whose "effectiveness is the result of a preparation so thorough and a technique so perfectly coordinated that the audience cannot see the wheels go around."

Brainstorm topics for your oral interpretation

You need to find a serious or humorous theme for your oral interpretation that is significant and relevant to you and your judges. Your theme should inspire you to conduct the necessary research on the authors and literature you select. Your will deliver your oral interpretation to more than one audience, so the theme you select should be potentially entertaining and interesting to a broad

---

Guidelines

Steps in the Creation and Presentation of an Oral Interpretation

Before the Tournament

1. Brainstorm themes and subjects for your oral interpretation.
2. Conduct a literary analysis of the texts you have selected.
3. Identify a theme and an argument to organize your cuttings.
4. Write the first draft of your interpretation.
5. Perform and practice your oral interpretation.

During the Tournament

6. Present your interpretation to the judges.
7. Listen to the other oral interpreters.
8. Make modifications in your oral interpretation as necessary.

After the Speech and Tournament

9. After the tournament, read your ballots and use the comments made by your judges to improve.
10. Conduct additional research and practice.

---

spectrum of people. As you select a theme for your oral interpretation, try to pick a significant subject and find literature that expresses the theme energetically.

You might also start in the opposite direction and think about the novels, short stories, and plays that you admire. Perhaps a common theme will emerge that connects the literature you read. Once you identify a theme, you can begin the process of selecting the material that will help you develop the theme.

As you search for a theme and literature, use the three touchstones discussed in chapter 10. First, the theme and material you select should have a broad-based appeal and a universal impulse. Some literature is restricted in its meaning and focus. This touchstone is particularly helpful, for you will present your oral interpretation to many judges and audience members with diverse views of the world. The literature you select should appeal to those who may not share your cultural background.

The second touchstone to use in selecting a theme and materials is to choose individualistic authors and unique materials. While you want to select material that has universal appeal, that appeal should be expressed in a novel manner.

For example, the film director and writer Spike Lee expresses universal themes in an innovative way.

You should also use a third touchstone that calls for literature that is rich, subtle, and open to suggestion. Such literature will encourage the judges who hear your interpretations to play an active role in your performance. How can your judges play an active role when you are the one who performs the oral interpretation? If your materials are rich, subtle, and open to suggestion, judges from any background and experience can appreciate it. Your goal is to allow your judges to use their life experiences to understand and appreciate your theme and material.

Searching for themes and literature requires brainstorming. With the three touchstones as your guide, brainstorming should provoke a wide-ranging discussion between you, your forensics teacher, and teammates on possible themes and literature for oral interpretation. During the brainstorming period, discuss every theme and literary work that even remotely sounds interesting. At this stage, you should write down the topics and literature that come to mind.

Use the theme and the literature you select to build an interpretative program. The theme and literature will work together to create a mood. If the mood brought forth by your literature is serious, you should enter the serious reading or memorized divisions. If the mood sparked by your program is humorous, you should enter the humorous reading or memorized division. Regardless of the category you choose, you need to find your topic through brainstorming.

Let us say the brainstorming session on topics for serious reading produced the following topics:

Checklist

The Results of a Brainstorming Session on Serious Reading

Potential Topics for Serious Reading

Love	Families	Friendship	War
Insanity	Nature	Hatred	Euthanasia
Conscience	Evil	Rebellion	Sports

All these topics have universal appeal. However, because these are such common topics, your forensics teacher might suggest that some of them are tired and overdone. Love and death may not make the best choices, for they are the most popular themes in serious oral interpretation. If you do choose these topics and develop a strong theme with good literature, then these judges might respond favorably. Your forensics teacher can help you make a wise choice from among the topics generated during the brainstorming session. Once a list of topics has been generated, you, your teammates, and your forensics teacher can select those that best meet the three touchstones of universal appeal, unique and individual expression, and rich, subtle, and suggestive content.

You might also start in a different direction and list the novels, short stories, plays, and poetry you have read and enjoyed. You may also ask your forensics teacher and other knowledgeable people about literature they cherish. You may find after the discussion and some careful reading on your part that the families theme has potential.

Let us say that you have read K. Kam's short story "Hopeland," Louise Erdrich's *Love Medicine,* August Wilson's play *Fences,* and Saul Bellow's novel *Herzog.* These four literary works develop the theme of family ties and conflict as they occur in Chinese-American, Native-American, African-American, and Jewish-American families. All the selections meet the touchstones used to evaluate good literature. First, each of these literary works evokes or brings forth a theme that is universal: family ties and conflict. Second, each of these literary works expresses this universal theme in a unique and distinctive manner. Third, each of these works are richly suggestive and invite audience participation and response.

Check with your teammates and your forensics teacher to see if they believe your selections will make a good program. If they give you a green light, then you need to analyze the literature you have selected. As you recall from the previous chapter, you should conduct an internal and an external analysis of your texts.

Conduct a Literary Analysis of Your Texts

You have decided to develop a program on family ties and conflict, and you have identified the literature you wish to interpret in developing this theme. Now you need to gain an understanding of the intellectual, emotional, and aesthetic meanings of the works of the authors. As you recall from the previous chapter, a literary analysis involves an internal analysis of the text and a contextualized external analysis of the text. To illustrate how to conduct an internal and an external analysis of a text, let us consider how K. Kam's "Hopeland" and August Wilson's play *Fences* might be subjected to a literary analysis. Kam's work is a short story; Wilson's work was written for the theater.

Literary analysis

An internal analysis involves a careful reading of the entire text from which you take cuttings. To achieve an understanding of the text, you need to look at the author's story. Taking this perspective, the first question you would ask is: What story and argument is K. Kam trying to create?

Checklist

How to Make Selections From a Novel, Short Story, or Play

Aim: To identify stories, passages, and other materials that will best represent the essence and the intellectual, emotional, and aesthetic meanings of the entire work.

Steps.

1. Read the entire work to gain an understanding the author's theme and argument.

2. Identify stories and passages that present the theme and argument with intensity and would help the judge gain an understanding of the author's theme and argument.

3. Excerpt and cut these stories and passages to meet the time limitations.

An Internal Analysis. To gain an understanding of the author's story and argument, you need to read the complete story, not just the selections you make from the text. You cannot truly understand your selections unless you realize how they relate to the whole work.

"Hopeland" is a short story written by a second-generation Chinese-American woman. The author is the narrator; she tells of her attempt to understand her parents. As immigrants, they endured much suffering to reach America, which they saw as "Hopeland." At the same time, the author finds her Chinese heritage—and China itself—difficult to understand. In "Hopeland" she regrets that her "parents' China still eludes her."

As you prepare to select and cut a literary work for your own interpretation, review the checklist on how to make selections.

Recall the questions discussed in the last chapter that you can ask in analyzing any piece of literature:

To whom is the persona (the character) speaking?

Where is the persona speaking?

When is the persona speaking?

About what is the persona speaking?

How is the persona speaking?

Why is the persona speaking?

These questions can help you uncover the intellectual, emotional, and aesthetic meanings of any piece of literature. However, you need more precise questions for the internal analysis of prose literature. (See the checklist.)

Checklist

How to Analyze Selections from Works of Prose

Who is speaking?

To whom is the narrator speaking?

About what does the narrator speak?

From where does the narrator tell the story?

When does the narrator tell the story?

Why is the story told?

Keep in mind that the use of a prominent narrator is the primary difference between prose and drama.

Who is speaking? The narrator tells the story. Unlike drama in which many characters may share the stage, in prose interpretations the narrator is in charge. A careful and through literary analysis of the narrator can help improve your interpretative performance. You should gain an understanding of the narrator's values and agenda, for they influence the story and your interpretation of the literature.

For instance, the narrator of "Hopeland" is K. Kam herself. She was born in Hong Kong and immigrated to the U.S. when she was two.

To whom is the narrator speaking? The narrator's audience is an important consideration. You perform the role of the narrator in you oral interpretation; therefore, you need to determine the audience to whom the story is directed. For example, in some stories, such as Kam's, the narrator speaks to a general audience; in other stories, the narrator addresses a specific person or audience.

About what does the narrator speak? The narrator of a story identifies and develops the author's themes and arguments intended by the author. The narrator can develop the plot and the meaning of the literature.

From where does the narrator tell the story? The location from which a narrator tells the story provides insight into the story's purpose and argument. The location of the story may affect how the story is told.

When does the narrator tell the story? The narrator will usually tell the story in past tense; although the narrator may move, on occasion, from the past to the present and future.

Why is the story told? Authors tell stories to advance a theme and an argument. A careful literary analysis of the literature you select should help you identify the theme and argument.

You must acquire an understanding of why the author chose the story, argument, and literary form you will perform. You need to go beyond and outside the text to gain complete answers. An external analysis of the literature complements your textual analysis and provides the extra information you need to make your oral interpretation a success.

An external analysis. The library has much information on the author, the story, the argument, and the literary form of the literature. Your goal is to discover the intellectual, emotional, and aesthetic meanings of your text. At this stage, you want to know how context and culture influenced the creation of the literature and how the author wished to influence the outside world in return.

Context and Culture of the Author and Work. First, you need to discover the context and cultural problems that shaped your literary selection. If you only read the text, you can not appreciate the full meaning of the literature. If you are to understand the essence of the selection at hand and the intellectual, emotional, and aesthetic meaning of the literature, then you must read what scholars and critics have to say about the particular author's work. To achieve an even better understanding, you should read articles and books that reveal how writers and literature work to achieve their goals. The *Book Review Index* and other reference sources can assist you as you compile a bibliography.

In addition to reading articles and other materials on the culture and context of your author and texts, you should consider reading articles and books on ethnic literature. For example, Minh-ha Trinh's *Woman, Native, Other* (Bloomington: Indiana University Press, 1989) is a scholarly book written by a Vietnamese woman on the influence of race, gender, and culture on literature. This book would give you profound insights into the works of nonwestern female writers.

Other books on prose literature can also provide insight. Ian Watt's *The Rise of the Novel* (Berkeley: University of California Press, 1957) offers a more traditional introduction to prose literature, and Elaine Showalter, *A Literature of Their Own* (Princeton: New Jersey: Princeton University Press, 1977), and Cherrie Moraga and Gloria Anzaldua, eds., *This Bridge Called My Back: Writings of Radical Women of Color* (New York: Kitchen Table, 1981) provide insight into women's literature and the writings of women of color. Together, these sources create a sound foundation upon which to build an oral interpretation.

Once you understand the cultures and contexts affecting the author and the novel, you need to learn more about the author and the author's intent. Any good literary analysis should include statements made by an author about what he or she intended by the artistic product.

Author's Intent. Once you have a good idea about how outside forces influenced the creation of the literary piece, you need to determine how the author's literature was a response to these forces. All prose, drama, and poetry is a response by an author to societal pressures and problems. K. Kam's short story "Hopeland" is an example of an emerging body of work by Asian American women. This work attempts to record and make vivid the experiences and histories of a neglected part of Asian American history: the stories of Chinese, Japanese, Korean, and Filipino women. While little biographical material is available on K. Kam, the brief note on the contributors to the *Making Waves* anthology reveals that she is an editor for *California Tomorrow* and that she has worked in education and social work.

How do you determine an author's intent? You can often find articles written by authors about their works and interviews in which authors respond to questions about their work. The best oral interpretations are those that reflect a deep understanding of the cultural contexts and the feelings and thoughts of the author. This holds true for the interpretations of dramatic literature as well.

Literary Analysis of Dramatic Literature

A good literary analysis of the cultural contexts and the author's intent gives you access to the novel's arguments and essence, and to the intellectual, emotional, and aesthetic goals of the author. A literary analysis of plays written for the stage requires an approach similar to the one taken in analyzing prose. However, dramatic literature tends to have a different form and focus than prose.

Remember that scripts written for the theater are in the present tense, de-emphasize the role of the narrator, and place more emphasis on the scenes that tell the story. These differences affect the way you perform the text. You still need to understand the culture and the context of the text and the author's intent.

For purposes of illustration, let us assume that you have selected August Wilson's *Fences* for interpretation. *Fences* is about family and conflict between generations; Wilson's play portrays the relationship and conflict between father and son. *Fences* is written in the present tense; there is no dominant narrator, and there is more emphasis on the scenes in which the characters perform their roles.

A literary analysis of *Fences* requires an internal and an external analysis of the drama.

An Internal Analysis. When you interpret dramatic literature, you need to read the entire play and then carefully excerpt or cut the materials you wish to use in your oral interpretation. As you read the play, take a global view of the themes, characters, and scenes. Every playwright attempts to make a statement, develop a theme, or make an argument. Before you can interpret the play, you must understand the playwright's statement, theme, or argument.

Fences is a two-act play and tells the story of the Maxon family. The Maxon patriarch, Troy, plays a central role in the drama. His wife, Rose, and sons, Cory and Lyons, also play major roles. Troy was an outstanding baseball player in the thirties and forties, but because of racism he did not have an opportunity to achieve his potential. His job as a garbage collector fuels his frustration, which in turn shapes his personality and his relationships with his family.

Let us assume that a scene from act two makes up part of your interpretative program. This scene develops a major climax of the play. The scene also captures the essence and the intellectual, emotional, and aesthetic meaning of the entire work. In this scene, Rose learns that Troy has fathered a child with another woman. In the conflict that follows, the anger and betrayal that has existed in their lives together is exposed. Using the questions suggested by Judy Yordon in *Roles in Interpretation,* we can analyze this selection from *Fences.* Yordon suggests that you use more specific questions in your analysis of dramatic literature. These questions, which are designed to reveal the meanings of plays, are as follows.

Who is speaking? You must understand the characters you interpret. You are responsible for identifying how the characters differ from one another. You can mark these differences by using the following categories: physical, social, psychological, and moral.

In this selection from *Fences,* Troy tells Rose about his affair and his pregnant girlfriend. August Wilson, the playwright, tells us that Troy is a "large man with thick and heavy hands. . . ." He drinks, "can be crude and almost vulgar, though he is cable of rising to profound heights of expression." Rose is ten years younger, attends church, doesn't drink, and works hard to keep house and take care of their children. This information can be used to flesh out the physical, social, psychological, and moral differences between the characters.

Who is being addressed? Before you interpret dramatic literature, you need to identify the audience to whom the characters are speaking.

In this scene, the characters speak to each other. Troy tells Rose that he has fathered a child with another woman. She responds with anger and despair. He is defensive.

About what do the characters speak? All literature is driven by an argument the author wishes to make. The characters in dramatic literature usually address this argument. As you learned in the previous chapter, the nature of the argument is often revealed during the crisis or the fulcrum of prose, drama, and poetry.

This scene of the second act is the crisis point of *Fences.* Troy and Rose speak about the child Troy will have with another woman. The conflict that results reveals their core values, the direction their marriage will take, and the argument of the play.

Where and when does the play take place? To analyze dramatic literature, you must be able to place the drama in its context. The place and date identified by the playwright will help you understand the meanings of the play.

The play takes place in the home of Troy and Rose Maxon. The play takes place in the 1950s. The scene is set in a middle-American urban industrial city and in an America deeply affected by racism.

How do the characters speak? A character's nonverbal and verbal patterns of communication reveal the character's values and purpose.

In this scene, the characters begin tentatively and then explode with anger. Because the characters are intimates (wife-husband), they use a language of intimacy.

Why are the characters speaking? A good literary analysis helps you identify the reasons why the characters are speaking. These reasons, in turn, can be traced to the theme and argument the playwright wishes to develop.

Fences tells the story of African American life, family, and marriage. In this scene, the husband and wife argue about the meaning of their marriage and the choices both have made. The play also makes an important argument about the black experience and about the impact of racism on the black family.

After completing an internal analysis of the text, you can complete an external analysis of the drama, its playwright, and the culture and context to which the play is a response.

An external analysis. To truly understand dramatic literature, you go beyond the text and research the playwright, the playwright's agenda, and the culture and context to which the playwright responds. The research process is similar to the one used in the external analysis of prose literature.

Context and Culture of the Playwright and Play. A simple reading of the play does not impart a full understanding of the problems and the cultural issues that August Wilson addresses in his play. Drama critics and scholars of theater write articles and books designed to illuminate the problems and cultural issues to which playwrights respond.

Many drama critics wrote reviews of *Fences,* and the play won a Pulitzer prize in 1985. *The Christian Science Monitor, the New York Times, The Nation,* and other publications of note carried reviews of the play and discussed its social importance. Reading these reviews would help you gain a better understanding of August Wilson and his play.

These reviews explain that August Wilson attempts in his work to represent the black experience in America. For example, in a October 16, 1984, article in *Christian Science Monitor,* Hilary DeVries observed:

Wilson's works also include the undeniable presence of racial anger, frustration, and even violence; but it is an emotional perspective from which the playwright refuses to write. "What is there to be angry about?" he asks. "If people ask me if my work is autobiographical, I say, 'Yes, 400 years' autobiographical.' " Wilson says blacks "have something that informs their sensibilities that is not the same thing that informs European sensibilities." Within their history, he says, in their transition from being African to becoming American, they have lost something central to their identity. It is this spiritual journey that is of most concern to him (p. 29).

August Wilson's plays are responses to racial anger, to the unique experience of African Americans, and to the problems of America. Wilson charts the transition from being African to being American. While this transition may represent a universal experience, African Americans and Chinese-American also possess a unique history and experience. The universality and the individuality of these experiences are captured in the "Hopeland" and *Fences.*

Before you could interpret *Fences,* you must understand the black experience in America. The "racial anger, frustration, and even violence" experienced and expressed by blacks are a result of the terrible consequences of racism. The central character in *Fences,* Troy Maxon, is a product of racism. His anger and frustrations represent the central theme of the play.

Act Two, Scene One of fences also involves Troy Maxon's wife, Rose. Although Troy Maxon is the central character, an understanding of this scene would also require a sensitive analysis of Rose and the feelings and thoughts of African American women. Rose does not accept Troy's actions willingly, and in this scene, she defends her integrity and dignity. An oral interpretation of *Fences* requires an appreciation and an understanding of the black experience in America, the consequences of racism, and the resulting anger and violence.

To gain an appreciation of the black experience, you might begin with Gunnar Myrdal's *An American Dilemma: The Negro Problem and Modern Democracy* (New York: Harper, 1944). This is one of the first major studies of racism in America. Andrew Hacker's *Two Nations: Black and White, Separate, Hostile, Unequal* (New York: Scribners, 1992) and Studs Terkel's *Race: How Blacks and Whites Think and Feel about the American Obsession* (New York: New Press, 1992) would give you more recent and well-documented accounts of the impact of racism on America.

Because *Fences* comes out of the ethnic theater tradition, you should read articles on ethnic theater to prepare for your oral interpretation. The journals *MELUS* and *New Theater Quarterly* publish articles on ethnic theater and plays that concern Chinese, African-Americans, Jews, and other ethnic groups. Once you understand the context and the culture of the playwright and the play, you can turn more directly to the playwright's purpose.

Author's intent. Playwrights intend to develop themes and arguments in their plays. Often, in interviews, articles, and books they describe their dramatic goals. An understanding of these goals is essential to proper interpretation of their work.

August Wilson has clearly defined the themes and arguments he wishes to advance in his plays. He has been interviewed by the *New York Times* and *The New York Times Magazine, Christian Science Monitor, Vogue, MELUS,* and by television journalist Bill Moyers. In an interview with the *Christian Science Monitor,* Wilson has discussed his vision of the theater and the arguments he advances in his plays: "I'm taking each decade and looking at one of the most important questions that blacks confronted in that decade and writing a play about it," he says. "Put them all together and you have a history."

Wilson is attempting to convey the history of African-Americans with his drama. His intent, according to his interview with the *Christian Science Monitor* is to "reexamine the past . . . in order to arrive at different choices," he says. "My generation knows so very little about our parents. There is no real sense of who we are until we discover who our parents are and the indignities they have suffered." An understanding of this intent reveals the argument Wilson wishes to advance in his plays.

You can follow the arguments and themes Wilson develops in his other plays to get a better sense of his intent. A careful reading of *Ma Rainey's Black Bottom, Joe Turner's Come and Gone, The Piano Lesson,* and his other plays provide insight into Wilson's patterns of argument and themes. You now see the importance of a careful literary analysis of the literature you select. Once you complete your literary analysis, you need to identify an argument you can use to organize your selections.

Identify a Theme and an Argument to Organize Your Selections into a Meaningful Format

By this point, you have brainstormed for themes and subjects for your oral interpretation, and you have conducted a literary analysis of the texts you selected. Next you need to identify the argument of your program and select a format that fits your material and your argument.

As you recall, oral interpretations are designed to present an argument and a theme. You draw the argument and theme of your oral interpretation from the literature you select. Your literary analysis helps you understand the author's intended argument.

The argument or theme August Wilson presents in *Fences* centers on the experience of an African-American family. Out of these experiences, Wilson's characters present arguments and themes concerning racism, frustrated dreams, and betrayal. *Fences* deals with issues of ethnicity and family conflict; therefore, they might be joined together in a program, or each might be the sole subject of an oral interpretation program.

The introduction

After you identify the argument and the theme of your program, you need to organize your selection in a meaningful way. The order you select depends on the literature in your program. Your program needs an introduction and, if you have included more than one selection, transitions. Your transitions should connect your selections and link them to the theme or argument.

As you learned in the previous chapter, the introduction to an oral interpretation program is essential. The introduction tells the judges who authored the

---

Guidelines

A Traditional Organizational Pattern Used in Interpretive Events

I.   Introduction: Argument, author[s], title[s], and justification.
     Transition and introduction of title and author of first selection

II. Selection One
     Transition and introduction of title and author of second selection

III. Selection Two
     Transition and introduction of title and author of third selection

IV. Selection Three

V.   Conclusion

---

selections, the titles of the selections, the argument and theme connecting the selections, and why the judges should listen.

Consider the following introduction to Kam's short story:

> We are a nation of immigrants; many of us are the sons and daughter of immigrants. The experience of those who have immigrated to America is strikingly similar, for those who are new to this country often face difficulties with language and customs. As immigrants learn English and American customs, they are often reluctant to share their histories with their American-born children. Often, these histories are filled with pain; and as often there are stories of joy and laughter. However, if parents and children do not share stories, precious cultural history is lost. And even when parents share these stories, their children do not completely understand. As an example, Asian American writer K. Kam in her short story "Hopeland," tells of her difficulties attempting to understand her parents' China.

This introduction introduces the author, the title, the theme, a brief literary analysis, and the argument. The author, title, and theme come in the first sentence. The brief literary analysis, gives the judge a useful explanation of the author and her work. Finally, the last two sentences capture the argument of the selection and the program.

Organizational format

You should place your literature into a purposeful order. The organizational format you select should fit the theme, the literature, and the expectations of the judges. The organizational pattern you use should also emphasize the theme and the variety of your literature.

The theme should be explicitly announced in the introduction and reviewed in the transitions. In addition, you may choose to place a selection that overtly addresses the theme in the first part of the program. You may place selections less directly related to the theme in the latter section of the program.

As you recall from the previous chapter, drama, prose, and poetry are organized by authors to reach stages of climax, or moments of crisis and resolution. In dramatic and prose readings, the movement to and from the climax reflects the playwright's organizational sense. For example, in *Fences* August Wilson creates several moments of climax. An interpretative program based on these works might include representative selections that include these moments of climax.

Transitions

Let us assume that your program includes more than one selection. Programs with more than one selection require transitions. Let us assume that your program includes selections from K. Kam's "Hopeland" and from Act Two, Scene One of *Fences*. Let us assume that the theme and argument of the program is the universal theme of family conflict and personal identity and that your first selection is "Hopeland." After you finish the first selection, you need to introduce the second selection and connect it to the first selection and to the argument of your program.

Here is an example of a transition:

> K. Kam's struggle to understand her heritage and personal identity are echoed in the relationship of Rose Maxon and her husband Troy in August Wilson's play *Fences*. August Wilson's dramas are an attempt to record the pain suffered by African Americans in the last 400 years. In Act Two, Scene One, Troy reveals that he has fathered a child with another woman. His justification and her response make vivid the universal themes of family conflict and personal identity.

This transition connects "Hopeland" to *Fences* and both to the theme of the program. Like the introduction, a transition provides the judge with the author and the title of the selection. Unlike the introduction, the transition must make a direct connection between the selections. The best oral interpreters spend much time on their introductions and transitions. After you identify your theme and argument, write an introduction and transitions, and place your selections into a meaningful order, you are ready to write the first draft of your interpretation.

Write the first draft of your interpretation

Your oral interpretation will go through many drafts and alterations during the course of the forensics season. As you write the first draft of your interpretation, you will write the introduction and transitions in your own words. Choose the selections you take from novels, short stories, and plays carefully. These selections, unlike the introduction and transitions, consist of words and ideas written by the authors you choose.

The first draft of a speech or an oral interpretation is an experiment. You should be ready and willing to make needed changes. As you write the first draft, make sure that you follow the rules of the tournament you will attend and that your program has a clear theme and argument. After you finish the first draft, you will be ready to practice and perform your oral interpretation program.

Perform and practice your oral interpretation

The first four steps are designed to help you learn your literature and to write a first draft of your program. Step five is the transition from literary study to oral performance. Your literary study gives you the insight and knowledge you need to interpret the literature for your judge.

Recall the fifth principle discussed in the previous chapter: the oral interpreter should purposefully use nonverbal and verbal messages to perform the literature. You communicate the theme and argument of your selections with your nonverbal and verbal messages. The nonverbal messages you use in your oral interpretation—posture, gesture, bodily movements, and use of the script—are essential to the interpretation of the literature.

Posture

In the previous chapter, you learned that the posture you use to interpret a character should fit the character's age, mood, and temperament, and the message the author wishes to communicate through the character. Your literary study reveals the information you need to make choices regarding a character's posture. For example, Troy Maxon, the lead character in *Fences,* is a big and a proud man. If you were interpreting the character of Troy Maxon, you would need to convey the strength and nobility of the man through your posture.

Gestures

The rules of the event may prevent you from using hand gestures. However, in the memorized category gestures are important. In the previous chapter, you learned that your gestures should convey the personal mannerisms of the character you perform. You would need learn about these patterns through observation and detective work.

Bodily movements

Again, the rules of the event may restrict the movements you are allowed to make with your body. Yet, you can convey many emotions with the muscles in your face and body. Rose Maxon, for instance, is angry in Act Two, Scene One of *Fences*. You could express this anger by clenching your facial muscles. If the rules allow for unrestricted bodily movements, you could convey Rose Maxon's anger through larger movements.

The script

The rules of the event may require you to read from, and to keep your hands on, the script. As you learned in the previous chapter, your script should blend into your performance. As you read from the script, make sure you turn the pages carefully, and that you do interpret from the page to the audience.

The verbal qualities of your voice—volume, pitch, stress, and rate—combine with nonverbal messages to communicate the theme and the meanings of the literature you select. Your literary study provides you with the information you need to make appropriate choices about the verbal qualities of voice.

Volume

Some characters call for soft voices—the narrator of "Hopeland," for example. Other characters, such as Troy Maxon, may require a loud voice. Turn first to the character and how the character is defined by the author, but also adjust the volume of your voice to the judge and to the situation. Your goal is to communicate the spirit of the character to the judge. Take into account your judge's situation and your judge's eardrums!

Clarity

As you present and perform the literature you have selected, speak as you think the character would speak. You need to help the judge understand what is being said. Clear and careful pronunciation and enunciation can help you communicate the intent of the character and literature. When James Earl Jones played Troy Maxon in the Broadway production of *Fences,* he displayed great vocal clarity in creating Troy Maxon. That was *his* interpretation.

Pitch

Because the voice is an instrument, and different people speak at different tonal levels, you will need to adjust your pitch to the character. The pitch levels of the characters you interpret help you and the judge understand who is speaking.

Rate

Finally, different characters speak at different rates. In Act Two, Scene One of *Fences,* Troy Maxon attempts to justify his infidelity. Rose Maxon doesn't accept his explanations. In an oral interpretation of this scene, you may wish to perform Troy Maxon's justification at a rapid rate—he may wish to overwhelm Rose with his words. You may wish to have Rose speak slowly and with anger. This difference in rate would help make a clear distinction between the characters.

After you make the necessary decisions about the nonverbal and verbal messages you plan to use to interpret your literary selection, you are ready to present your interpretation to your judges at the speech tournament. Your judges will provide you with useful instruction on the strengths and weaknesses of your interpretation. In addition, you can learn much by listening to the interpretations of your competitors.

Present your interpretation to your judges

By the time you arrive at the tournament, your oral interpretation program should be in good order. You have at least two or three opportunities to present your interpretation to judges. While you may have practiced your interpretative program many times, make sure that you present the literature as if it were the first time. Judges give you higher scores if you appear to be sincerely interested in and inspired by your material.

Don't be too concerned about mistakes you might make. Often, the judge will not know if you forgot a sentence or a paragraph of your interpretation unless some change in your face or body reveals the mistake. If you do make a mistake, don't stop speaking. Many beginning and experienced interpreters make mistakes. The goal is to continue speaking and to finish making your point.

Listen to the other oral interpreters

Before and after you present your program, listen carefully to the interpretations of your competitors. As you know, you should be a good audience member. This means treating the other speakers as you would want them to treat you. If you hear a speaker present an idea or a perspective with which you disagree, do not give the speaker negative nonverbal reactions. Remain a civil and a polite audience member.

You can learn much from the interpretations delivered by your competitors. Take notes on what they do well and how they organize and present their interpretations. Their programs can provide you with clear examples of effective and not-so-effective oral interpretations. After the tournament is over, you may wish to use these examples as models for improving your oral interpretations.

Modify your oral interpretations as necessary

Your oral interpretation should be in a constant state of evolution and change. You may decide after your first round that some minor modifications need to be made. For example, you may decide to change the wording of your introduction or use a different transition. You should, however, wait to make major changes in your oral interpretation until the tournament is over. Take time to think through any major alterations in your program. Make sure to talk with your forensics teacher or an experienced team member if you think your oral interpretation needs significant change.

After the tournament, read your ballots and use the comments made by your judges to improve

When the tournament is over, your forensics teacher will give you the ballots your judges wrote in reaction to your oral interpretation. These ballots tell you how your judges ranked and rated you and your program in comparison to your competition, and they record what your judge felt were the strengths and weaknesses of your interpretation. With the help of your forensics teacher, read these ballots and identify the comments made by your judges that you can and should use to revise and improve your oral interpretation.

Seek out patterns and recurring statements in the ballots. If, for example, all the judges commend you for your understanding of your literature, then you know your literary analysis was complete. If two of your judges suggest you should make a clearer distinction between the characters you present, then focus on developing better distinctions during your practice sessions.

Your ballots should be of great use to you, but use them with care. Your forensics teacher can help you to discriminate between helpful comments and those that may not be as useful. Because you may have the same judges at the next tournament, you need to read your ballots for insight into the feelings and beliefs of your judges. With their views in mind, you can work to revise and better adapt your interpretations to your judges.

Conduct additional research and practice

Your program should change after every tournament. Some sections of your interpretation may remain the same; other sections may need major or minor revisions. You must conduct additional research and practice even if you took first place at a tournament! Additional research and practice keep your program up-to-date and your delivery sharp.

Continue to practice your program throughout the forensics season. Your practice sessions should resemble, as much as possible, the tournament environment. As you practice, identify specific improvements you wish to make. After delivering the same speech a number of times, some speakers lose interest in their programs. Concentrate on making specific improvements in the content and delivery of your program, and your continued commitment to improving your program will help you retain the energy you need to succeed.

An Excerpt from Prose Literature

In almost every case, a direct excerpt is better than cutting, for when you cut or delete sentences from an author's work, you might alter its meaning. If you need to cut the literature you have selected, follow the guidelines discussed in the previous chapter. The following excerpt is taken from K. Kam's "The Hopeland."

> I try to imagine my mother as young girl, small and frail with a quite heart, shiny black hair cropped to prevent her from indulging in hours of vanity before the mirror. I laugh when she tells me some pranksters in her village filled a large vat with dung and it a fire under it, boiling the smelly contents until they exploded.
>
> But the funny stories are always followed by somber ones that will not let me forget the horrors my parents must have endured. I hear only bits and pieces. My mother tells of drunken soldiers banging on the doors of houses nearby, dragging out screaming girls and raping them in the night. She watched an angry crowd of villagers haul a traitor to the top of a hill, where they hanged him for selling secrets to the enemy. There were victims forced to kneel on broken glass and the hunted ones who chose suicide. During the land raids, she stared mutely as soldiers smashed windows and shot down old women barricading doorways with their bodies to protect young ones inside. During one onslaught, she hid underneath a bed as a soldier entered her house and held a bayonet to her mother's throat.
>
> I am disturbed, yet intrigued. I listen to the stories, casting characters and writing the script, but my mental exercise is only a game. My parents' China still eludes me.

Locate the climax of this selection as you read this excerption from "The Hopeland." As you have learned from the literary study of the author K. Kam and the culture and context to which her short story responds, she expresses in her writings the pain and joys of Chinese-Americans. In this selection, the following passage appears to be the climax, for it captures the theme of the novel and the intent of the author.

> I am disturbed, yet intrigued. I listen to the stories, casting characters and writing the script, but my mental exercise is only a game. My parents' China still eludes me.

The argument of this selection reflects the three themes highlighted in the introduction and is supported by the "evidence" in the three paragraphs: that there was humor and horror in the homeland of origin and that children of immigrants will have difficulty understanding the stories of their parents.

In interpreting and performing this selection, you would need to use nonverbal and verbal communications to interpret the intellectual, emotional, and aesthetic meanings of K. Kam's work. In works of prose, the narrator is the center of the story. In this case, K. Kam is the narrator. A literary analysis of "The Hopeland" would give you insight into how the story might be interpreted. In interpreting the characters, you will need to make choices about how you will present their messages.

These choices will fall into two categories. First, you need to make some choices about posture, gestures, body movements, and the script. Second, you need to make some choices about the vocal qualities of the two women.

Nonverbal Considerations. To perform "The Hopeland," you would need to use the nonverbal patterns and gestures of a first-generation Chinese immigrant in portraying K. Kam's mother. Ms. Kam, the narrator, would exhibit the gestures and the bodily movements of an American-born and raised woman. The judge should know by observing the nonverbal messages that she is American-born. However, if you included passages that quote her father, then you would need to reflect in your nonverbal behavior the actions of a native-born Chinese man.

The rules of the event may require you to read from, and to keep your hands on the script. If so, your script should blend into your performance. For example, you might hold the script in different positions when you read the three paragraphs. If you compete in the memorized category of oral interpretation, your body, rather than the script, will convey your interpretations of the character.

Verbal Qualities. The verbal qualities of your voice will combine with the nonverbal messages to communicate the theme and the meanings of this selection. A literary study of K. Kam and "The Hopeland" will provide you with the information you will need to make choices about the verbal qualities of voice.

Focusing on verbal qualities of voice—volume, clarity, pitch, and rate—will help you speak as you think the character would speak. When K. Kam states that her "parents' China eludes me," you may choose to interpret these words in wonder and slight frustration. The characters' vocal qualities would also differ in clarity, pitch, and rate. You need to adjust and adapt these qualities to your vision of the character's personality and goals in your selection.

An excerpt from dramatic literature

We have considered a scene from August Wilson's *Fences* as an example of dramatic literature. As you recall, dramatic literature, unlike prose literature, tends not to position a narrator at the center of the interpretation. Rather, the characters share a stage. This is the case in Act Two, Scene One of *Fences*. When you read the following excerpt, think about how you would interpret the characters of Troy and Rose Maxon:

Rose: You should have stayed in my bed, Troy.

Troy: Then when I saw that gal . . . she firmed up my backbone. And I got to thinking that if I tried . . . I just might be able to steal second. Do you understand after eighteen years I wanted to steal second.

Rose: You should have held me tight. You should have grabbed me and held on.

Troy: I stood on first base for eighteen years and I thought . . . well, goddamn it . . . go for it!

Rose: We're not talking about baseball! We're talking about you going off to lay in bed with another woman . . . and then bring it home to me. That's what we're talking about. We ain't talking about no baseball.

Creating an Interpretative Performance of *Fences*

A literary analysis of August Wilson's plays and of *Fences* reveals much about how you might interpret the characters of Troy and Rose Maxon. Troy sees life as a baseball game and sees his affair as an attempt to "steal second." Rose refuses to see life as a baseball game: "We're not talking about baseball." She zeroes in on what is, to her, the real issue.

The argument in this selection has to do with the "life is baseball" attitude. At the root of August Wilson's plays is the impact of racism on African-Americans. Troy Maxon was denied, because of his race, the opportunity to excel in baseball. The idea of "stealing second" is, in part, a response to his life's frustrations. However, Rose will have none of it. The climax of the passage is "We're not talking about baseball! We're talking about you going off to lay in bed with another woman. . . ."

Nonverbal Considerations

In putting this selection into performance, you need to use nonverbal and verbal communication to perform the roles of Rose and Troy Maxon. You need to use posture, gestures, and body movements in an interpretative performance of these two characters. Because Troy is a big man, your posture must reflect his size.

Rose is resisting Troy's characterization of his affair, and her gestures and body movements should reflect her refusal to accept his justification. Troy is on the defensive, so his movements and gestures should mirror his intent to defend his actions. Troy and Rose are involved in an argument; the nonverbal messages of anger, defensiveness, and verbal attack are essential if the meaning of the selection is to be communicated.

Verbal Qualities

The verbal qualities of your voice will combine with the nonverbal messages in an interpretation of *Fences*. A literary study of August Wilson and *Fences* provides you with the information you need to make choices about the verbal qualities of voice.

Verbal qualities of voice—volume, clarity, pitch, and rate—help you speak as you think Rose and Troy Maxon would speak. When Rose Maxon cries out "We're not talking about baseball!" you should perform this sentence with a voice filled with anger and hurt. Troy Maxon's voice should sound notes of apology and defense. A careful analysis of nonverbal and verbal communication can produce a faithful interpretation of this selection.

CONCLUSION

The oral interpretation of prose and dramatic literature is an art that requires careful literary study of the text and an energetic performance of exciting literature. In this chapter, you have learned how to select and analyze literature for competitive oral interpretation. If you follow the steps outlined, you will be proud of your understanding and your interpretation of prose and dramatic literature.

As with other forensics events, your oral interpretation should be designed to present a theme and make an argument. This theme and argument should come from the literature you select. Many resources can help you discover good literature with a theme that intrigues you.

Your programs should consist of literature that you love and that moves you. If you don't like the literature you interpret, or if you tire of your program, find new material. A vast universe of wonderful and exciting literature awaits you. Don't settle for selections that do not inspire you or your audience.

CHAPTER TWELVE

Interpretation of Poetry

The educational aim of oral interpretation is for the student to gain an understanding of prose, drama, and poetry. As with prose and dramatic literature, competitors need to gain an understanding of their poets and poems through a careful literary analysis and performance of this literature. Judges expect competitors to understand the intellectual, emotional, and aesthetic meanings of the poems.

The best oral interpretations of poetry are a result of a careful literary study of the poets and poetry and guided performance of the poetry. You might think that poetry cannot be evaluated. However, literary scholars have identified some yardsticks for judging the worth of poetry. The best poetry programs are those that have a universal appeal, express this appeal in a unique fashion, and invite audience participation. Poetry programs should develop themes, make arguments, and move audiences.

Scholars of poetry have identified three kinds of poems. Narrative poems tell stories in which narrators and characters speak. Dramatic poems center on one character who faces a conflict. Lyric poems are characterized by language and images that spark deep emotions and feelings.

Poetry does share the basic characteristics of prose and dramatic literature. Most poets intend to tell a story, communicate a message, and make an argument about the world. Poetry is distinguished from prose and dramatic literature by its compactness, emotional intensity, and its focus on sound and rhythm. The content and structure of poetry meld together to achieve its effect.

This chapter explains the specific steps you should take in selecting good poetry, constructing a poetry program, and performing the poems you have selected. Before you read on, you should read or reread chapter 10, which outlines the basic principles that apply to all divisions and categories of oral interpretation. After you have a good understanding of these principles, you can begin to take the steps necessary to create a successful poetry program.

The first step you should take in creating a poetry program is to understand and follow the rules of the event.

Guidelines

Rules for Poetry Reading

Purpose: The primary purpose of poetry reading is for the student to communicate the intellectual, emotional, and aesthetic meanings of poetry as they relate to an organized central theme.

Length: Readings are limited to five (5) minutes with thirty (30) seconds grace. Contestants who violate the time limit will be disqualified.

Procedures

1. All programs will have a central or unifying theme.
2. Many tournaments require no fewer than three poems or cuttings from three poems and that at least three poems are not less than eight lines.
3. The interpretation is to be read from a printed text. Frequent references are to be made to the text during the performance.
4. Contestants will keep both hands on the manuscript and stand in one place when the text is presented. Appropriate physical movements and gestures can be made during introductions, transitions, and moments when the text is not the focus.
5. Contestants can use facial, verbal, and vocal modes of communication.
6. The original work of the student is often permitted.

You must understand and follow the rules for these events. In particular, pay attention to the time limits. Judges are quite about strict enforcing the time limits, and you may be disqualified if you violate them. With the rules for competitive poetry reading in mind, we can now explore what happens in the poetry round. You need to know how to read the tournament schedule and to find out where your competitions will take place.

The Poetry Round

The tournament schedule lists times you will present your interpretation. As you can tell (and if the tournament permits), you may choose to compete in more than one interpretative event. For example, you might compete in extemp in pattern A and in poetry in pattern B. At some tournaments you might do two events in the same pattern. This is called "double entering." For example, the sample tournament schedule on the next page might allow a student to compete in both impromptu and poetry. If you compete in both events, then you present your impromptu and your poetry reading in the same hour. Let us assume that you have entered the poetry competition. As you can tell from the schedule, poetry is in pattern B.

You will present your poetry interpretation three times on Friday at 1:30, 5:30, and 7:00. If you do well in these three rounds, you may present your poetry reading at 10:30 (semifinals) and at 1:30 (finals) on Saturday.

When you arrive at the tournament, find out where the tournament staff is posting so that you know where your rounds are scheduled to take place. Most tournaments post the panels in each event, listing the rooms and judges. (See the following checklist.)

Let us assume that you are speaker two in the first round of novice poetry reading.

You need to find Dickinson Hall. Your forensics teacher may give you a map of the campus, or you may need to ask for directions. Try, if possible, to arrive ten to fifteen minutes before the round starts. When the judge and the other competitors have arrived, speaker one (Browning from St. Vincent Millay) will be the first to speak. When Browning and the other four competitors speak, be a good audience member. Pay attention to the oral interpretations of your competitors and provide positive reactions whenever possible. Remember that all the speakers are trying hard to interpret poetry that means much to them.

As you listen to your competitors, try to identify what they do well and what you can learn from their interpretative programs. You might ask yourself: What literature did they pick? Why did they choose to interpret those particular poems? How do they introduce their program? What organizational pattern do they use? What transitions did they use? How did they present and deliver their poems? The answers to these questions may help you to understand what distinguishes the strong interpretative program from one that needs significant improvements.

SAMPLE SPEECH TOURNAMENT SCHEDULE

PATTERN A EVENTS   PATTERN B EVENTS
Extemp   Impromptu
Radio Commentary   Expository speaking
Expos   Humorous Interp
Serious Interp   ADS
                              Poetry

THURSDAY, Feb. 27
    11:00 - 12:00 Registration
    12:30 - 1:50 SENIOR LD debate, Round I
     2:00 - 3:20 JUNIOR LD and ALL CX debate, Round I
     3:30 - 4:00 ALL DEBATE, Round II
     5:00 - 6:20 ALL DEBATE, Round III
     6:30 - 7:20 Break
     7:30 - 9:00 ALL DEBATE, Round IV

FRIDAY, Feb. 28
     8:00 - 9:30 CX Debate, Round V
     8:30 - 9:30 Registration for schools with IEs only
    10:00   EXTEMP DRAW
    10:30 - 11:30 Pattern A, Round I
    12:00   EXTEMP DRAW
    12:30 - 1:30 Pattern A, Round II
    1:30 - 2:30 Pattern B, Round I
     2:45 - 3:30 LD Debate, Round V (both JR & SR)
     4:00   EXTEMP DRAW
     4:30 - 5:30 Pattern A, Round III
    5:30 - 6:30 Pattern B, Round II
     6:30 - 7:00 Break
    7:00 - 8:00 Pattern B, Round III
     8:15 - 9:45 ALL DEBATE, Round IV
     9:00   IE Semifinal Postings

SATURDAY, Feb. 29
     7:30   UNIVERSITY CENTER Opens
     7:45   Debate Outrounds Postings
     8:00 - 9:30 ALL DEBATE, Octo-finals
    10:00   EXTEMP DRAW
    10:30 - 11:30 IE Semifinals, Pattern A & Pattern B
    12:00 - 1:00 ALL DEBATE, Quarter-finals
     1:00   EXTEMP DRAW
    1:30 - 2:30 IE Finals, Pattern A & Pattern B
     3:00 - 4:30 ALL DEBATE, Semifinals
     5:30 - 7:00 ALL DEBATE, Finals
    8:00   Awards

Checklist

Postings
Poetry reading
Novice Division
Round One
Judge: R. Frost
Room: 128 Dickinson Hall

Speaker One: Browning, St. Vincent Millay team
Speaker Two: **YOU**, Jefferson team
Speaker Three: Bacon, Wallace team
Speaker Four: Eliot, Donne team
Speaker Five: Cummings, Whitman team
Speaker Six: Milton, Brooke team

Guidelines

A Traditional Organizational Pattern Used in Poetry Programs

I. Introduction: Theme, author[s], title[s], and argument
    Transition and introduction of title and author of first poem

II. Selection One
    Transition and introduction of title and author of second poem

III. Selection Two
    Transition and introduction of title and author of third selection

IV. Selection Three

In organizing a poetry reading, you need to create an introduction that provides the judge with the title(s) and the author(s) of your cuttings. Judges also expect clear transitions between your selections, as shown above.

Your poems should be connected by a central, unifying theme and an argument. This theme will help you decide how to organize your selections. The transitions you use are of great importance, for they help to remind your judges how the selections are connected by the theme.

When it is your turn to perform your oral interpretation, you should walk from your seat to the front of the room. You should walk with confidence and position yourself so that all the members of your audience can see you. Once you have positioned yourself, you pause and open your text. Most competitors place their text in a black notebook and open the notebook before they begin.

Judges' Expectations

Judges look for student interpreters to select high-quality poems, to have important themes and arguments, coherent and well-connected cuttings, and an effective style and delivery. Most judges believe that a solid understanding of the poetry and a well-developed performance technique are equal in importance. Unfortunately, some competitors overemphasize performance and fail to develop a good understanding of the poetry. This chapter analyzes how you should conduct a literary analysis of your poetry selections so that you achieve a good understanding of the poetry you select.

Judges ask themselves at least five questions when evaluating your poetry programs: Did you follow the rules? Did you identify a relevant and consequential theme and argument? Did you organize and provide transitions for your selections? Did your interpretations reveal an understanding of the literature you have selected? Did your delivery enhance the effect of the literature? Let us take each of these questions in turn.

Did you follow the rules?

Judges expect you to know and to follow the rules of this event. Depending on the rule violation, judges may penalize you for failing to comply with the rules. For example, you may be disqualified if your poetry reading is overtime.

The rules for district and state tournaments may differ from those used by school-sponsored forensics tournaments. For example, the poetry reading you present at a district tournament may need to contain the same selections as the one you present at the state tournament. Make sure to check with your forensics teacher for the rules used by individual tournaments.

Did you identify a relevant and serious theme?

Judges reward interpretations that center on a topic or theme of some consequence. The theme you select should be meaningful and pertinent to you and your judge. Experienced judges have heard many poetry readings: the theme you develop should arouse their interest and inspire them to listen.

How do you know if you have selected a relevant and consequential theme? Your judges consider your theme important if it reveals and develops a broad and basic truth and experience; if it speaks to this truth and experience in a unique manner; and if the poems you select are rich, profound, and of the highest quality.

Did you organize and provide transitions for your selections?

You need to organize your poems for your judge. Judges want to hear poetry programs that have a clear and purposeful order. The words you use to introduce your theme and the sentences you use to create transitions between your cuttings are key to helping your judge understand your poetry program. In addition, the order of your selections should reflect a purpose. You may wish to begin with a powerful but depressing poem and end with a soothing poem. The choices you make in organizing and ordering your materials depend on the theme and the mood you wish to develop.

Did your interpretations reveal an understanding of the poetry you have selected?

Your judges expect you to exhibit an understanding of the poetry you have selected. You have a responsibility to understand the backgrounds, the cultures, and the impulses of the poets whose work you interpret. The library research you conduct and the literary analysis you perform should help you gain a thorough appreciation of the poems you perform.

Did your performance enhance the effect of the poetry?

Most judges look for a delivery style that fits the poetry. Because your goal is to share the meaning and the experience of your poetry with your judge, your delivery should reflect the mood, tone, and the spirit of the poetry program. For example, if you read a poem about a prisoner who is anticipating parole, your delivery should mirror the emotional vibrations of the poem. The best oral interpreters of poetry adjust the volume, the pace, and the tone of their delivery to their theme, materials, judge, room, and speaking situation.

Creating and Presenting Your Poetry Program

With the judges' expectations in mind, let us move to the following steps you must take to create an oral interpretation.

These steps are designed to help you select, develop, and present your oral

---

Guidelines

Steps in the Creation and Presentation of a Poetry Program

Before the Tournament

1. Brainstorm for poets, poetry, themes, and subjects for your poetry reading.
2. Conduct a literary analysis of the poets and poems you have selected.
3. Identify a theme and an argument to organize your poems into a format that puts your program into a meaningful order.
4. Write the first draft of your poetry program.
5. Perform and practice your poetry program.

During the Tournament

6. Present your poetry program to your judges.
7. Listen to the other competitors present their poetry programs.
8. Modify your poetry program as necessary.

After the Speech and Tournament

9. After the tournament, read your ballots and use the comments made by your judges to improve and modify your poetry program.
10. Conduct additional research and practice as necessary.

---

interpretation of poetry. Each step is important if you are to create an oral interpretation that effectively communicates the intellectual, emotional, and aesthetic meanings of the poems you have selected.

Brainstorm topics and subjects for your poetry program

You need to find a theme for your poetry reading that is interesting and significant to you and your judges. The theme you select should inspire you to conduct the necessary research on the authors and literature you have selected. You will deliver your poetry program to diverse audiences, so select a theme that will engage a broad spectrum of people. As you select a theme for your oral interpretation, try to pick one that is socially significant and find poems and poetry that express the theme with energy and animation.

You might also start in the opposite direction and think about the poems you have read and enjoyed. Perhaps a common theme will emerge that connects these poems. Once you identify a theme, you can begin to select material that will help you develop the theme.

As you search for a theme and literature, use the three touchstones discussed in chapter 10 in making your decisions. First, the theme and poems you select should have a broad-based appeal and a universal impulse. Some literature is restricted in its meaning and focus. This touchstone is particularly helpful if you wish to present poetry to a general audience with diverse views of the world. The poems you select should appeal to those who may not share your personal experiences or cultural background.

Poems that speak to the universal human condition appeal to more audience members than those that speak to a particular feeling or concern. For example, the poetry found in the Christian Bible, the Jewish Torah, and the Islamic Koran shed light on problems that all humans face. The more secular poetry of Adrienne Rich, T.S. Eliot, Gwendolyn Brooks, and many others also sounds emotional notes to which many people respond.

The second touchstone you can use to select a theme and poems is the individuality expressed by the theme and the poets you choose. While you want to select material with universal appeal, you also want selections that address a universal theme in a novel manner. The durable poetry of Robert Frost, Elizabeth Browning, William Shakespeare, and Anne Sexton express universal themes that clearly reflect the distinctiveness of the poets. You should feel free, however, to seek out new poets and poetry.

You should also use a third touchstone that calls for poetry that is rich, subtle, and open to suggestion. Such literature encourages your judges to play an active role in your performance. How can your judges play an active role when you are the one who reads the poetry? If your materials are rich, subtle, and open to suggestion, then judges can draw on their own experiences, background, and feelings in responding to the poetry, giving it greater meaning for them. Your goal is to bring your judges' life and experiences into contact with your theme and material.

The search for themes and good poetry requires some brainstorming. With the three touchstones as your guide, the brainstorming is designed to provoke a wide-ranging discussion between you, your forensics teacher, and teammates on possible themes and literature for a poetry reading. During the brainstorming period, you discuss every theme, poet, and poem that even remotely sounds interesting. At this stage, you should write down all the topics and poems that come to mind.

Brainstorming for Subjects

Let us say the brainstorming session on topics for a poetry reading produced the following responses listed in the following checklist.

Checklist

Potential Topics for Poetry Reading

Misfortune	Love	War	Peace
Cultural Identity	Children	Depression	Magic
Aging	Disgrace	Ghosts	Animals

All these topics have potential universal appeal, but because they are such common topics, your forensics teacher might suggest that some of them are tired and overdone. Death, for example, may not make the best topic, for it is a very popular theme for poetry readings. If you do choose this topic and develop a strong theme with good poetry, then the judges might respond favorably. Your forensics teacher and teammates can help you make a wise choice from the list of topics generated during the brainstorming session. Select a topic that meets the three touchstones of universal appeal, unique and individual expression, and rich and subtle expression.

Brainstorming for Poems

You might also start in a different direction and list the poets and poems you have read and have enjoyed. You may also ask your forensics teacher and other knowledgeable people about the poets they read and the poems they cherish. You might also want to consult an anthology of poems so that you have a number of choices. Perhaps you find after the discussion and some careful reading that the families theme has potential.

Let us say that you have read Maya Angelou's book *I Know Why the Caged Bird Sings* and the collections of her poetry, *Just Give Me a Cool Drink of Water 'fore I Die, Oh Pray My Wings Are Gonna Fit Me Well*, and *On the Pulse of Morning*. As a celebrated, award-winning poet, her poetry meets the touchstones used to evaluate good literature. First, her poems set forth universal themes. Her poems speak of the agony suffered by those who lack power. They also discuss the failure of the American dream and the hope of an America at peace with its diversity. Second, her poems express these universal themes distinctly and in a voice you know belongs to Maya Angelou. Third, her poems are richly suggestive and invite audience participation and response.

From a careful reading of her poems, you decide on the theme of multicultural identity. This theme is expressed in her poems "Africa," "America," and "On the Pulse of Morning." You should check with your teammates and your forensics teacher to see if they believe this theme and the three poems will make a good program. If they agree with your choices, then you will need to conduct a literary analysis of the poems you have selected. As you recall from

---

Checklist

Questions to Ask in the Internal Analysis of Poetry

Who is speaking? And to whom is the speaker speaking?

About what is the speaker speaking?

When and were does the speaker speak?

How does the speaker speak?

Why does the speaker speak?

---

chapter 10, a literary analysis of the poems you have selected requires you to conduct an internal and an external analysis of your texts.

Conduct a literary analysis of the poems you have selected

Once you have decided to create a poetry reading showcasing the poetry of Maya Angelou, you need to understand the intellectual, emotional, and aesthetic meanings of her poetry. As you recall from chapter 10, a literary analysis involves an internal analysis of the poems you read and a contexualized external analysis of the poet and poetry. To illustrate how you should conduct an internal and an external analysis of a text, let us consider how Maya Angelou's poems might be subjected to a literary analysis.

Literary analysis of Maya Angelou's poem "America"

An internal analysis would involve a careful reading of the entire poem. To achieve an understanding of a poem, you need to look at the story the poet tells. As you read Maya Angelou's poem "America," try to identify the theme she develops and the argument she makes.

An Internal Analysis. Recall the questions, discussed in chapter 10, that you can ask in analyzing any piece of literature. These questions can help you to uncover the intellectual, emotional, and aesthetic meanings of a piece of literature. We will ask the following questions of the poem "America."

Who is speaking? And to whom is the speaker speaking? To answer these questions, you need to know how to classify the poem you will read. Three types of poems exist—lyrical, dramatic, and narrative. If a poem is classified as lyrical, the speaker tends to be the poet or a poet-substitute. Dramatic poems are told by characters who are definitely not the poet. Narrative poems are told by narrators and characters.

"America" is a lyric poem. The poet, Maya Angelou, is the speaker. She

America
by
Maya Angelou

The gold of her promise
  has never been mined

Her borders of justice
  not clearly defined

Her crops of abundance
  the fruit and the grain

Have not fed the hungry
  nor eased that great pain

Her proud declarations
  are leaves on the wind

Discover this country
  dead centuries cry

Erect noble tablets
  where none can decry

"She kills her bright future
  and rapes for a sou

Then entraps her children
  with legends untrue"

I beg you
Discover this country.

sou: (French) a coin, now practically worthless.

is addressing this poem to a general audience. Most likely she is addressing an American audience, for she states the vision of America ("The gold of her promise") and the reality of America ("has never been mined") are inconsistent. This statement of inconsistency makes up the argument of the poem.

About what is the speaker speaking? Maya Angelou makes a clear argument in this poem. She considers the promise of America and the injustice, hunger, and hypocrisy that need to be discovered by the audience. Maya Angelou seems motivated in this poem to expose the corruption of the American dream and soul.

When and where does the speaker speak? This poem makes an argument about an America of today. While the dreams and promises were made in the past, the present is filled with nightmares and broken promises. The speaker seems to understand America and its stated traditions. The speaker also seems to look forward to a day when people will truly "discover" America and put its dreams and promises into place.

How does the speaker speak? The sounds of words often communicate the meaning of poetry. In addition, these sounds are often intended by poets to lead an audience to a fulcrum, or climax. Together, the sounds and the fulcrum determine how an audience will react to the poet's theme and argument.

Poets use meter (a measured rhythmic pattern) and imagery to create their poems. A number of rhythmic patterns and images are available to the poet. Entire books have been written in which these patterns and images have been classified and analyzed. To limit our investigation, let us focus on the work of Maya Angelou. What rhythmic patterns and images can you identify in the poem "America?"

Meter. A careful scan of the poem reveals the poem's rhyme scheme. The words that rhyme in this poem are at the ends of the lines:

The gold of her promise
    has never been *mined*

Her borders of justice
    not clearly *defined*

Her crops of abundance
    the fruit and the *grain*

Have not fed the hungry
    nor eased the great *pain*

This kind of rhyme scheme is known as an end rhyme.

The rhythmic pattern detected in the tenth stanza offers a way to organize the poem. A stanza is a division of a poem composed of two or more lines. The stanzas used to construct the poem "America" are organized around juxtapositions or comparisons and contrasts. When the first and second lines of the stanza are placed side by side, you can tell the promise outlined in the first lines are betrayed by the reality of the second lines.

Promise	Reality
The gold of her promise	has never been mined
Her borders of justice	not clearly defined
Her crops of abundance	Have not fed the hungry
fruit and grain	nor eased the pain

The rhythmic pattern of the poem involves an ending rhyme and stanzas that alternate the American promise with the American reality.

Imagery. Poets also use imagery to communicate their themes and arguments. Poets create imagery with words and sounds that attract the senses. Poetic imagery can also be the result of figurative language. Figurative language is allusions and figures of speech.

Take the first stanza in the poem "America."

The gold of her promise
has never been mined

The word "gold" sparks a visual image of bright wealth and riches. The reader and audience of this poem visualizes a golden promise. Because it is in the first line of the poem, the audience will use this image to frame and define the rest of the poem. The next line shifts the imagery to the pits of a gold mine. The line "has never been mined" places the golden promise below ground in a place yet to be excavated.

The fifth stanza uses the imagery of the wind:

Her proud declarations
are leaves on the wind

The golden promise of the first stanza and the "proud declarations" of the fifth stanza are reduced to leaves blowing in the wind. Because most people have seen leaves blowing in the wind, the imagery is powerful and appealing. To this point in the poem, the audience knows that the gold is unmined and the proud declarations are as leaves on the wind.

The Fulcrum. There is a moment of crisis and resolution in many poems, known as the fulcrum. You will need to identify and communicate the fulcrum to your judge for it is a defining moment of the poem. In the poem "America," the fulcrum occurs between the ninth and tenth stanzas. Stanzas one through nine develop the failure of the American promise: The gold of the promise is unmined; justice is unclear; the abundant crops are not used to feed the hungry. The final stanza shifts from complaint to call for action as the audience is called to "Discover this Country."

Discovering a poem's meter, imagery, and fulcrum will help you read the poem to your judge. Poets use a number of words and sounds, rhythms and images to achieve their goals. As you gain more knowledge of the mechanics of poetry, you will become a better reader of poetry. The best poetry readers understand how poems work. You can gain an understanding of how poems work by reading articles on poetry and by a careful literary analysis of the poets and poetry you love.

Why does the speaker speak? You need to know why poets write poetry. What motivates and inspires poets to use words and sounds, meter and imagery to communicate themes and arguments? All poets have reasons for writing poetry. Your task is to discover these reasons and use them to gain a better understanding of the poems you read. After you complete an internal analysis of the poems, you need to conduct an external analysis of the poet and the poem. This involves studying the culture and the context of the poet. To illustrate how such a study can be accomplished, let us ask: Why did Maya Angelou write the poem "America?"

An external analysis. The research process you follow is similar to the one used in the external analysis of prose and dramatic literature. First, you want to put the poet and the poetry in their context and culture. You will need to conduct library research on the poet, the poet's agenda, and the culture and the context to which the poet responds.

Context and Culture of the Poet and Poetry. A quick read of the poem "America" does not reveal the background and experiences of the poet, Maya Angelou. She is an award-winning poet who was invited by President Bill Clinton to read a poem at his inaugural. She is also the author of five works of autobiography and five collections of poetry. Her work has been discussed by literary critics and scholars of poetry.

These critics and scholars detail how African American poets write poetry that celebrates African American traditions and condemns the racist attitudes that have prevented African American progress. Her poetry reflects and responds to her experience as a woman and an African American. Reading outside sources can help you understand how her poetry works and what motivates it.

Like the plays of the African American playwright August Wilson, the poems of Maya Angelou deal with the consequences of racism. To understand her poems, you need to learn much about racism in America. Many books and articles address the issue of racism in America. The books you should read to understand August Wilson's plays would also help you to understand Maya Angelou's poems: Gunnar Myrdal's *An American Dilemma: The Negro Problem and Modern Democracy* (New York: Harper, 1944); Andrew Hacker's *Two Nations: Black and White, Separate, Hostile, Unequal* (New York: Scribners, 1992); and Studs Terkel's *Race: How Blacks and Whites Think and Feel About the American Obsession* (New York: New Press, 1992).

Poets write in response to their culture and context. The poem "America" is a response to the American culture and context and to the pain and anger of an African American writer. Once you understand the culture and context of American racism, you can consider what Maya Angelou intends to accomplish with her poems.

Author's Intent. Poets develop themes and arguments with their poems. Often, in interviews, articles, and books they describe the goals they hope to accomplish with their poems. An understanding of these goals is essential to proper interpretation of their work.

Maya Angelou has clearly defined the themes and arguments she hopes to advance in her poems. In her autobiographies she tells the story of her life. Before you read the poetry of Maya Angelou, you should read or reread *I Know Why the Caged Bird Sings, Gather Together in My Name, Singin' and Gettin' Merry Like Christmas, The Heart of a Woman, and All God's Children Need Traveling Shoes*. In addition, you should be familiar with her volumes of poetry: *And Still I Rise; Just Give Me a Cool Drink of Water 'fore I Die; Oh Pray My Wings Are Gonna Fit Me Well; Shaker, Why Don't You Sing?;* and *I Shall Not Be Moved*.

Her autobiographies and volumes of poetry attest to her drive to expose American racism, her need to celebrate her African heritage, and her belief that America can create a new beginning and a new morning. She worked for Dr. Martin Luther King, Jr. as the Northern Coordinator for the Southern Christian Leadership Conference, formed a close relationship with Malcolm X, and is now a professor at Wake Forest University.

In her autobiography *All God's Children Need Traveling Shoes,* she writes of her dual existence as she returned to the United States after living in Africa:

> Many years earlier, I, or rather someone very like me and certainly related to me, had been taken from Africa by force. This second leave-taking would not be so onerous, for now I knew my people had never completely left Africa. We had sung it in our blues, shouted it in our gospel and danced the continent in our breakdowns. As we carried it to Philadelphia, Boston and Birmingham we had changed its color, modified its rhythms, yet it was Africa which rode in the bulges or our high calves, shook in our protruding behinds and crackled in our wide open laughter.

Maya Angelou's belief is that "I knew my people had never completely left Africa." At the same time, she sees the impact African Americans have made on America. Her poem "America" communicates her unhappiness with America's treatment of African Americans, but you will find her poem "On the Pulse of Morning," communicates a hope that America can keep its promises by accepting its multicultural reality. Once you have completed an internal and an external analysis of the poet and her poems, you can begin to organize your poetry reading.

Organizing Your Reading

Identify a theme and an argument to organize your poems into a format that puts your reading into a meaningful order. By now you have brainstormed for themes and subjects for your poetry reading, and conducted a literary analysis of the poets and poems you have selected. After you complete the literary

---

Guidelines

A Traditional Organizational Pattern Used in Poetry Programs

I. Introduction: Theme, author[s], Title[s], and Argument
    Theme and Argument: Multicultural identity; America must keep its promise
    Author: Maya Angelou
    Titles: "Africa," "America," "On the Pulse of Morning"
    Transition and introduction of title and author of first poem

II. Poem One: "Africa"
    Transition and introduction of title and author of second poem

III. Poem Two: "America"
    Transition and introduction of title and author of third selection

IV. Poem Three: "On the Pulse of Morning"

---

analysis, identify the argument of your reading and select an organizational pattern that fits the material and the argument.

Identifying the Theme and Argument

As you recall, all oral interpretations are designed to present an argument and a theme. You will draw the argument and theme of your oral interpretation from the literature you select. Your literary analysis helps you determine what argument the poet is advancing. For example, the argument and theme of the poem "America" concern the experience of African Americans and the broken promises made by America. The theme of multilcultural identity and the argument that America needs to keep its promises are expressed in her poems "Africa," "America," and "On the Pulse of Morning." You might choose these three poems for your program. You would design your poetry reading to communicate this theme and make this argument to the judge.

The Introduction

After you identify the argument and theme of your program, you need to place your selection into a meaningful order. That order depends on the poetry and the organization of your reading. At a minimum, your reading should have an introduction. If you include more than one selection, you need strong transitions that connect the selections and link them to the theme or argument such as the following.

Maya Angelou, teacher, author, poet, has written a host of poems in which she communicates her unhappiness with America's treatment of African Americans and the hope that America can keep its promises by accepting its multicultural reality. As an African American, she believes her people never completely left Africa. At the same time, she expresses her pride in the contributions made by African Americans to American culture. In her three poems, "Africa," "America," and "On the Pulse of Morning," she displays the pain of racism and the dream of a new morning in America.

This introduction gives the name of the poet, the titles of the poems, the theme, a brief literary analysis, and the argument of the poetry reading. The brief literary analysis is drawn from her autobiography, and the last two sentences capture the argument of the selection and the program.

Organizational Format

You should place your literature into a meaningful and purposeful order. The organizational format you select should fit the theme, the poems, and the expectations of the judges. This organizational format or pattern shown on page 276 should help you to bring out and communicate the essence of the poetry

You should explicitly announce the theme in the introduction and review it in the transitions. In addition, you may choose to place a poem that overtly addresses the theme in the first part of the program. Other selections, that may address the theme less directly, may be better in the latter section of the program. You might place the poem "Africa" first, for it captures the rhythms and images of Maya Angelou's country of origin. "America" could be the second poem you read, for it communicates the American betrayal. "On the Pulse of Morning" might be the third and last poem, for it conveys her sense of hope in the American promise. The organizational pattern should help to strengthen the theme and the argument of the poetry reading.

Transitions. Let us assume that your poetry reading includes more than one poem. Poetry readings with more than one poem will need transitions. If, for example, your poetry reading included the three poems of Maya Angelou, you would need transitions between the three poems.

Here is an example of a transition between the poem "America" and "On the Pulse of Morning."

> In "America" Maya Angelou speaks of a country whose gold of the promise is unmined, whose justice is unclear, and whose abundant crops are not used to feed the hungry. In "On the Pulse of Morning," she looks, with hope for a new pulse and a new beginning. In this poem, she urges Americans to move beyond their fear and embrace the land and the diversity of its peoples.

This transition connects the second and third poems and both to the argument of the reading. Like the introduction, a transition provides the judge with the author (if it is a different author) and the title of the selection. Unlike the introduction, the transition must make a direct connection between the selections. The best oral interpreters spend much time on their introductions and transitions. Once you identify your theme and argument, write an introduction and transitions, and place your selections into a meaningful order, you are ready to write the first draft of your interpretation.

Write the first draft of your interpretation. Your poetry reading will go through many drafts and alterations during the course of the forensics season. As you write the first draft of your poetry reading, you will write the introduction and transitions in your own words. The selections you take from poems should be made with great care. These selections, unlike the introduction and transitions, should consist of words and ideas of the poets you feature.

The first draft of a poetry reading is an experiment. You should be ready and willing to make needed changes. As you write the first draft, make sure that you follow the rules of the tournament you will attend and that your program has a clear theme and argument. After you finish the first draft, you are ready to practice and perform your poetry reading.

Perform and practice your poetry reading. Once you have developed an understanding of your poetry and completed a first draft of your program, you are ready to practice the oral reading of your poetry. Your literary study gives you the insight and knowledge you need to read your poetry for your judge.

Recall the fifth principle discussed in chapter 10: The oral interpreter should purposefully use nonverbal and verbal messages to perform the literature. You will communicate the theme and argument of your selections with your nonverbal and verbal messages. The nonverbal messages you use in your oral interpretation—posture, gesture, bodily movements, and use of the script—are essential to the performance of the literature you have selected.

Posture. In the previous chapter, you learned that the posture you use to read a poem should fit the mood, temperament, and the message the author of the literature wishes to communicate through the poem. Your literary study provides the information you need to make choices regarding the poem's form and purpose. For example, the poem "America" is an angry poem; "On the Pulse of Morning" is a hopeful poem. You would want to communicate anger and hopefulness with your posture as you read these poems.

Gestures. The rules of the event prevent the use of hand gestures. The poetry is to be read from a printed text. Frequent references are to be made to the text during the performance. The text or notebook can be used to help you communicate the mood of the poetry. You might choose to move your text or notebook to underscore a word or sound.

Bodily Movements. Again, the rules of the event restrict the movements you are allowed to make with your body. Yet, you can convey many emotions with the muscles in your face and body. You might express the anger that is at the center of the poem "America" by the tightening of the muscles in your neck and face.

The Script. The rules of the event may require you to read from, and to keep your hands on, the script. As you learned in the previous chapter, your script should blend into your performance. As you read from the script, make sure that you turn the pages with care, and that you interpret from the page to the audience.

Poems convey their messages through words and sounds. The verbal qualities of your voice—volume, pitch, stress, and rate—combine with the nonverbal messages to communicate the theme and the arguments of the poems you select. Your literary study of the poet and poetry offer you the information you need to make choices about the verbal qualities of voice.

Volume. Some poems call for a soft voice; others may require a loud voice. While you should turn first to the poem and the intent of the poet, you should also adjust the volume of your voice to the judge and to the situation. Your goal is to communicate the spirit of the poem to the judge. Take into account the size of the room and the comfort of your judge.

Clarity. As you present and perform the poetry you have selected, you should speak as you think the character would speak. You do need to help the judge understand what is being said. Clear and careful pronunciation and enunciation can help you communicate the intent of the character and literature. If you do not recognize some of the words used in a poem, make sure to look up the meanings of such words in the dictionary.

Pitch. Because the voice is an instrument, and different people speak at different tonal levels, you need to adjust your pitch to the mood of the poem. A low pitch tends to suggest seriousness and intensity. Because "On the Pulse of Morning" is an upbeat poem, the pitch you use to deliver it might also be upbeat. The mood of the poem "America" is despair, so the pitch you use to read this poem might be at a lower octave.

Rate. Finally, different poems and different stanzas and lines within the poem should be read at different rates. Again, you should adjust the rate to the form and the mood of the poem. As you approach the fulcrum of a poem, you might want to slow down to give the change in mood and tone an additional emphasis. Take the fulcrum of the poem "America":

She kills her bright future
  and rapes for a sou
Then entraps her children
  with legends untrue
I beg you
Discover this country.

The first eight stanzas of the poem might be read, with some anger and emotion, at normal rate of delivery. The rate of delivery might be reduced when the line "with legends untrue" is read, and the last two lines might be read at a slow and intense rate.

After you have made the necessary decisions about the nonverbal and verbal messages you will use to interpret the poetry you have selected, you need to present your interpretation to your judges at the speech tournament. Your judges will provide you with useful instruction on the strengths and weaknesses of your poetry reading. In addition, you will learn much by listening to the poetry readings of your competitors.

Present your poetry reading to your judges

By the time you arrive at the tournament, your poetry reading should be in good order. You will have at least two or three opportunities to present your poetry reading to judges. While you may have practiced your poetry reading many times, make sure you read you poems as if it were the first time. Judges give you higher scores if you appear to be sincerely interested in and inspired by your poems.

Don't be too concerned about mistakes you might make. Often, the judge will not know if you forgot a word or a stanza of your poetry reading unless you reveal the mistake through some change in your face or body. If you do make a mistake, don't stop speaking. Many beginning and experienced poetry readers make mistakes. The goal is to continue speaking and to finish your reading.

Listen to the other competitors

Before and after you present your program, you should listen carefully to the poetry readings of your competitors. As you know, you should be a good audience member. This means that you should treat the other speakers as you would want them to treat you. If you hear a speaker present an idea or a perspective with which you disagree, do not give the speaker negative nonverbal reactions. Remain a civil and polite audience member.

You can learn much from the poetry readings delivered by your competitors. Take notes on what they do well and how they organize and present their poetry readings. Their programs can provide you clear examples of effective and not-so-effective poetry readings. After the tournament is over, you may wish to use these examples as models for improving your poetry readings.

Modify your Poetry Reading as Necessary

Your oral poetry reading should be in a constant state of evolution and change. You may decide after your first round that some minor modifications and changes might need to be made. For example, you may decide to change the wording of your introduction or use a different transition. You should, however, wait to make major changes in your poetry reading until the tournament is over. You will want time to think through any major alterations in your program. Make sure to talk with your forensics teacher or an experienced team member if you think your poetry reading needs significant change.

Read Your Ballots

After the tournament, read your ballots and use the comments made by your judges to improve. When the tournament is over, your forensics teacher will give you the ballots your judges wrote in reaction to your poetry reading. These ballots tell you how your judges ranked and rated you and your program in comparison to your competition. These ballots record what your judge felt were the strengths and weaknesses of your poetry reading. With the help of your forensics teacher, read these ballots and identify the comments made by your judges that you should use to revise and improve your poetry reading.

You should seek out patterns and recurring statements in the ballots. If, for example, all the judges commend you for your understanding of your poetry program, then you know that your literary analysis was complete. If two of your judges suggest that you should work on clarity and energy, then you would want to devote a part of your practice sessions to these suggestions.

Your ballots should be of great use to you, but use them with care. Your forensics teacher can help you to discriminate between helpful comments and those that may not be as useful. Because you may have the same judges at the next tournament, read your ballots for insight into the feelings and beliefs of your judges. With these feelings and beliefs in mind, you can work to revise and better adapt your poetry readings to your judges.

Conduct Additional Research and Practice

Your program should change after every tournament. Some sections of the poetry program may remain the same; other sections will need to be slightly or completely revised. You should conduct additional research and practice even if you took first place at a tournament! Additional research and practice keep your information up-to-date and your delivery sharp.

Continue to practice your program throughout the forensics season. Your practice sessions should resemble, as much as possible, the tournament environment. As you practice, identify specific improvements you wish to make. After delivering the same speech a number of times, some speakers lose interest in their programs. If you concentrate on making specific improvements in the content and delivery of your program, you can retain the energy and commitment you need to make your poetry program a success. With these steps in mind, let us briefly consider some model examples of oral poetry reading.

Model Oral Poetry Readings

Maya Angelou's poems have served us well to this point, so let us consider how the three poems discussed would be placed into a program.

An Abbreviated Model of a Poetry Program

Maya Angelou's "Africa," "America," and "On the Pulse of Morning."

Model Introduction

Maya Angelou, teacher, author, poet, has written a host of poems in which she communicates her unhappiness with America's treatment of African Americans and the hope that America can keep its promises by accepting its multicultural reality. As an African American, she believes her people never completely left Africa. At the same time, she expresses her pride in the contributions made by African Americans to American culture. In her three poems, "Africa," "America, and "On the Pulse of Morning," she displays the pain of racism and the dream of a new morning in America. First, a cutting from "Africa":

Africa

Thus she had lain
sugar cane sweet
deserts her hair
golden her feet
mountains her breasts
two Niles her tears
Thus she has lain
Black through the years

Over the white seas
rime white and cold
brigands ungentled
icicle bold
took her young daughters
sold her strong sons
churched her with Jesus
bled her with guns.
Thus she has lain.

Transition

Maya Angelou's vision of Africa recalls great loss and great glory. In this cutting from "America," she condemns America for its hypocrisy and pleads for people to discover the real country in which we live.

_____

America

The gold of her promise
    has never been mined

Her borders of justice
    not clearly defined

Her crops of abundance
    the fruit and the grain

Have not fed the hungry
    nor eased that great pain

Her proud declarations
    are leaves on the wind

_____

Transition

In "America" Maya Angelou speaks of a country whose promised gold is unmined, whose justice is unclear, and whose abundant crops are not used to feed the hungry. In "On the Pulse of Morning," she looks with hope for a new pulse and a new beginning. In this cutting from her poem, which she read at the 1993 inauguration of President Clinton, she urges Americans to move beyond their fear and sculpt the land into a country that embraces the diversity of its peoples.

_____

On the Pulse of Morning

Women, children, men
Take it into the palms of your hand
Mold it into the shape of your most
Private need. Sculpt it into
The Images of your most public self
Lift up your hearts

Each new hour holds new chances
For a new beginning
Do not be wedded forever
To fear, yoked eternally
To brutishness

Reading the poetry of Maya Angelou

A literary analysis of Maya Angelou's poetry can tell you much about how you might read her poems. While she is a hopeful poet, she does not ignore the ugly realities of American life and culture. As you read her poetry, you would want to locate a mood and a tone somewhere between hope and despair.

Nonverbal Considerations

In reading the poetry of Maya Angelou, you need to adjust your nonverbal and verbal messages to the mood and the intent of the poems. You can convey much of the mood and tone of the three poems through your posture, gesture, bodily movements, and use of the script. The first poem, "Africa," calls for an angry but buoyant posture. This poem seems to portray the survival of Africa, even though the white Europeans had "bled her with guns."

The second poem, "America," might call for nonverbal messages of despair, anger, and great frustration. The third poem might be delivered with nonverbal messages of guarded hope and optimism. You can communicate anger, buoyancy, frustration, and guarded hope with the posture you adopt, the muscles you relax and tighten, and the way you move your body and script.

Verbal Qualities

The verbal qualities of your voice will combine with the nonverbal messages to communicate the theme and argument of your poetry reading. A literary study of Maya Angelou and her poems provides the information you need to choose the proper verbal qualities of voice.

Verbal qualities of voice—volume, clarity, pitch, and rate—help you interpret the mood and tone of the poetry. When you reach the fulcrum of the poem "America," your voice will, through its volume, pitch, and rate, call for the audience to "discover this country." Consider this passage from "On the Pulse of Morning":

Lift up your hearts
Each new hour holds new chances
For a new beginning

> Do not be wedded forever
> To fear, yoked eternally
> To brutishness

———

You may want to raise the pitch of your voice when you read "lift up your hearts" and reduce the pitch when you read

———

> Do not be wedded forever
> To fear, yoked eternally

———

You and your forensics teacher can decide how you should read your poetry. While there is no one right or wrong way to read poetry, there are some guidelines that you can follow in creating the best readings possible. Once again, your careful and thorough literary study and analysis of the poems you read will help you make the right choices.

CONCLUSION

The oral interpretation of poetry is an art that requires the careful literary study of the poems and an energetic reading of a poetry program. In this chapter, you learned how to select and analyze poems for competitive poetry reading. If you follow the steps outlined in this chapter, you will be proud of your understanding and reading of poetry.

As with other forensics events, you should design your poetry reading to present a theme and make an argument. This theme and argument should come from the poems you select.

There are many resources that can help you discover fine poetry. Your poetry readings should consist of poems that you love, poems that move and inspire you. If you don't like the poems you read, or if you tire of your poetry program, find new material. There is a vast universe of wonderful and exciting poetry. Don't settle for selections that fail to inspire you or your audience.

APPENDIX

Reader's Theatre

Reader's Theatre (or multiple interpretation) is an individual event offered at some forensic tournaments. Reader's Theatre programs, which involve between three and eight interpreters, are designed to present a theme and an argument about an important issue, theme or idea. Reader's Theatre programs consist of selections from prose, dramatic, and poetic literature. Unlike the interpretative events discussed in Chapter 8, 9 and 10, reader's theatre is a team event and you will need to work with the other students in your program to form a troupe.

Reader's Theatre Programs

Your troupe will prepare and present a program before judges at forensics tournaments. Judges will evaluate your troupe's program using the general standards discussed in Chapter 10. Your judges will also rank and rate your program in comparison to those presented and performed by troupes from other schools.

How should you and your teammates (your troupe) create a Reader's Theatre program? How are Reader's Theatre programs judged? Fortunately, the same principles and guidelines outlined and discussed in the last section of *Creative Speaking* can be applied to help you and your teammates create an effective Reader's Theatre program. Because Reader's Theatre is a team event, the principles and guidelines discussed in this chapter will be presented in terms of group performances.

The best Reader's Theatre programs are those that present an interesting and compelling theme or argument about a topic of universal concern. Reader's Theatre troupes have conducted research on and performed such themes as "Unrequited Love," "Graduations," and "TV Comedies and the American Culture." As with any interpretative event, you and your troupe will need to conduct a careful literary analysis of the texts selected for your program. Additionally, your troupe will need to communicate this theme to your audiences.

The goal of a Reader's Theatre program is to communicate a theme and an argument to audience that reveals the intellectual, emotional, and aesthetic (artistic) meanings of good literature to an audience. The rules for Reader's Theatre will vary from tournament to tournament. Most tournaments will, however, use similar rules. The guidelines on page 285 are drawn from the rules used in Michigan (in connection with interscholastic competition at the high school level).

Judges will expect your troupe to follow the rules of the particular competition. The rule most frequently violated is the time limit. Make certain you and your troupe are aware of the limitations. Also, make sure everyone knows the exact location of the tournament and, specifically, how to get to the assigned room. Know the schedule and be punctual.

There are some specific steps that your and your teammates will need to take to create a Reader's Theatre program, as shown on page 286.

As a group event, you and your teammates will need to be clear on the roles the troupe members will assume. The group will need to identify the theme or "argument," discover fitting and effective literature, conduct a thorough literary study of the selections, and create a moving performance.

As with group work in other classes, you and your teammates will need to clarify the roles and responsibilities of the individuals who will participate in

Guidelines

Reader's Theatre

Purpose: The primary purpose of any form of oral interpretation is for the student or students to communicate the intellectual, emotional, and aesthetic meanings of good literature. Reader's Theatre should help students learn the art of developing and performing a unified and coherent program of good literature that presents an important theme and argument to an audience. The Reader's Theatre event should help students develop an appreciation for literature that can be interpreted and performed by a group.

Length: Reader's Theatre programs are often limited to ten to fifteen minutes.

Procedures

1. The interpreters will present an introduction that explains the theme, argument, plot, scene, author, or other characters.

2. The texts and materials used shall come from cuttings of materials that can be discovered in the public realm. Published novels, short stories, plays, or poetry are appropriate for use in Reader's Theatre programs. Original scripts, or a photocopy of the pages from the original sources, should be available to judges.

3. Acting and materials associated with acting are not allowed in Reader's Theatre.

4. The use of a manuscript is often optional.

5. Selections used in previous years' competition should be avoided.

the performance. Your forensics teacher or coach may advise or direct your troupe in preparation for performance and competition.

What Judges Expect from Reader's Theatre

In Chapter 10, the principles necessary for good and effective oral interpretations of literature are outlined. Judges of interpretative events and Reader's Theatre or multiple interpretation will use these principles when they evaluate Reader's Theatre programs. With these principles in mind, you and your teammates can identify what judges will expect.

Guidelines

Step One: Agree on roles, responsibilities, and rights of the troupe members.

Step Two: Brainstorm for themes and subjects for the troupe's program.

Step Three: Conduct a literary analysis of the texts the troupe selects.

Step Four: Identify a theme and an argument to organize the selections and cuttings into a format that puts the troupe's selections into a meaningful order.

Step Five: Write the first draft of the troupe's program.

Step Six: Perform and practice the program.

Judges will expect to hear a Reader's Theatre program with a topic, theme, or argument that unifies the literature you and your teammates perform

The selections that make up the Reader's Theatre program should contribute to the development of a theme. For example, you and your teammates might develop a program dedicated to the topic, theme, and argument about the richness of cultures in America.

Judges tend to give higher rankings and ratings to Reader's Theatre programs that present well-developed and interesting ideas and themes. How do you and your teammates develop topics and select literature that will appeal to judges? Scholars of oral interpretation have identified three standards critics and judges use in the evaluation of the themes, literature, and performance of oral interpretation programs.

First, the themes, literature, and performance of good literature should provide a universal appeal. Keep in mind that what might be interesting, intriguing, and funny to you and your teammates may not be interesting, intriguing, and funny to judges. However, this does not mean you and your teammates should always select themes and literature that are very popular and widely-known and loved.

Note that the second standard you and your teammates can use to select a theme and material is the uniqueness and the individuality expressed by the theme and the troupe has selected. While the material for Reader's Theatre should have universal appeal, you and your teammates will want that appeal expressed in a fresh and novel manner. As your troupe works to create a Reader's Theatre program, think how it can be adapted to the values, beliefs, and preferences of your judges, as much as you know them.

When the themes and selections of Reader's Theatre are performed effectively, your troupe is inviting audience participation, which is the third standard you and your teammates can use in creating successful Reader's Theatre. Such literature will encourage the judges who hear your troupe's Reader's Theatre program to participate emotionally and intellectually.

Judges will expect you and your teammates to understand the literature your troupe selects and performs

Forensics is an activity designed to encourage knowledgable speaking. Some judges of oral interpretation and Reader's Theatre are concerned that students spend too much time practicing and perfecting their performances and not enough time analyzing their selections. Beyond the skills of performance you and your teammates will learn competing in Reader's Theatre, your troupe should also learn how to study and appreciate good literature. Two types of literary analysis are suggested for interpretation of literature.

First, an internal anaylsis involves a careful reading of the entire text from which you and your troupe will take cuttings. To achieve an understanding of the text, your troupe will need to look at the entire story told by the author of the texts you select. Regardless of the materials used in a Reader's Theatre, all will tell a story about something.

Second, you and your teammates will need to conduct an external analysis of the literature used in your Reader's Theatre program. You and your teammates will need to discover the context and cultural problems that affected and shaped the literature you and your teammates have selected.

In many ways, you and your teammates will have to develop the tools required of the literary critic. You and your teammates will have to make choices from a wide range of poems, plays, short stories, and novels. The choices your troupe makes will depend on their particular likes and dislikes. By reading the criticism of literary critics, you and your teammates can learn how to create and apply benchmarks for the evaluation of literature.

Judges will expect an introduction, transitions, and an organizational pattern

The introduction, transitions and organizational format should feature the central theme and the argument of the Reader's Theatre program.

The Introduction. At a minimum, the introduction should provide the judges with the authors and the titles of the selections and the themes connecting the selections.

The introduction should accomplish two specific goals. First, the program should give the judge enough information to gain an appreciation and an understanding of the literature. Often, information about the author and title may not be enough. Your troupe's literary study may reveal pertinent biographical information on the authors whose selections you use in your program. This biographical information should help you, your teammates, and the judge/audience understand the meaning of the literature.

The second goal of the introduction is to specify the theme and the argument of the program and to justify the troupe's selection of literature. This is critically important element of the introduction, for judges will need to know the intellectual, emotional, and artistic claims the troupe will make and why the literature helps your troupe make these claims.

Organization. Regardless of the literature you and your teammates select for the program, your troupe will need to write an introduction, provide necessary transitions, and create a fitting organizational pattern. Most interpretative literature share some basic characteristics. Dramatic, prose, and poetry literature all tend to reach stages of climax or moments of crisis and resolution. Teachers of oral interpretation encourage their students to organize their selections and their programs around these moments of crisis and resolution.

The Reader's Theatre troupe should purposefully use nonverbal and verbal communication to perform the literature

The delivery and performance of an oral interpretation must be true to the meaning of the literature. Yet, the presentation of an interpretation is also a creative act. You and your teammates should provide a unique interpretation of the literature selected for performance. The choices the troupe makes when members move, gesture, speak, breathe, etc., will influence how judges and audience understand the literature and the performance. The best oral interpreters are careful to communicate their interpretations so that literature itself is preserved and the audiences can appreciate the emotional, intellectual, and aesthetic essence of the literature.

The rules of oral interpretation and Reader's Theatre limit the range of nonverbal and verbal messages available to you, depending on the rules of the individual competition. These rules, generally, restrict the use of broad ranges of movement, stages, costumes, and props that stage actors depend upon. As a result, the troupe is limited to bodily action, voice, and if the rules permit, a few props or costumes. While these rules do restrict the troupe's options, you and your teammates will be surprised by the skills the troupe will develop in communicating with the body and voice.

Study of the literature itself will help the troupe prepare and practice the nonverbal and verbal communication necessary for the performance of the literature. An important result of this literary study will be a series of insights into how the narrator, characters, lines, etc., should be performed. Your literary study will help you to communicate with your body and your voice the intellectual, emotional, and artistic meanings of the literature you have selected.

The following are performance elements that your troupe needs to address.

Posture. The posture your troupe assumes will send messages to the judge and audience about the theme and argument of your program. The troupe should stand in a central location so that all members of the audience can see and hear the program. Whenever possible, use a posture which feels and looks comfortable. Troupe members should assume postures that will allow them to move and gesture. Above all, your posture should reflect balance and tone, as the literature dictates. The troupe's posture should contribute to and enhance the message it intends to send to its audience.

Unlike the public speaking events in which competitors will represent their own ideas and convictions, your Reader's Theatre troupe will play the roles and speak the words of other people. When your troupe interprets and performs characters found in prose or dramatic literature, the portrayal of these characters should be reflected in the posture your troupe members adopt. For example, if one of the troupe members interprets a character known for her pride, then the posture assumed should communicate pride. People who are proud tend to stand and exude confidence and strength.

The posture your troupe adopts in interpreting a character should fit the character's age, mood, temperament, and the message the author of the literature wishes to communicate through and with the character. Your troupe's literary study will reveal the information necessary for you to fit your understanding of the literature with your performance of the literature. For example, a very old person would call for a different posture than a very young person. An angry character would call for a different posture than one that is happy.

Gestures. Your literary analysis helps you and your teammates to choose the gestures that best fit the personal mannerisms of the characters the troupe will portray.

Bodily Movements. Again, the rules of the event may restrict the movements you are allowed to make with your body. Yet, your troupe can convey many emotions with the muscles in the face and body.

The Script. The rules of the event may require you to hold and/or read from a script. In such competition, your script should blend into your performance. As troupe members read from the script, make sure that they turn the pages with care and communicate effectively during the performance.

Verbal Qualities. Volume, clarity, pitch, stress, and rate combine with your nonverbal messages to communicate the theme and the meanings of the literature selected by your troupe. Your troupe's literary study of the author, characters, and the selection itself, will provide the information needed to make choices about the verbal qualities of voice.

Regarding volume, the troupe should turn first to the literature and analyze the spirit of the character to determine appropriate speaking volume. At the same time, the troupe needs to take into account the place of performance and the proximity of the judge(s) or audience.

As the troupe presents and performs the literature it has selected, each member should speak as he or she thinks the character would speak. However, the troupe needs to help the judge understand what is being said. Clear and careful pronunciation and enunciation can help you communicate and help the judge understand the intent of the character and literature.

Because the voice is like an instrument, and different voices speak at different tonal levels, members of your troupe will need to adjust their vocal pitch to the characters they perform.

Regarding the rate of speaking, most conversations occur at a rate of 150-185 words per minute. Speakers who talk at rates exceeding 185 words per minute will tend to irritate and confuse most audiences. However, speakers who talk at rates below 150 words per minute risk irritation and boredom. As with the other aspects of good speaking, your troupe should strive for balance—unless the literature calls for a rate of speaking that is imbalanced.

There are many other suggestion that scholars and teachers of oral interpretation and Reader's Theatre offer to students regarding the nonverbal and verbal messages needed to interpret literature. Your troupe should feel free to experiment with nonverbal and verbal messages in the performance of a Reader's Theatre program. At the same time, the troupe should not deviate from the meanings found through a careful literary study of the selections.

Conclusion

Reader's Theatre is a group or ensemble event. As a group event, the selection of a theme and an argument, the necessary research, and the performance of the program will all be the result of a collective effort. When Reader's Theatre programs are successful, they are successful because all the participants contribute to the creation and the performance of fine literature. As you work with others to write and present your program, you will learn much about the art of multiple interpretation and the significance of collective effort.

After an actual performance for competition, go over the ballots and judges' critiques. Use them to assess, improve or modify your Reader's Theatre performance for the next competition. Above all, enjoy this creative and challenging interpretative event.

ACKNOWLEDGMENTS

"Africa" and "America" from OH PRAY MY WINGS ARE GONNA FIT ME WELL by Maya Angelou. Copyright © 1975 by Maya Angelou. Reprinted by permission of Random House, Inc. Excerpt from ON THE PULSE OF MORNING by Maya Angelou. Copyright © 1993 by Maya Angelou. Reprinted by permission of Random House, Inc.

Excerpts from "Hopeland" by K. Kam from MAKING WAVES, published by Asian Women United. Reprinted by permission of Beacon Press.

Excerpts from student speeches by Chris O'Keefe (After-dinner Speech, pp. 99–102) and Jay Lane (Informative Speech, pp. 117–120) from 1987 CHAMPIONSHIP DEBATES AND SPEECHES, Volume 2, edited by John K. Boaz and James R. Brey. Published in 1987 by Illinois State University, Normal, Illinois. Copyright by the American Forensic Association. Reprinted by permission of the publisher.

Excerpts from student speeches by Suzie Sprague (Extemporaneous Speech, pp. 134–136), Cort Sylvester (Impromptu Speaking, pp. 113–115), and Betsy Heffernan (Persuasive Speaking, pp. 81–84) from 1989 CHAMPIONSHIP DEBATES AND SPEECHES, Volume 4, edited by Christian L. Reynolds and Larry Schnoor. Published in 1989 by the Speech Communication Association, Annandale, Virginia. Copyright by the American Forensic Association. Reprinted by permission of the publisher.

Excerpts from (radio) speech by Daniel Schorr: © Copyright National Public Radio® 1993. The news commentary by NPR's Daniel Schorr was originally broadcast on National Public Radio's "Weekend Edition" on June 13, 1993, and is used with permission of National Public Radio. Any unauthorized duplication is strictly prohibited.

Excerpts from FENCES by August Wilson. Copyright © 1986 by August Wilson. Used by permission of Dutton Signet, a division of Penguin Books USA Inc.

NTC LANGUAGE ARTS BOOKS

Business Communication
Business Communication Today! *Thomas & Fryar*
Handbook for Business Writing, *Baugh, Fryar, & Thomas*
Meetings: Rules & Procedures, *Pohl*

Dictionaries
British/American Language Dictionary, *Moss*
NTC's Classical Dictionary, *Room*
NTC's Dictionary of Changes in Meaning, *Room*
NTC's Dictionary of Debate, *Hanson*
NTC's Dictionary of Literary Terms, *Morner & Rausch*
NTC's Dictionary of Theatre and Drama Terms, *Mobley*
NTC's Dictionary of Word Origins, *Room*
NTC's Spell It Right Dictionary, *Downing*
Robin Hyman's Dictionary of Quotations

Essential Skills
Building Real Life English Skills, *Starkey & Penn*
English Survival Series, *Maggs*
Essential Life Skills, *Starkey & Penn*
Essentials of English Grammar, *Baugh*
Essentials of Reading and Writing English Series
Grammar for Use, *Hall*
Grammar Step-by-Step, *Pratt*
Guide to Better English Spelling, *Furness*
How to be a Rapid Reader, *Redway*
How to Improve Your Study Skills, *Coman & Heavers*
NTC Skill Builders
Reading by Doing, *Simmons & Palmer*
Developing Creative & Critical Thinking, *Boostrom*
303 Dumb Spelling Mistakes, *Downing*
TIME: We the People, *ed. Schinke-Llano*
Vocabulary by Doing, *Beckert*

Genre Literature
The Detective Story, *Schwartz*
The Short Story & You, *Simmons & Stern*
Sports in Literature, *Emra*
You and Science Fiction, *Hollister*

Journalism
Getting Started in Journalism, *Harkrider*
Journalism Today! *Ferguson & Patten*
Publishing the Literary Magazine, *Klaiman*
UPI Stylebook, *United Press International*

Language, Literature, and Composition
An Anthology for Young Writers, *Meredith*
The Art of Composition, *Meredith*
Creative Writing, *Mueller & Reynolds*

Handbook for Practical Letter Writing, *Baugh*
How to Write Term Papers and Reports, *Baugh*
Literature by Doing, *Tchudi & Yesner*
Lively Writing, *Schrank*
Look, Think & Write, *Leavitt & Sohn*
Poetry by Doing, *Osborn*
World Literature, *Rosenberg*
Write to the Point! *Morgan*
The Writer's Handbook, *Karls & Szymanski*
Writing by Doing, *Sohn & Enger*
Writing in Action, *Meredith*

Media Communication
Getting Started in Mass Media, *Beckert*
Photography in Focus, *Jacobs & Kokrda*
Television Production Today! *Kirkham*
Understanding Mass Media, *Schrank*
Understanding the Film, *Bone & Johnson*

Mythology
The Ancient World, *Sawyer & Townsend*
Mythology and You, *Rosenberg & Baker*
Welcome to Ancient Greece, *Millard*
Welcome to Ancient Rome, *Millard*
World Mythology, *Rosenberg*

Speech
Activities for Effective Communication, *LiSacchi*
The Basics of Speech, *Galvin, Cooper, & Gordon*
Contemporary Speech, *HopKins & Whitaker*
Dynamics of Speech, *Myers & Herndon*
Getting Started in Public Speaking, *Prentice & Payne*
Listening by Doing, *Galvin*
Literature Alive! *Gamble & Gamble*
Person to Person, *Galvin & Book*
Public Speaking Today! *Prentice & Payne*
Speaking by Doing, *Buys, Sill, & Beck*

Theatre
Acting & Directing, *Grandstaff*
The Book of Cuttings for Acting & Directing, *Cassady*
The Book of Scenes for Acting Practice, *Cassady*
The Dynamics of Acting, *Snyder & Drumsta*
An Introduction to Modern One-Act Plays, *Cassady*
An Introduction to Theatre and Drama, *Cassady & C*
Play Production Today! *Beck et al.*
Stagecraft, *Beck*

For a current catalog and information about our complete line
of language arts books, write:
National Textbook Company
a division of NTC Publishing Group
4255 West Touhy Avenue
NTC Lincolnwood (Chicago), Illinois 60646-1975 U.S.A.

Behold

———

I Do a

———

New Thing

———

The Seattle School
2510 Elliott Ave.
Seattle, WA 98121
theseattleschool.edu